Government in Canada

COMPARATIVE MODERN GOVERNMENTS

General Editor: Max Beloff

Gladstone Professor of Government and Public Administration,
University of Oxford

Government in Canada

THOMAS A. HOCKIN

Associate Professor, Department of Political Science,
York University, Canada

W · W · NORTON & COMPANY · INC ·
NEW YORK

Library of Congress Cataloging in Publication Data
Hockin, Thomas A   1938-
  Government in Canada.
  (Comparative modern governments)
  Bibliography: p.
  Includes index.
  1. Canada—Politics and government—1945-
I. Title.
JL65.1975.H63   320.4'71   76-5846
ISBN 0-393-05532-9
ISBN 0-393-09294-1 pbk.

Printed in the United States of America

1 2 3 4 5 6 7 8 9 0

Contents

Contents

Editor's introduction

The series of which this volume forms part is intended as a contribution to the study of contemporary political institutions in a number of countries both in Europe and in the rest of the world, selected either for their intrinsic importance or because of the particular interest attaching to their form of government and the manner of its working. Although we expect that most readers of such a series will be students of politics in universities or other institutions of higher or further education, the approach is not wholly that of what is now technically styled 'political science'. Our aims have been at once more modest and more practical.

All study of government must be comparative, in that the questions one asks about one system will usually arise from one's knowledge of another, and although we hope that anyone who has read a number of these volumes will derive some valuable general ideas about political institutions, the notion that politics is a suitable subject for generalization and prediction is alien to the empirical spirit that animates the series.

The authors are concerned with government as an important practical activity which now impinges on the life of the citizen in almost every sphere. They seek in each individual country to ask such questions as how laws are made and how enforced, who determines and in what manner the basic domestic and foreign policies of the country. They seek to estimate the role not only of elected persons, presidents, ministers, Members of Parliament and of lesser assemblies but also of the officials and members of the armed forces who play a vital role in different ways in the different societies.

But government is not something carried out for its own sake; ultimately the criterion of success and failure is to be found in its impact upon the lives of individual citizens. And here two further questions need to be asked: how does government conduct itself in regard to the citizen and what protection has he through the courts or in other ways against arbitrary action or maladministration? The second question is how the citizen can in fact make his influence felt upon the course of government, since most of the countries that will be discussed in these volumes claim to be democratic in the broadest sense. And this inquiry leads on to a discussion of political parties and the various interest-groups or pressure groups which in modern states form the normal vehicles for self-expression by citizens sharing a common interest or common opinions. To understand their working, some knowledge of the role of the press and other mass-media is clearly essential.

The study of such aspects of politics has recently been very fashionable and is sometimes styled the behavioural approach or the investigation of political culture. But our authors have kept in mind the fact that while the nature of a country's formal institutions may be explained as the product of its political culture, the informal aspects of politics can only be understood if the legal and institutional framework is clearly kept in mind. In the end the decisions are made, except where anarchy or chaos prevails, by constituted authority.

We would like to feel that anyone suddenly required for official or business or cultural purposes to go to one of these countries hitherto unknown to him would find the relevant volume of immediate use in enabling him to find his way about its governmental structure and to understand the way in which it might impinge upon his own concerns. There is a great deal to be said for a guide-book even in politics.

Nevertheless no attempt has been made to impose uniformity of treatment upon these volumes. Each writer is an authority for his particular country or group of countries and will have a different set of priorities; none would wish to treat in the same way an old-established and highly-integrated polity such as that of France or the United Kingdom and a vast and heterogenous political society still searching for stable forms such as India.

Preface

This book is an introduction to the shape and influence of government at the Federal level in Canada. It also sketches the relevance of some of the more important economic and political forces to the Canadian system of government. Like others in this series, it endeavours to communicate to non-professional as well as to professional observers of Canadian government. It is also written for non-Canadians. The book analyzes the relevance of Canadian government within some general themes which concern students of comparative government and which make Canada's government particularly interesting. It addresses itself above all to the questions non-Canadians often ask of Canada: how, given its multi-culturalism and economic cleavages, has Canada been able to hold together and enjoy considerable political stability. This book tries to cast some new light on these questions by focusing not primarily on the nature of Canadian society, thereby assuming that government is little more than the artifact of society, but by emphasizing the dynamic of government in Canada, its leadership, its activities. It suggests, in short, that government often does as much integrating and penetrating of society as society does of government.

I wish to thank Professor Beloff for his help and advice and my wife for her invaluable assistance. I also wish to thank McClelland and Stewart Ltd of Toronto for permission to draw upon two parts of two chapters of my *Canadian Condominium* for background in this book. My debt to the insights and work of others is great. I am especially indebted to the writings of J. Corry, J. Ellul, J. Blondel, S. Beer, A. Cairns, E. Black, D. Smiley and the stimulating conversation, bibliographic suggestions and research of my colleagues at York University and elsewhere, especially David Hoffman, George Szablowski, Rich Schutz, Gerald Wright, Robert Presthus, David Bell and Douglas Verney. The Treasury Board kindly allowed me to reproduce one of the figures. Of course none of these people is in any way responsible for the faults or interpretation in this volume.

T.A.H.

ELLESMERE ISLAND

ARCTIC OCEAN

ALASKA

BANKS ISLAND

Resolute

Arctic Bay

Port Ross

Fort McPherson

Inuvik

VICTORIA ISLAND

YUKON

Fort Good Hope

Cambridge Bay

Dawson

NORTHWEST

Whitehorse

Yellowknife

TERRITORIES

Chesterfield

Fort Nelson

Fort Smith

BRITISH COLUMBIA

ALBERTA

Uranium City

Fort St John

Churchill

Prince Rupert

McMurray

MANITOBA

Prince George

Grande Prairie

Thompson

Edmonton

Prince Albert

Jasper

The Pas

Banff

Calgary

Saskatoon

VANCOUVER ISLAND

Vancouver

SASKATCHEWAN

Victoria

Lethbridge

Regina

Winnipeg

PACIFIC OCEAN

Brandon

UNITED STATES OF AMERICA

Source: Information Canada, Ottawa 1972.

Government in Canada

1 The Canadian State: Its Development and Influence

In the mid-1960s, Canadian author Kildare Dobbs suggested in his book *Canada* that his country was 'a society rather than a nation'. He suggested that Canadians as a whole were antithetical to the 'Hegelian idea of the superiority of the state to the sum of its parts'. He saw that Canadian politicians were willing to compromise and to mediate. In Canadians he saw a tendency to mind their own business; a people innocent of 'lawlessness and gang-rule', living in a 'society in which power is decentralized'. It was 'a good country', one in which the human spirit 'flowers in quiet'.

Ten years later the insight in this description is far from obsolete. This book explores the Canadian state and suggests that, if much of this un-Hegelian quality in Canadian society persists, the state has played, and is increasingly playing, its own somewhat autonomous, role in holding Canada together and in defining the nature of society. A state need not be Hegelian to do these things. It can be subordinate to society in two different senses: it tries to adjust to some of society's needs; and it recognizes that most of the individual's self-development cannot be the responsibility of the state. Nevertheless the state's own internal needs will push it to become somewhat superordinate to society. The very nature of its activity helps to define and appropriate parts of society. What has developed in Canada is, not as yet a tightly integrated, but an increasingly integrated, Federal* and provincial state system. This system may now be as formative in defining

*'Federal' is capitalized when it refers to the central (once known as the 'Dominion') level of government in Canada. Federal is not capitalized when it comes before 'Parliament' since 'Parliament' refers only to the upper and lower

what Canada is, or will be, as are the autonomous patterns of society itself. If the state network in Canada has not yet become an all-consuming leviathan, its activities must be recognized if Canada's hitherto rather surprising political stability, modicum of integration and persistence as a nation are to be understood.

Just before this century began, Canada's prime minister Sir Wilfrid Laurier declared that 'the twentieth century belongs to Canada'. Clearly this has not happened: but neither has the Canadian experience been a failure.

In what sense was the century to belong to Canada? Canada has not become a great imperial or colonizing power. This older idea of greatness has not been Canada's. In fact what limited world role Canada has played has been made possible precisely because it is one of the few wealthy Western nations not suspected of such ambitions. Canada's world role this century has oscillated between isolation and voluntarist schemes of peacekeeping, alliance participation and involvement in supranational institutions. Canada has not become a noisy nationalist power but instead has inveighed against such manifestations in others. If greatness means hegemonial leadership, then Canada, to be sure, is not a great power and neither this century, nor any international constellation within it, belongs or will belong to Canada. This old idea of Asian and European greatness, and the motivation behind the bipolar power struggle of today, is not Canada's.

Other European and American ideas of greatness also elude Canada. The country has not developed a coherent set of political ideas that it feels must be promulgated and proselytized throughout the world (unless Canada's suspicion of nationalism can be dignified as such a mission). Nor has Canada witnessed a massive demographic increase across those regions of the country which in Laurier's time were little more than expanses of howling wilder-

---

legislatures and the crown at the Federal level. Provincial assemblies are known as 'legislatures'.

'Government' is capitalized when it refers to the political executive, e.g. 'the Trudeau Government'. It is not capitalized when it refers to the whole governmental machine, the political executive, the public service, boards and commissions, etc. I have not used the term 'state' in any formal sense in this book. It refers not only to the 'government' but also to ministerial and prime ministerial political aides, parliamentary secretaries, and Members of Parliament and Senators who in effect sustain and protect the government. This is the 'Federal state'. The 'Canadian state' is the Federal state together with its counterparts at the provincial and municipal levels.

ness. At the end of the last century only 12 per cent of the country's population inhabited the immensity between the Great Lakes and the Pacific Ocean; today the proportion has crept up to 25 per cent. Canada's great northern wilderness remains thinly populated. In Laurier's time, Canada demographically was a narrow strip of territory hugging a railway route not far north of the southern border. Today with more railways as well as other modes of transportation, over four-fifths of Canada's population live within a strip reaching no farther north than two hundred miles from this border.

Canada has been called the world's smallest large nation. Although Canada's population has grown from five to twenty-two million in the last seventy-five years, this is not much of an increase for the world's second largest geographic nation. Also, Canada, although rich in natural resources, has felt itself to be capital poor and now finds that it is not only sparsely populated around much of its resource base but that a large portion of it is foreign-owned.

Turning to political rather than economic and demographic development, a case might be made that Canada has failed to progress since the time of Laurier. At that time the fundamental political challenges facing Canadians included Canada's relations with the United Kingdom and the United States and, internally, relations between French and English Canada, and relations between the Dominion and the provincial governments. The contents of these concerns have changed, but their contours persist.

Yet this brief check-list of failure will not do. One suspects in fact that Laurier would be astonished by the capacity Canada has shown in this century to grow in both wealth and in political viability. Canada has slowly yet persistently disengaged itself from the mother country without incurring either civil war or national fragmentation and without indulging in the usual nationalist rhetoric of new societies. Fate has placed the country between this century's two most powerful nations, yet Canada has not been squeezed out of playing useful roles on the world scene. Indeed, Canada's options in international affairs may increase if it continues to try to ameliorate its economic dependence on foreign investment. By the end of this decade – Canada's Economic Council of Canada tells us – the country's Gross National Product, which now approaches that of China, will surpass it and Britain's as well. The discovery and development in this century of enormous deposits of iron ore, coal, oil and nickel, together with huge increases in wheat, sawmill, pulp, paper and water power production, have made Canada one of the leading exporters in the world and have helped, together with a some-what protected manufacturing sector, to give Canadians the fourth or fifth highest per capita income in the world.

Nor will an image of political stasis suffice. Laurier had to wrestle with the growing power of provincial governments but never with provincial seats of power and responsibility as vast as those now found in Quebec City, Toronto, Edmonton and Victoria today. The provinces (especially Quebec, Ontario, Alberta and British Columbia) are not 'overgrown municipalities', as some observers predicted in 1869. It can be suggested also that the influence and responsibilities of Manitoba, Saskatche-wan, even Nova Scotia and New Brunswick, far exceed what most Canadians expected at the beginning of this century. Yet this development has been paralleled by a transformation in the scope and penetration of Ottawa's role in national life that would astound Laurier, to say nothing of the authors of the British North America Act who launched the confederation in 1867. This parallel process has greatly affected Canadian society, so that it is difficult to describe or assess any problems or opportunities in Canadian life without acknowledging the importance of govern-ments, at both levels. What is more, this steady penetration, and even definition, of much of Canadian life by governments has occurred without giving rise to more than a few occasions of severe political instability. Nor have the growth of governments and the growing interdependence and integration of provincial and Federal governments in planning, policy-making and execu-tion – for all the speeches about conflict – been retarded since Laurier's time. If these are manifestations of political integration then Laurier might very well be quite impressed. In order to understand what has happened, and why, this chapter will sketch some of the key social and constitutional developments.

(1) *Some Constitutional Fundamentals*

Canada consists of ten provinces and two northern territories. The Canadian federal union was created on 29 March 1867 when the British Parliament passed the British North America Act. The official birth of the Canadian Confederation was on 1 July 1867 when New Brunswick, Nova Scotia and Canada (now Quebec and Ontario, before 1840 known as Upper and Lower Canada or Canada West and Canada East) united to form what was called the 'Dominion of Canada'. Other provinces joined later: Manitoba in 1870, British Columbia 1871, Prince Edward Island 1873, Saskatchewan 1905, Alberta 1905, the Northwest Territories 1870, the Yukon Territory 1898, and Newfoundland 1949. In essence the British North America Act granted control to the Federal parliament over defence, trade, criminal law, postal services, banking, the armed forces, transportation, and foreign affairs. Provincial legislatures were granted jurisdiction in matters of property and civil rights, education and health, as well as matters of purely local interest. These jurisdictions and levels of government will be discussed at length in chapter 2.

Canada's governmental system did not, in 1867, emerge from a vacuum; political and constitutional developments in British North America before confederation helped to form much of the framework and the assumptions of Canadian government. Foremost perhaps was the inheritance of a parliamentary tradition. In 1758 Nova Scotia was granted an Assembly, followed by New Brunswick, Prince Edward Island, the Province of Upper Canada and, in 1791, Lower Canada. The granting of more or less popularly elected Assemblies established that male British North Americans had inherited the right to elect their own members to a lower House of their own. (Women did not receive the right to vote until after World War I.) This House had to share, or balance, its power with the governor (the British-appointed viceroy) and the Upper House. In the period from the turn of the nineteenth century to the beginning of the 1830s it became apparent that the 'balanced constitution' – the balance among the Assembly, the governor's appointed 'Executive' or 'Legislative' Council and the governor himself – was not working and was not likely to work. In a number of provinces the Council and the Assembly refused to admit the right of the other to make

5

ultimate decisions on supply. During stoppages and threatened stoppages of supply, only the governor – by use of his separate financial account and civil list – could govern. Finally, after much debating but very little fighting, a series of agreements were reached in the various provinces. These were based in part on a recommendation of a Benthamite and Whig-dominated Westminster Select Committee giving the Upper Canadian Assembly predominance over supply. Nevertheless, some important patronage and executive powers, and a small separate fund, remained with the governor. This provoked some brief armed conflict in the Canadas. Very soon a report by Upper Canada's governor Lord Durham followed in 1838, recommending the political union of the predominantly English-speaking Upper Canada and the predominantly French-speaking Lower Canada. They were joined to form the Province of Canada in 1840. Durham also recommended 'responsible government'. This was not immediately accepted but from 1840 to 1848 the governor's patronage power was attacked in the provinces of Canada, New Brunswick and Nova Scotia. Eventually his executive power was appropriated by the groups that could command a majority in the Assembly. From the 1830s to 1848 governors appealed to the people in general elections, campaigning 'above party' (but in effect as party leaders urging something less than responsible government). This appeal to the electorate worked in the end to confirm that power resided, in part at least, in the people, and not solely in the Crown. As the governor's supporters lost in elections in the late 1840s, the leaders of the Assemblies took over executive power in Nova Scotia in 1847, and in United Canada in 1848. The principle of responsible government had taken hold: this is the principle that the Assembly has the right to have an executive in which it has confidence and which can therefore command a majority in the Assembly. This popular theory of government, however, was linked to monarchial ideas of a central executive. Hence an important principle of government remained in the province of Canada throughout this long constitutional and political journey to responsible government. A centralized energizing executive, enjoying central command over the budget, and in charge of proposing policy as well as administering it, was never completely shattered (although shaken for a brief period from 1854 to 1864). Whether the executive was dominated by the governor or by the leaders of the Assembly, it remained the central and energizing agency of government.

As S. H. Beer has shown in Britain, the Old Tory notion of the monarch reflecting the national interest and the legislature reflecting individual and local interests helped to entrench the idea of a central initiating executive to give national leadership and to provide national protection[1]. This principle of central initiation and control was carried forward in the province of Canada as the governing party leader and his cabinet appropriated the old central initiating responsibilities of the governor. Responsible government without this monarchial heritage could just as easily have led to a weak, passive executive which would be little more than a vague coordinator of the separate and decentralized initiatives of parliamentarians. In fact in New Brunswick, for example, where American notions of local democracy ran deep, this variant of responsible government thrived during the first part of the nineteenth century.

This principle of a central initiating executive in the Canadas remains perhaps one of the more potent forces contributing to the executive's predominance in the Canadian state system. Today provincial as well as Federal governments are led by central initiating executives, even under minority Governments. This principle has contributed to a state apparatus enjoying powerful resources for internal development, largely unencumbered by parliamentary interference. It has also led to the development of nationally integrative policies and decision-making processes to counterbalance the naturally decentralized forces of Canadian society. Their impact will be evident in every chapter of this book.

The tradition of a collective central energizing executive as the key engine of the state was also carried forward in Canada in the principles that the prime minister, with the help of his ministers, is to assume the leadership: in scheduling many of the activities of Parliament; in drawing up a budget; in formulating and implementing the broad policies of government; in proposing expenditures; in levying taxes; and in proroguing Parliament (if it is clear that the governor-general cannot find another person who can command a majority in the House). Also similar to British tradition is the principle in Ottawa, and in the provinces, of 'cabinet solidarity'. This implies that all ministers assent to the decisions of the cabinet as a whole and are answerable to Parliament for the work of their portfolio.

Another concomitant of British influences is Canada's bicameral legislative system: the popularly elected House of Commons and the appointed Senate. Many of the rules and procedures of the two Canadian Houses are borrowed from Westminster. Bills may originate in either the Senate or the House, except money bills, which can originate only in the House of Commons. Bills must pass both Houses and receive Royal Assent before becoming law. As at Westminster, most public bills originate in the House of Commons; but in contrast to Westminster, the Canadian Senate does not enjoy the right of 'suspensive veto'. It must pass, amend or defeat bills sent to it from the Commons. As at Westminster, differences between both Houses are usually settled without serious conflict, mostly in favour of the Commons. Another similarity to British practice is the official position given to the Leader of the Opposition. Usually he is the leader of the party with the second largest number of seats in the House of Commons. He has been given a special salary since 1905 to fulfil his role in the work of Parliament.

Very early in Canada's constitutional development another vital principle was established: the framework was set for the persistence of French Canada. The Quebec Act of 1774, passed by the British Parliament, established the right of French Canadians to retain their language and religion. Although these rights frequently provoked misgivings in English Canada and in Westminster, (notably in Lord Durham's report of 1838 which called for the eventual 'Anglicization' of the French Canadians), they have persisted ever since. The Constitutional 'Anglicization' Act of 1791 went further. It implicitly recognized the cultural and linguistic differences in British North America and accorded the French Canadians the right to their own legislature.

Another enduring context set by the British inheritance on Canadian government and politics is the British tradition of common law which, among other things, protects certain fundamental 'rights' and 'freedoms'. It is this tradition, and not the enunciation of rights in a constitutional document, which protects liberties in Canada.

In 1960, some of these rights received formal recognition when a Canadian Bill of Rights was passed by Parliament. This Act is simply a statute, and hence it is not entrenched in the Constitution, nor does it affect the power of the provinces in the field of civil rights. (Many of these rights are receiving full protection, however, in the provinces.) The Official Languages Act of 1969 also gives the French and English languages equal status for all purposes of the Parliament and government of Canada.

(2) *Canadian Political Ideas and the Canadian State*

Canada's political attitudes and its system of government have been shaped by and given shape to a host of other social, economic and ideological patterns. The Canadian government's citizenship booklet for introducing prospective immigrants to Canada describes some of the forces this way.[2]

The historic political traditions of Western Europe, the habits of the peoples who settled in the country, the early colonial status of Canada, and the presence of a dynamic society to the south were among these influences, added to and altered by the Canadian environment.

The greater part of government was based on British law, traditions and habits of mind, including the principle that the citizenry has a right to representative political institutions. The political and cultural traditions of France which found expression in Quebec not only affected the government of that province but also had an influence on the nature of the federal government created in 1867. Similarly, the experiences of the United States, especially in governing a large country, were examined and considered by Canadians.

This is a suggestive but somewhat obscure introduction for the Canadian immigrant hoping to comprehend the vast and complex forces that have helped to make Canada what it is in the latter third of the twentieth century. The 'political traditions of Western Europe' and 'the habits of the peoples who settled in the country' add up to a host of influences too varied to summarize here, but a few interpretations are worth introducing for a foreign observer. First, the argument about European influence. Louis Hartz argues that 'new societies', like Canada and the United States, are 'fragments' of Europe, hence they necessarily unfold in a way dissimilar from the whole, that is, from Europe.[3] The full scope and character of the European drama cannot be expected to recur in the fragment, the new society. The European dynamic of feudalism with its corporate solidarity, giving way to the rationalist bourgeois Whigs with their liberal formulations, then Whiggery being assailed by the Jacobin, who inspires but eventually fears the Socialist, this unfolding and familiar drama of the European whole, can seldom be faithfully re-enacted by the fragment. One reason for this is that the new society may not begin with a social and political organization faithfully similar to the European whole. Hartz shows, in *The Liberal Tradition in America,* how socialism becomes remote as a political ideal in the United States because the corporate memory and preconditions did not exist. The United States began as a liberal individualist state and remains one. To some extent Canada also fails to develop politically in the familiar European way because, in English-speaking Canada, society began as a construct not devoted solely to corporate and monarchial imperatives but to a fair measure of individualist imperatives as well. This suggests that Canada, outside of Quebec, will unfold in ways not only somewhat dissimilar from Europe but dissimilar also from the United States, because socialist and tory sentiments are admissible and natural, if far from all-commanding, in Canada. These latter sentiments and styles, and the naturalness with which they are held, continue to distinguish English Canadians from Americans. French Canada evolved differently from France, even though it began with a pre-revolutionary corporate tradition, because it was cut off from France after the British conquest of 1759 and thus escaped many of the anti-corporatist and libertarian ideals of the French Revolution. Based upon these beginnings, it can be suggested perhaps that the Canadian political mentality is much more open and supportive to the notion of state action for national and provincial development than is the American.

Yet all new societies begin to resemble each other more than older societies in one vital sense: their fortification by nationalism. In the new nation, the tendency to generalize national experience as a new and authentic standard becomes compelling. In fact this is almost the vocation of the ideologue in the new society; he defines the new nation. He even gives up much of his identity as a 'radical' or 'liberal' or 'conservative' to receive the national emotion, to appeal to all. To some extent this has happened even in Canada. This brand of nationalism is well known in Quebec, yet it has been far more muted in English Canada. Here English Canada differs somewhat from the strident nationalism in some African states and in the United States. The ideologue as nationalist exists, but not as an anti-mother country nationalist. Canada's first prime minister evoked the greatness of a new trans-continental nation, hospitable to English and French; but he saw Canadians as loyal to the British Crown. Canada's (second Liberal and first French-Canadian) prime minister had already in 1886 as a young Member of Parliament made a famous speech out-lining the irrelevance of European 'liberalism' in a Canadian setting; as prime minister he kept Canada firmly within the British Empire. Lester Pearson saw the importance of Canada to the survival of the British Commonwealth and to peace-keeping throughout the world, but he believed sufficient national feeling existed to enable Canada to accept a new national flag. Well known too are John Diefenbaker's vision of the Canadian north, his loyalty to the monarchial tradition, and his insistence on equality for all Canadians, not simply Canadians of British or French background.

These themes hardly qualify as fully developed theories of society and government. A European might reject them as little more than a cosmetic. Certainly they are not greatly satisfying to ideologists of the class struggle, but they do reflect the impulse of a new society to define itself, however tentatively.

Generalizations of national experience as props for feelings of nationhood are not therefore totally absent in Canada at the Federal level, but they are bound to strike most new societies, and more nationalist older societies, as unusually pragmatic and un-inspiring. The muted form of nationalism in much of Canada can no doubt also be traced to the unideological nature of many of Canada's first and later settlers.

Notable in Canada is the tendency since the eighteenth century for immigrants to appear to value economic well-being as highly as, if not higher than, political symbols. One distinguished Canadian historian, suspicious of any generalities about Canadian political attitudes, suggests that immigration, especially in the eighteenth and nineteenth centuries, to the 'edge of the Canadian forest', was motivated in most cases by the immigrant's desire to improve his economic livelihood.[4] Driving the first English, Scottish, Irish and many French settlers to British North

America were not so much political or religious motives (as with the American Puritans for example) but economic motives. Nation-building 'deep into the forest' has been pursued less for its own sake than for economic necessity. This thesis may also help one to understand the pragmatic political attitudes of some of Canada's twentieth-century immigrants. Twentieth-century Canadian immigrants – eastern European, Italian, Portuguese and other peoples who came from outside the two charter groups, the English and French – do not seem to have generated intense political dissent. Since their economic situation is on the whole better than it had been in their original homeland, their relative economic deprivation compared to other Canadians may, therefore, be less resented for the first few generations than students of their condition might suspect.[5]

The citizenship pamphlet quoted earlier also mentioned as important influences on the Canadian state and society, the 'political and cultural tradition of France which has found expression in Quebec'. Here one finds a host of vital influences on Canada's political history but the citizenship pamphlet's formulation is a bit misleading. French Canada has been abandoned by France since the conquest in 1759 and Quebec has had to fight for itself since this closure. Although some historians of French Canada, such as Michel Brunet, emphasize that economic ambition has always mattered as much to *les Québecois* as has the survival of a French Canadian culture, most historians emphasize the corporate memory, the clerical, and now secular, sense of mission and identity in this province. 'While English Canadian history was being dessicated with economics, French Canadian history was enriched with passion, immediacy and purpose . . .', writes one historian.[6] It is not surprising that many English Canadians resignedly agree with Chester Martin's pungent description of English Canadian history as a 'tough and intractable business', a story not of vision but of baffled pragmatism.[7]

Yet even if English Canadian history has been largely 'dessicated with economics', some non-economic themes of self-justification, of a sense of being in the vanguard of civilized society have emerged in the past. English Canadian feelings of identity, of a 'sense of power' as members of the British Empire, was strong from 1880 to 1920. Another English Canadian theme, by no means unanimously held, yet promoted by the Conservative Party in the nineteenth and part of the twentieth century, is a deep suspicion, even moral distrust, of American political institutions. (Yet this did not stop Canada from engaging in a host of continental agreements with the United States after the Second World War up to the present.)

Since the mid-1950s, when most of the props for this English-Canadian self-justification seem to have disappeared, another more inclusive notion has tentatively appeared. This is the 'mosaic' concept of Canada which rejects the 'melting-pot' idea many ascribe to the United States. The mosaic is an idealization of reality which implies that members of different ethnic communities are able to retain their ethnic identity and yet participate to the full in national life.[8] This concept reflects the fact that the Canadian state cannot be the ultimate expression of a particular culture, coterminus with a certain region, as may have occurred under Anglo-Canadian leadership in the first fifty years after Confederation. This new idealization of Canadian reality is not without important implications for the state. Both Federal and provincial governments now are engaged in multi-cultural, not simply bicultural, support for the arts for example. The mosaic concept also supports the notion that the state should encourage indigenous cultural expression to prevent Americanization. It can also serve as a lever for increasing the viability of French-Canadian culture across Canada.

Yet for all this diversity, there is one historic tendency which has been relevant to most of Canada since the eighteenth century : She is a conservative country that has not been afraid to employ the state. The British North America Act prescribes that one of the fundamental duties of the Federal Parliament is to promote 'peace, order and good government'; Canadian social opprobrium against violence is well known. Another generalization put forward by outside observers is that Canadians like strong government, both at the provincial level and in Ottawa. Although Canadians have been affected by some of the revolutionary and self-governing traditions of the United States, these have not led to the American system of checks and balances but to strong executive government. This solution was evident both before and after responsible government was granted, almost as a reaction to the excesses of the American tradition. On the western frontier the political organization which grew out of the frontier experience was not designed to secure popular control of the population over their affairs. Outside authority dominated. This led to local protests and uprisings, yet in the process of gaining local control, the frontiers began by failing to provide the conditions for effective democratic control over their own leadership.[9]

An authoritarian tradition in Quebec, the lack of a revolutionary history, the use of the Royal Canadian Mounted Police to police the opening of Canada's west (in vivid contrast to the American 'wild west'), and much of Canada's constitutional, economic and political thought, also show a blend of conservatism and faith in the state. In Canada, judges are appointed not elected; Crown attorneys are not subject to election or dismissed when parties alternate in office; the public service is expected to serve non-partisanly. And perhaps the greater reserve and restraint of Canadians explains the existence of fewer citizens' movements and individualistic crusades against government actions in Canada compared to the United States.

(3) *The Canadian Constitution: An Introduction to its Impact on Federalism*

Regardless of the society's liking for strong governments, one might suspect that a federal division of powers within the state system could emerge as an important restraint on the growth of the state as a whole and diminish its influence in Canadian national and provincial life. And to some extent this may have occurred in Canada. A constitution need not necessarily deny the supremacy of Parliament or entrench a bill of rights to restrict the state. It can also restrict the state by delimiting the legislative competence of the various levels of government. The influential British legal scholar A. V. Dicey once suggested that 'Federal government meant weak government'. He also argued that a Federal government could not effectively interfere with the natural development of the economy. Let us look at Canada's written and unwritten federal Constitution to provide an introductory response to his first proposition and a partial response to his second.

First, however, the limits of the British North America Act as a constitutional document should be recognized. The written parts of the Canadian Constitution can be found primarily in the British North America Act of 1867, yet the Act as written in 1867 has been directly amended many times as well as having been indirectly amended by the United Kingdom Parliament, the Parliament of Canada and the provincial legislatures. The BNA Act is an Act of the United Kingdom Parliament and can therefore be directly amended only by that Parliament. Yet Westminster no longer chooses to wield this power in a way contrary to Canadian wishes. Its power now is purely formal. Also fallen into disuse are the royal power to disallow any Federal law within two years of its passage and the Federal power granted in the Act to disallow any provincial laws. The ultimate court on disputes concerning the interpretation of this Act was the Judicial Committee of the Privy Council in Great Britain until 1949. In that year the Supreme Court of Canada took over this role. The Judicial Committee of the Privy Council and the Supreme Court of Canada have redirected the original impact of various sections of the original Act. Administrative arrangements and political decisions reached by Federal and provincial governments have affected the practical effect of a number of sections of the Act. Also altering the practical effect of the Act far beyond the intentions of the original authors have been developments in transportation, communications, business organization, tax yields, and the impact of the two world wars.

It must be remembered that this Act was not intended to be a Constitutional document in the sense that the Constitution of the United States is such a document. The BNA Act is merely a British statute passed for the purpose of confederating three of Britain's colonies in British North America. Not surprisingly, it is detailed on practical matters of concern at the time, and silent on many large matters. No ringing 'we the people' prefaces the British North America Act. It is instead a pragmatic arrangement between the provinces, beginning with the phrase: 'The provinces ... have expressed their desire to be federally united into one Dominion under the Crown of the United Kingdom and Ireland with a Constitution similar in principle to that of the United Kingdom.' Later the Act goes on to complete the 'confederation business deal' with references to lumber dues, financial grants to New Brunswick, etc. In essence the Act was an agreement worked out by the Canadian and maritime politicians of the day and was occasioned in large measure by the collapse of the political system in the old province of Canada. The incapacity of any Ministry in that province from 1854 to 1864 to retain a legislative majority for much more than a year finally led to a grand coalition of parties or 'factions' in that province which was to attempt to negotiate a Confederation agreement with Nova Scotia, New Brunswick and Prince Edward Island. With the help of various subsidies, railway pledges, hopes of a larger market, and hopes of greater military safety, New Brunswick and Nova Scotia were enticed into the Confederation. Prince Edward Island joined six years later. The Act, however, should not be understood as a document which ended the ethnic or, one might say, the 'national', conflict between French and English Canadians in the province of Canada. It simply transposed these conflicts to a larger political arena, the new Parliament of Canada.

The BNA Act was in no way meant to be a comprehensive constitutional framework. It was concerned with providing solutions to those problems with which the conventions and practices of British constitutionalism could not deal. Small wonder then that the Special Joint Committee of the Senate and the House of Commons on the Constitution of Canada, in its final report in 1972, commented that:

> ...the measure of the inadequacy of the British North America Act is that it does not serve Canadians fully as either a mirror of ourselves or as an inspirational ideal. As enacted in 1867 it did not attempt explicitly to set forth any values or goals at that time except to adopt 'a Constitution similar in Principle to that of the United Kingdom'. Whatever values it recognizes are implicit in that statement, or have to be inferred from the governmental structure and division of powers it establishes.

The Americans, like the French during their revolution, believed in the efficacy of statements of abstract principles. Both apparently believed these statements were essential not only for national cohesion but for an inspired consensual political community. In contrast, the politicians who brought the Canadian confederation into being mirror the prejudices of Edmund Burke against this approach. Canada's founding fathers were pragmatic. They felt lofty statements of principles and goals unnecessary. Though devoted to some principles of individual liberty such as freedom of the judiciary and freedom from arbitrary power they did not develop these ideas in the British North America Act. The rights of British citizens were, for them, sufficient. It was assumed that these rights would be enforced through the common law, through the cultural tradition of respect for freedom, and it was assumed that the Opposition in Parliament would be zealous as well.[10]

A key British inheritance implicit in the Act is the doctrine of the 'Supremacy of Parliament'. This principle is imported into Canada not without some dilution. In Canada, the federal Parliament can make any law it wishes, or repeal any law it wishes, on matters of Federal jurisdiction: the courts have no authority to declare illegal any statute passed by the federal Parliament that is clearly within Federal jurisdiction. In practice this supremacy is limited by the cultural and political restraints on the Federal government. These prevent political executives from using Parliament in reprehensible ways (such as eradicating the Opposition, or restricting freedom of speech, or denying traditional procedures of the courts). It is true however, that the courts have built up rules of statutory interpretation which they expect the federal Parliament to have in mind when it passes an Act (such as the assumption that a statute shall not have retroactive effect). It is important not to overestimate the effect of judicial interpretation, however, because it is only in the event of lack of clarity in the wording of the Act that the courts can resort to techniques of interpretation to bring about what they regard as a just result. The concept of parliamentary supremacy involves the notion that, if the words of the Act are clear, they must be given full effect. It is possible to conclude, as does one Canadian student of this subject, that although the courts have been able to control legislative power somewhat through the principles of statutory interpretation and through their power to decide whether legislation falls within Federal or provincial jurisdiction, that 'judges have never been willing bluntly and openly to substitute their view of policy for that of the legislators. The subordinate role assumed by the court and their relationship to Canada's legislatures constitutes one of the most fundamental differences between Canada's constitutional system and that of the United States.'[11] Another restriction established by judicial interpretation in Canada is the court's rule that the federal Parliament and provincial legislatures cannot delegate power to each other. Yet even this restriction appears easy to avoid because it might be possible for a Federal government to delegate powers to a list of named people who incidentally could be members of the Federal, or a provincial, legislature. No provision was made in this statute for an amendment process, and no agreement on one – except for unanimity of all the provinces and the federal Parliament – has been reached since. Another omission is that, although there is now a final Court of Appeal or Supreme Court for Canada, the British North America Act did not originally provide for one. It was assumed that final appeals would go to the Judicial Committee of the Privy Council in London. Nor is any reference made in the Act to what at the time Walter Bagehot would have called, the 'efficient' parts of the British Constitution, such as the office of prime minister, the cabinet, and the political parties.

The British North America Act has affected, and has been affected by, the growth of the state in important areas of public policy. First, it is vital to recognize that the division of powers outlined in the British North America Act clearly gives more power to the federal Parliament than to the provincial legislatures, and this obviously favours a system in which Parliament would be the dominant authority. (The division of power as set out in sections 91 and 92 can be seen in the appendix to this book, pp. 235–40.) The 'peace, order and good government' clause, the federal Parliament's power to disallow provincial legislation, the explicit grant of residual power to the federal Parliament, and the nature of the power given to the federal Parliament in sections 24, 58, 59, 90, 93, 94, 95 and 96, all indicate that the federal structure was to be heavily centralist.

Well-known to all students of Canadian constitutional law, however, is the fact that this centralist emphasis was altered to a large extent by many decisions of the Judicial Committee of the Privy Council. The committee extended provincial authority by expanding provincial jurisdiction under the provinces' 'property and civil rights' power and its powers under Section 92 : 16 (see Appendix). The Judicial Committee also developed the principle that the provincial legislatures were not subordinate to the federal Parliament but were as sovereign in their jurisdiction as was the federal Parliament in its jurisdiction. After '105 years of judicial interpretation and of legislative and administrative practice, we now have [in the words of the Final Report of the Special Joint

Committee of the Senate and the House of Commons on the Constitution of Canada in 1972] a Constitution where the legislative power is about equally divided between the provincial legislatures and the federal Parliament'. This assessment by Federal parliamentarians may be biased. It should be read along with the perceptions of a number of provincial legislatures that since 1940 the Federal government on the whole has grown more powerful than provincial governments through its use of its spending powers (which will be discussed below) and its more generous tax base. To assess who has power, one must take into account the fact that each province's relations with Ottawa differ. Several provinces now have, and always have had, special constitutional *provisions* without having special legislative *powers* compared to other provinces. For example, Quebec is allowed to use its civil law system in the area of 'property and civil rights' since this falls under the area of private law which is under provincial jurisdiction for all provinces. There are also Federal-provincial legislative *provisions* which apply in some provinces, although these do not give any province special legislative *powers*.

Beyond this distinction an examination of the unfolding of the constitutional division of powers between the Federal and provincial governments reveals that Canada was not established with many hermetically-sealed legislative powers for each level of government. Instead, consultation and tacit acknowledgement between the two levels was built into the federation from the start.

The most penetrating, yet apparently unassailable, right of the federal Parliament has been its power to make payments to individuals, institutions and provincial legislatures for all manner of purposes, including purposes for which it does not necessarily have the *substantive* power to legislate. The Canadian constitutional provisions concerning this spending power can be found primarily in the power which stems from the division of legislative jurisdiction as stipulated in sections 91 to 95. The courts have interpreted in favour of the Federal spending power primarily on the basis of section 91(1A) which gives the Parliament of Canada authority to legislate in respect of 'the public debt and property', and section 91(3) which permits 'the raising of money by any mode or system of taxation'. The Federal government, therefore, has been able to make expenditures for any purpose as long as the legislation authorizing the expenditure does not constitute an invasion of provincial jurisdiction. This use of the spending power of Parliament has been challenged by a number of provincial governments, but it remains a fact that Parliament makes these payments both conditionally and unconditionally. Such payments now represent more than 30 per cent of Federal government expenditures and more than half the revenues of some provincial governments. (In the Constitutional proposals of the Federal government in the late 1960s, entitled *Federal Provincial Grants and Spending Powers of Parliament,* the Federal government reaffirmed its right to make payments to individuals, institutions and provincial governments, but it did suggest certain restrictions on its power to make conditional payments to the provinces. It indicated that the Federal government no longer need exercise its power to decide unilaterally when a shared-cost programme with the provinces ought to be initiated.)

Ottawa's use of the Federal spending power has spawned the many conditional and unconditional grants to the provinces. In many instances these grants have forced provincial governments to alter their priorities in order to adjust to Federal priorities. Quebec therefore has opted out of certain joint programmes. Pursuant to the Established Programmes Act (transitional agreements) Quebec receives a portion of its compensation by receiving more of the income tax paid to Ottawa by its citizens than do other provinces (the units of compensation are called 'tax points'.) Even the Parliamentary Committee Report of 1972, quoted earlier, admitted that the aim of these conditional payments 'is to influence the provincial governments so that some of their services will take the national interest into a greater account and, especially, to enable them to achieve standards regarded as a minimum for Canada as a whole.'

The formulae for these grants are widely different, depending on the programme. Table 1 shows the respective formulae used in calculating the amounts to be paid to each provincial government for three key programmes. These amounts are always equivalent to 50 per cent of the total national costs for each of the programmes (in the case of assistance to post-secondary education, the proportion is slightly higher) but the formulae take into account either average provincial or average national costs or

Table 1
Factors Determining the Federal Grant

Programme	Average Provincial Cost	Average National Cost
Health insurance	0 per cent	50 per cent
Hospital insurance	25	25
Post-secondary education	50	0

both. These programmes have been the most expensive shared costs programmes for the Federal and provincial governments.

Moving to the federal Parliament's other powers to legislate, one finds the usual Federal powers over banking, criminal law, foreign affairs, defence, trade and the postal services, enjoyed by most central governments, set out in section 91 of the British North America Act. The declaratory clause in the Act sets out a number of other areas of legislative competence for Parliament 'for greater Certainty but not so as to restrict the Generality of the foregoing Terms of this section'. Through this declaratory clause the Act states that the legislative authority of Parliament extends to the enumerated classes of subjects 'notwithstanding anything in this Act'. Then follows the enumeration outlined in the appendix. After this enumeration of exclusive Federal powers comes the crucial 'deeming clause'. The intent of this clause was to ensure that the enumerated classes of matters of section 91 took precedence over section 92(16) in the provincial list of powers. The Judicial Committee of the Privy Council in its history of interpretation did not, however, pay much attention to this until the 1930s when it began a rehabilitation of this general power. This rehabilitation continued in various decisions of the Supreme Court of Canada after it became the court of final resort in 1949. As a result, various areas of public policy such as broadcasting, regulation of the national capital district, and some labour relations powers have been assigned to the Federal level under this general power. The parliamentary committee on the Constitution was able to feel sufficient confidence to report in 1972 that 'the General Power is therefore no longer a merely residual power nor is it likely to become so again'.

Another resource of the Federal power is the power of Parliament to pass measures for 'the raising of Money by any Mode or System of Taxation' (section 91(3)). Because of this, provincial legislatures were to be confined primarily to direct taxation. Interpretations of this constitutional provision have been broad, and have permitted considerable flexibility. Now there is virtual and complete accessibility for both levels of government to any tax field (with the exception that provincial governments seem to be denied access to the indirect sales tax). This accessibility has occurred because for some time the presently established Federal tax fields are generating more revenues than are the usual provincial and municipal tax fields. This has led to considerable provincial pressure on the Federal government to allow more tax room to the provinces. To date, the Federal government has preferred to respond to provincial needs by its use of conditional and unconditional grants and through equalization grants.

Turning to provincial powers it is interesting to note that one of the distinguishing features of the Canadian division of powers is the fact that provincial legislatures have always had considerable responsibility for social security. Paragraphs 6, 7 and 8 of section 92 gave the provinces exclusive authority over public and reformatory prisons, hospitals, asylums and charities as well as municipal institutions (paragraphs 11 and 28 of section 91 gave legislative authority to the Canadian Parliament in respect of marine hospitals and penitentiaries). The British North America Act was amended in 1941 to transfer to Parliament exclusive power over unemployment insurance. In 1951 Parliament was granted concurrent legislative power with respect to old age pensions. In 1964 this was extended to cover survivors' and disability benefits in respect of age. Ottawa's penetration into the welfare field has also increased through shared cost programmes with the provinces.

Education, however, has always been dominated by provincial jurisdiction. The provisions of the British North America Act for education make the jurisdiction of the provinces clear. However, the final report of the Joint Parliamentary Committee on the Constitution reflects the inclination of Federal Governments to try to make its influence felt here as well. 'Since the passing of the Act great changes have taken place in the character of the population and in economic, technological and social conditions, which have produced a progressive, affluent, urban-oriented society. Consequently the Federal government has had to assume an indirect and limited role in education.' So even in education the Federal government has begun to play a role. Some provinces, particularly Quebec, are in favour of a return to full provincial jurisdiction over education and oppose any interference by Federal authorities. But, the federal Parliament's pursuit of its legitimate constitutional powers in culture, research and training institutes has led to heavy indirect Federal funding of education regardless of provincial disquiet.

Let us now examine some of the less clear-cut areas of legislative power in Canada.

Communications. In 1867 'communications' meant telegraph lines, the post and transportation. Thus the British North America Act deals with this subject only in section 92(10) (a) and (b). In 1932, the Judicial Committee of the Privy Council, relying on the doctrine of the Federal general power, held that regulation and control of radio communications was within the exclusive jurisdiction of Parliament. Since that time, Parliament has regulated radio and subsequently television. The Province of Quebec in 1945, however, passed its own Broadcasting Act, authorizing the creation of a provincial broadcasting system. The Federal government refused to issue a broadcasting licence to the province or to a corporation owned by the province. Finally, in 1968, a new Federal Broadcasting Act, following the recommendations of a Royal Commission, suggested that facilities should be provided within the Canadian Broadcasting System for educational broadcasting. There has, then, been some evolution from exclusive Federal control of the field of communications to acceptance by the Federal government that provinces might share Federal facilities in the field of educational broadcasting. In 1969, the Quebec Government introduced an Act to update the 1945 Act (which had remained on its statute books after the Federal rebuff). The 1972 Joint Parliamentary Committee Report summarizes developments since 1969 :

Although the Bureau was granted wide powers, programmes produced by it were required still to be transmitted by federally licensed stations. Following this legislation, the Federal government cancelled its plans to establish a federal educational broadcasting agency and moved towards the recognition of a provincial role in educational television.

The principal constitutional problem has not been provincial rights in the field of education as such, but rather what type of broadcasting constitutes education. Ontario and Alberta were as interested as Quebec in arriving at a solution, and in 1969 the secretary of state and the council of ministers of education worked out a definition acceptable to all for purposes of implementing the new policy.

Trade and Commerce. Another major field of public policy in any federal state is the regulation of trade and commerce. It is well known that in the United States the Federal power over commerce has been a major instrument of Federal economic leadership and control. Nor is the United States unique. In Australia, for example, the Constitution gives paramountcy to Commonwealth over state legislation in matters of 'trade and commerce with other countries and among the states'. In Canada the language of section 91(2) of the British North America Act, granting 'regulation of trade and commerce' to the federal Parliament, suggests that Parliament has control over the whole field. The Judicial Committee of the Privy Council's interpretations defined this clause very strictly, making no distinction between trade *and* commerce and interpreting the power of regulation as not including the power of prohibition. One Federal lever over trade within Canada, however, is Parliament's power to designate grain elevators, mill and feed warehouses 'for the general advantage of Canada' under sections 91(29) and 92(10)(c) in order to gain a measure of control over the grain trade. It has even been suggested that 92(10)(c) is an open-ended power, and that this allows the Federal government to declare any work to be for the general advantage of Canada or for the advantage of two or more provinces. An appropriate bargain with the provinces, therefore, would be to eliminate this open-ended power and to equip the federal Parliament instead with more adequate and specific powers to control the instrumentality of trade and commerce. It is unclear how this matter will be resolved, if ever.

Environmental Protection. A major area of public policy in the latter third of this century centres on control over the pollution of air and water. Federal and provincial sources in the British North

America Act for controlling pollution are varied. Provincial sources stem from their jurisdiction over 'property and civil rights' or over 'municipal institutions in the province' or over 'local works and undertakings' or its control over 'all matters of a merely local or private nature in the province'. Federal jurisdiction, on the other hand, usually follows from its power over 'the criminal law', 'navigation and shipping', 'seacoast and inland fisheries' and 'the regulation of trade and commerce'. The Federal minister of the environment reported that in the two years up to May 1972 the Federal government attained 184 successful convictions under the Fisheries Act and the Shipping Act.[12] It is obvious now that an increasing number of environmental problems cannot be solved within any of these narrow compartments and they have led to a number of *ad hoc* joint federal-provincial actions. For example, the proposed huge Quebec James Bay Hydro Development is a matter of provincial environment concern through its jurisdictions over wild life, forestry and river management, whereas certain Federal powers over migratory birds, navigable waters, fisheries and Indian Affairs involve Ottawa. The Federal minister explained Federal leverage this way:

... we in Ottawa are offering our expertise. In addition to expertise in environmental protection, we are offering the services of our experts in the related fields of fisheries, migratory birds, oceanography, forestry and meteorology. I am glad to say that these offers are being accepted. Some of our people are already hard at work alongside key personnel from Quebec in assessing those elements of the local ecology that might be affected by a big hydro project in that area. Several other Federal government departments are pooling their resources to assist other related problems.[13]

At the Federal level, more than thirty Acts are concerned with environment protection. Many of these grant very broad powers to government. Other pieces of legislation giving equally generous grants of powers to government exist at provincial levels.

Criminal Law and Economic Regulation. A vital instrument for regulation or prohibition in any federal state is the lever provided by control over criminal law. Because of the limitations which the Judicial Committee of the Privy Council placed upon the Federal government's 'general' power and the 'trade and commerce' power, it is the criminal law power in section 91(27) that has turned out to be one of the Federal government's more comprehensive powers. It is important to note, however, that the provinces have jurisdiction when it comes to imposing punishment and imprisonment. Together with its jurisdiction over provincial prisons, provincial governments have power over the *administration* of justice in general in the province. In effect, then, there is a situation resembling concurrent jurisdiction over criminal law, although it seems clear from various cases that when the two levels conflict Federal paramountcy is usually confirmed. Also, the existing Federal power over procedure in criminal matters is wide, and no doubt establishes complete Federal control in all prosecutions under criminal legislation. What is more, the Federal government is able to take the position that the administration of justice by the provinces now exists because of Federal tolerance rather than as a constitutional right.

Canada's provinces have considerable power in the fields of economic regulation – in insurance, the marketing of natural products, manufacturing, the service and distributive trades, and labour relations. Yet Ottawa can use the criminal code to act in some of these areas, for example in the field of restrictive trade practices. Although it has de-emphasized the criminal law here in the past twenty years, Parliament has dealt with restrictive trade practices primarily through the use of its criminal law power. The regulation of competition, truth in advertising, price maintenance, and the conditions under which firms might combine, consolidate or be absorbed has been considered on the whole to be dominated by Federal regulation.

When it comes to the marketing of securities in Canada, it is a different story. While Canadian securities markets and financal structures are in effect national, the jurisdiction to regulate them in Canada is provincial. What is more, there is a marked lack of uniformity in laws and regulations from province to province. Consequently, not only is there a lack of protection for the investor in many situations, but various provinces can use weak securities law or enforcement to entice corporations to incorporate in their province. The major devices used to regulate security trading are through the licensing of investment dealers and through laws which require information to be disclosed to the public. The Federal government introduced stiffer regulations on the latter in 1970 through its criminal law power to prohibit fraudulent dealing in securities, but at present most of the regulation is carried out by provincial securities commissions. The courts have not accepted the argument that the federal Parliament could exercise more jurisdiction here through its use of the trade and commerce clause or through its power over the Post Office. As the Joint Parliamentary Committee on the Constitution noted in 1972, Canada has been unable to accept the American argument that there should be a national jurisdiction for security regulation, because of the fear that Federal control over securities might simply draw capital resources from the smaller urban centres and regions to the major markets in Toronto, Montreal and Vancouver.

A Note on Canada's Integrated Judiciary. Canada's judicial system, whilst federal, is unlike the United States' vertically parallel state and federal courts: the jurisdictions of Canada's courts are in essence divided horizontally. In Canada a piece of litigation can progress from provincial to Federal courts. The Supreme Court of Canada is the court of final resort and it generally hears appeals from provincial supreme courts. The two main types of law in Canada are: criminal laws, which deal with crimes such as murder, arson, rape and theft – these are laws enacted by the federal Parliament, and apply to all of Canada, and the Federal government is responsible for bringing the accused to trial; and civil laws, enacted largely by the provinces since they generally arise within the province's jurisdiction for 'property and civil rights'. As a result these laws vary from province to province. Quebec's law, for example, has been codified under the model of the French civil code. As noted earlier, the highest court of final resort was once the Judicial Committee of the Privy Council in London. Its role as highest court is now filled by the Supreme Court of Canada (although this court was established in 1875 appeals could still be made to the Judicial Committee in London up to 1949). The Supreme Court sits in Ottawa and it is made up of nine judges – the chief justice of Canada and eight puisne judges. Judges are appointed to the age of seventy-five years. The Supreme Court is the general court of appeal but it usually hears only criminal appeals in the case of capital offences, appeals from the highest provincial court in civil matters above a certain amount of funds, cases from the highest provincial court on a constitutional reference where provincial law admits and, dramatically dissimilar from the United States, matters referred to it by the Federal government for opinion.

The Federal Court was set up by the Federal Court Act of 1970. It consists of the Trial Division, which as a court of original jurisdiction now does the work of the old Exchequer Court. This dealt with disputes based on the board, tribunal and commission decisions arising out of the Excise Act, Customs Act, Income Tax Act, Patent Act, Shipping Act and National Defence Act, Immigration Act and new areas of responsibility since the 1970 reforms, such as jurisdiction in matters relating to bills of exchange, promissory notes, aeronautics and works and undertakings extending beyond the limits of a province which previously were exclusive to provincial courts. An appeal is granted from the final judgement of the Trial Division to the Appeal Division of the federal court on matters of natural justice or on errors in law or fact. From there an appeal is given, on certain matters, to the Supreme Court of Canada without leave of either the Appeal Division or the Supreme Court.

Below the Federal level is the provincial court system. The lowest level of the hierarchy here is the magistrates' courts, which are appointed by the provinces and which deal with breaches of traffic laws, petty theft and minor domestic cases. Then there are circuit, county or district courts, which have jurisdiction within a county or district and may deal with criminal and civil cases. These are presided over by a judge, appointed and paid by the Federal government. Division courts are also established in some provinces for hearing civil cases (usually excluding tort actions such as libel, slander and actions concerning estates of deceased persons). These are presided over by a judge, but the procedure is informal, geared to speedy resolution of disputes. Some provinces also have surrogate courts for each county or district, whose jurisdiction includes most testamentary matters. Finally the provincial supreme courts are the high courts of justice. There is one in each province, known as the Supreme Court, or the Superior Court or the Court of Queen's Bench. This court hears appeals from lower courts within the province and has unlimited jurisdiction in both civil and criminal cases. The Supreme Court can, as in the case of

Ontario, divide itself into a Court of Appeal and a High Court. Salaries are set by Federal statute and paid by the Federal government although the courts themselves are established and administered by the province.

The independence of the Federal judiciary in Canada is protected by the following: no minister of the Crown is held accountable in Parliament for the actions of the judiciary; judges' salaries are specified in a separate statute and are distinct from the departmental estimates; appointments to the judiciary are for lengthy tenure; and, most important of all, a large consensus of opinion in Canada seems to preserve the notion that the judiciary should remain free from external political coercion.

(4) *Dicey's Argument Re-examined*

When one examines the great decisions on the divisions of power between the two levels of government, and the *ad hoc* arrangements both levels of government have worked out, it becomes clear that, although there are some real impediments to concerted state action in a number of areas, Federal-provincial collaboration is possible and necessary on a host of policy issues. In fact, many jurisdictions have become increasingly porous. It is difficult, for example, to find many provincial legislative prerogatives so exclusive that Ottawa (through its spending power on allocative policy and through the criminal code on regulatory policy) cannot affect provincial activity and priorities to some degree. Even though A. V. Dicey has argued that Federal government means 'weak government', that power divided means power diluted, these arguments are far from confirmed in Canada.

Here, not only have both levels of government collaborated to allow the state to act but the courts have also assisted. The potential for overlapping and for concurrency in legislative activity did not become apparent until after the Second World War. Since that time, the courts have allowed large areas of legislative overlapping, by finding for most pieces of impugned legislation a legitimate compartment in the distribution of legislative powers. The courts have also taken an extremely narrow view of the bases for 'conflict'. Now only rarely will the Supreme Court of Canada find that Federal and provincial legislation in the same area actually conflict. In short, except for some selected clear restrictions on

29

Federal activism in a few thorny areas of regulatory policy, Canada's constitutional development has increasingly revealed the ability of the over-all state system in Canada to grow, in spite of Dicey's pessimism about federal Constitutions. We will explore this further in the next chapter. We have also seen that the political and economic attitudes of most Canadians, together with Canada's constitutional development, have not been antithetical to the idea of strong state action when required. The development of the strong central executive and of legal Parliamentary supremacy, together with attitudes favourable to state-initiated nation-building schemes, to the state's economic leadership, and to the state's maintenance of 'peace, order and good government', all provide a framework for the growth of the state in Canada. We will trace some of the results of this in chapters 2 and 3.

2 Collaboration and Coexistence: The State Network for Province-Building and Nation-Building

Part of the foregoing chapter introduced the effect of Canada's Constitution on the activity of the state. Yet to concentrate on the Constitution will not take us far if we wish to understand all of the forces that help to create both a nation-state and provincial communities in Canada. This chapter will introduce some of these other forces.

The provinces have not been left to develop spontaneously. As we have seen, the Federal government has involved itself increasingly in provincial life. But equally important for understanding the impact of the state on Canadian society, provincial governments have not allowed provincial societies to languish. They have acted to help define the nature of provincial society. Many dimensions of 'province-building' merit attention in a book on Canadian government.

(1) *The Provinces and Province-Building*

The substance of provincial government activity is as important for defining Canadian society as is the activity of the Federal government. Also, the relationship of the provinces with the Federal government is important for understanding the texture and the character of the Canadian political system. This understanding, however, is always difficult in Canada because political rhetoric promoted by partisan advocates of provincial or Federal causes too often obscures the mass of collaboration and functional coexistence in Federal-provincial relations. One useful measure of the potency of each level of government is respective levels of expenditure. Yet even this can be misleading, since in the Canadian federal system, the Federal government finds itself spending billions of dollars for purposes and projects over which in effect the provinces have closer administrative and technical influence than does the Federal government (health, welfare and post-secondary education are examples). In contrast, provincial governments have found themselves under an obligation to spend millions of dollars for various activities because the Federal government has persuaded them to carry out such activities through shared-cost enticements. Finally, if one wishes to delve even deeper and take a look at the fabric of Federal-provincial consultation on joint programmes, it is not easy to know for sure which level of government, in the short run or the long run, will eventually emerge as the more influential in a policy area if the statutory framework under which joint programmes are to be pursued remains unchanged.

This much said, the continuing influence and very real power of most provincial governments has been and is likely to remain strong in the Canadian federation for decades to come. First, provincial governments perform substantial economic functions. How substantial is revealed in part when the level of provincial spending is combined with local or municipal spending and compared to Federal spending. (About one-half of combined 'provincial and local' spending is accounted for by 'local and municipal' expenditures. It must be remembered however, that a sizeable portion of this 'local and municipal' spending – about three-quarters of the total – is provided for by provincial government grants.[1] It must also be remembered that, unlike the provinces' relation to Ottawa, local governments are legal creatures of provincial legislatures. Therefore, both legally and financially, provincial control over local activity is substantial). Provincial and local spending combined has surpassed Federal spending each year since the mid-1960s. Equally significant a large portion of Federal spending is made up of funds shifted to the provinces for expenditures on provincial activities which provide for little Federal control of standards, i.e. secondary education, hospital construction, medical care and various welfare programmes.[2]

The total budgets of Ontario and Quebec together equal about

GOVERNMENT SECTOR REVENUE AND EXPENDITURE
BY LEVEL OF GOVERNMENT

NATIONAL INCOME AND EXPENDITURE ACCOUNTS BASIS
(Quarterly, Seasonally Adjusted at Annual Rates)

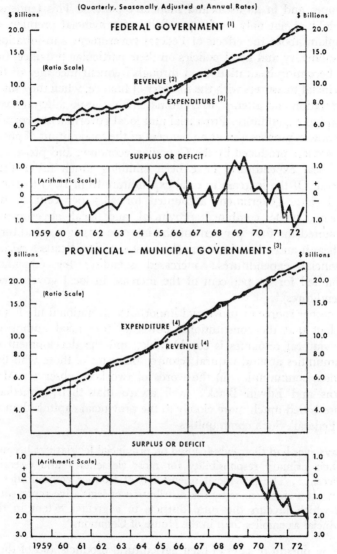

FEDERAL GOVERNMENT [1]

REVENUE [2]

EXPENDITURE [2]

SURPLUS OR DEFICIT

PROVINCIAL — MUNICIPAL GOVERNMENTS [3]

EXPENDITURE [4]

REVENUE [4]

SURPLUS OR DEFICIT

(1) Excludes Canada Pension Plan and Quebec Pension Plan
(2) Includes transfers to other levels.
(3) Includes Hospitals.
(4) Excludes all inter-governmental transfers except Federal to Provincial and Municipal.

Source: see note 1, p. 32

three-fifths of the Federal budget. It is not surprising that because of the increased costs of their responsibilities provincial governments are demanding a greater voice in Federal distribution of revenues and in its fiscal and monetary policies. This tendency is exhibited not only in the proclivity of provincial premiers to complain about the effects of Federal government anti-inflationary monetary and fiscal policies on their particular province, but it is becoming institutionalized through frequent meetings of the provincial treasurers with the minister of finance, when they share information and attempt to coordinate policy, especially on levels of capital expenditure. Provincial and local government expenditure now comprises almost 20 per cent of the total output of goods and services produced by the Canadian economy, and provincial and local expenditures have been climbing much faster than Federal. Of the increase in total expenditure from 1960 to 1969, the Federal government accounted for 38.7 per cent of the increase, while combined provincial and local governments accounted for 61.3 per cent of the increase (rising expenditures for health and education were the most significant causes raising provincial expenditures: increased spending for education accounted for 45 per cent of the increase in local government expenditures).[3]

Another source of provincial importance in national life lies in the fact that the constitutional power of provincial authorities over natural resources is considerable, and the development of communities around natural resource bases make those who live in these communities (in the words of two keen observers Alan Cairns and Edwin Black), 'well aware that their immediate future is tied much more closely to the provincial capitals than to the Federal'. Such communities

have ever had their eyes focused on provincial legislatures because of their primary responsibility for most elementary and essential services. ... The provincial orientation of frontier communities is given extra significance by the distribution of legislative representation which favours the rural districts to a greater extent in the provincial assemblies than in the House of Commons.[4]

Also, in pursuit of sales of their agricultural products and of their natural resources, the provinces have even opened missions in foreign capitals.

34

Another, but less comprehensive, measure of the importance of provincial and local governments is their number of employees. The Canada Yearbook shows that on 31 December 1970 the total number of Federal government employees reached 378,986 and that provincial (not local) employment probably equalled this amount. If civilian, not military, employment is considered, provincial governments now employ more personnel in total than does the Federal government.[5]

The tendency of each province to develop around a key metropolitan centre, with few counter-pulls to cities outside the province, may in fact give rise to considerable allegiance to the provinces as political units. This experience, according to the Canadian historian J. M. S. Careless, contributes to 'limited identities' in Canada.[6] Canadian experience to date, therefore, may be in contrast to the American experience of the growing homogeneity of political attitudes through urbanization. Since the turn of the century, the four western provinces have also been distinguished from Canada's other provinces by their high proportion of foreign-born inhabitants (although the foreign-born population of Ontario has been growing since the Second World War as well). Also, the conflict between the interests of primary versus secondary industry in Canada has tended to be reflected in part by provincial boundaries. Conflicts arise, for example, between those provinces oriented to primary industry, such as British Columbia and Alberta, and a province such as Ontario which is geared more to services and secondary industry. A further source of conflict, articulated primarily by the maritime provinces, is the other regional economic cleavage in Canada, the per capita income differential, which has diminished very little over the past forty years, and remains one of the more compelling reasons for the maritimes feeling somewhat alienated from the more wealthy provinces in Canada.

Despite improved communications, Canada's great distances still require considerable bureaucratic and political decentralization, and this also helps to contribute to the persistence of local identities. Such loyalties are obvious in the case of Quebec. But they seem to remain strong in all parts of Canada. For example, in a nationwide survey of Canadian attitudes carried out at the end of 1969 by a daily newspaper, the following patterns were exposed:

35

In the maritimes, no less than 52 per cent of the people thought of themselves first as Nova Scotians or New Brunswickers or Prince Edward Islanders, and only afterwards as Canadians. 34 per cent of the people in the prairie provinces declared their local loyalties stronger than their national ones; 28 per cent of the British Columbians felt their land within the mountains more important than Canada; only in Ontario, which identifies with the concept of Confederation more closely than in the other regions, was the fraction of local patriots negligible.[7]

It is clear, then, that since 1867 Canadians have been engaged not only in nation-building but in province-building as well. The existence of separate provincial governments has elicited, even in Ontario, as intense a pattern of communications and associational activity within provincial boundaries as across them. As Black and Cairns have noted, 'mechanisms set in motion by the creation of political institutions permit provinces such as Saskatchewan and Alberta, which possessed little sociological legitimacy at their birth, to acquire it with the passage of time and the creation of a unique provincial history'.[8] Some provincial government activity provides the major source of employment for some professional groups and for those involved in certain types of technical work. This helps further to contribute to the importance of provincial governments as sources of power in the Canadian condominium, and to the maintenance of regional and provincial identities. In spite of this, the collaborative network with Ottawa has widened greatly in the last forty years. Since much of this collaboration is brought about by technological, industrial and other economic forces, these features of provincial communities deserve a brief introduction.

(2) *Some Economic and Social Characteristics of the Provinces*

Any account of the significance and nature of province-building in Canada should include an introduction to the economic patterns and aspirations of each province. A brief summary risks caricaturing what are far more complicated realities, yet to prevent an impression of homogeneous patterns and aspirations it is important to note briefly some of the more dominant economic characteristics of each province.

As an economic unit, British Columbia (just over 2 million in population) is heavily dependent both directly and indirectly on resource extraction. Over one-half of the value of industrial output is in four groups of industries: fish-packing, wood products, paper products and primary metals (mainly lead, zinc and aluminium smelting industries which involve very little processing). In the rest of Canada, for example, these four industry groups account for less than 25 per cent of total industrial output. Manufacturing industries contribute less to the value added of the provincial economy than other wealthy provinces (47.8 per cent compared to Ontario's 71.9 per cent and Quebec's 67.9 per cent in 1970).[9] Canada's secondary manufacturing sector is weakly represented in this province and its service sector is auxiliary to the resource-centred industries. Wages and incomes in the province are high compared to the rest of Canada, almost $10 more per week (industrial composite) than Ontario which comes second. These wages have made British Columbia a magnetic force attracting population. The provincial government has often complained that it should have at least more informal control over immigration because the influx of people that it attracts further reduces its per capita wealth, and increases the services it must provide. This province's Government has also complained that it is senselessly discriminated against in Federal regional disparity programmes and in 'roads to resources' programmes. Perhaps the best-known provincial complaint, however, is the Canadian tariff. To quote the provincial premier's perhaps overstated summary in 1968:

Under the national policy of tariffs, they [the eastern industries] have an umbrella over all the markets east and west and they get that protection and sell their goods everywhere. But British Columbia does not get the benefit of selling in the rest of Canada in the protective market. We are on the extreme west. We sell our merchandise . . . on competitive world markets.[10]

In fact, British Columbia's forest industry exports face, in general, rather low tariffs in their major markets, the United States and the United Kingdom. Except for lead and zinc, the same is true for its exports of most minerals. The fishing industry's external restraints are not so much tariffs as international bilateral fishing agreements, which limit the catch of such major species as halibut

37

and salmon in the North Pacific. Yet it is accurate to insist that, under free trade, the province would no doubt purchase foods and various manufacturing goods at reduced prices.

British Columbia has a larger proportion of organized labour than any other province. This force, in conflict with the province's confident expansionist business community, has made for an ideological party rivalry between the free-enterprise oriented Social Credit Party and the vigorous CCF-New Democrats to the left, who finally assumed power in 1972 after over two decades of Social Credit rule.

Since the early 1950s Alberta (population just over 1.6 million) has enjoyed a buoyant if somewhat undiversified economy. It is the main source of crude oil and natural gas for the domestic market east of the Ottawa river and for markets recently opened up in the United States. Alberta has been the scene of a number of potent 'third' party movements in protest to Ottawa; first the Progressive Party in the 1920s and then the Social Credit Party. This latter party took over control of the provincial government and contested Federal seats with conspicuous success until the mid-1960s. In 1971 the Progressive Conservatives ended over thirty-five years of Social Credit rule in the province. Now, however, Alberta attracts over one-half of the total investment in the three prairie provinces, and if it appears less alienated from Ottawa, its distrust of the Federal Liberal Party has grown since 1956, and its tradition of support for individualism remains. It also enjoys a strong agricultural sector and its large reserves of coal and timber are attracting substantial investment.

Saskatchewan (almost one million population) has always been heavily dependent on its grain production. The Federal government has had to institute various wheat stockpile reduction programmes to decrease the naturally high output of wheat in that province. The decline in the enforced cutback of wheat production has been partly offset by increased production of other grains such as barley, rapeseed, flaxseed and other feed crops. Foreign sales to the Soviet Union and the People's Republic of China were vital to the health of the wheat economy in the 1960s and early 1970s. This province also enjoys a fairly diversified agricultural base (cattle and hogs predominate). Its mineral, petroleum and metals production have been increasing steadily. These have helped to compensate for the over-optimistic assessments of growth in the 1960s for the potash industry. The province's tradition of cooperative farm ventures and pioneering agrarian socialism is expressed in its support for the Cooperative Commonwealth Federation, now the New Democratic Party. Provincial Governments reflect sensitivity to the demands of farm families and to the needs of the working class. The New Democratic Party Government in the province also promises to watch carefully the extent to which development of industries and resources in the province involve excessive sell-outs to foreign interests.

Manitoba, with a slightly lower population than Saskatchewan, is Canada's 'gateway to the west'. It has enjoyed a dramatic and fascinating history as the seat of the Hudson's Bay Company, and the scene of the French and Métis uprising against the Federal authorities soon after Confederation. Countless other events give Manitoba's provincial history a distinctive identity. The French and Ukrainian populations rival those of British extraction for power and influence. Winnipeg has declined somewhat in its influence as a transportation hub leading to the prairies and to British Columbia. A recent example of this decline is the fact that Air Canada moved its head office and many other facilities to Montreal in the late 1960s. Manitoba is a province of small and large businesses, and many of its efforts to open large industrial and extractive enterprises, such as the forest products development at the Pas, have been plagued by problems. Mining has been the most expansionist industry in recent years in the province. Cash receipts for farm output are less than half for Alberta and Saskatchewan, but are rising slowly. Manitoba provides another somewhat classic ideological party confrontation in that as a province of small businesses it has been able to sustain a vigorous Progressive Conservative party and an equally vigorous CCF, now the New Democratic party. The province has also produced potent working-class movements in this century, especially in Winnipeg.

Ontario (over eight million population in 1971) is the most privileged province in Canada in terms of its geographical location

39

with regard to both domestic markets and to the important middle-location American markets. It has been governed since 1944 by the Progressive Conservative party. The distortions of the tariff barrier are little resented by this province because many of Ontario's industries are located in the province because of the tariff. Yet the provincial Government began to worry in the early 1970s about the extent of foreign ownership in the province and the extent to which the tariff and the branch plant profile of Ontario has discouraged specialization and product differentiation from the parent. Still, Ontario Governments have remained conscious of the two edges of the sword of economic nationalism since over one-third of Ontarians are directly employed by foreign-owned firms. As one of the richest of the Canadian provinces in terms of income, the province does not depend on Federal government regional economic expansion programmes, but benefits instead from Federal expenditures for other national programmes (such as an impending second international airport at Toronto). Ontario subsidizes less-developed regions by way of the Federal equalization grants and taxation, providing approximately 45 per cent of the total tax revenue flowing into the national treasury.[11] Not infrequently, Ontario complains about its tax burden. Only 16 per cent of provincial revenues in 1969 came from the Federal government, compared with, for example, 56 per cent for Prince Edward Island and Newfoundland.[12] The response from non-Ontarians is that Ontario benefits from the tariff which shelters its industry at the expense of the maritime and western provinces, both of which in most cases must sell abroad at competitive world prices. In fact this 'regional inequities' argument has been used to support other provinces' claims, ranging from regional national transportation subsidies to special tax concessions to primary producers, and to equalization payments to lower per capita income provinces. In 1967, Ontario accounted for 52 per cent of all wages paid in Canadian manufacturing industries. Ontario's per capita income in 1969 was $3,368 compared to Canada's $2,913.[13] Ontario also has a huge and productive mining industry. For all of Ontario's advantages however, the province is not without its internal economic problems. Distribution of development is uneven; encouragement of investment in the province has concentrated benefits in the urban areas and there have been continual complaints about provincial and Federal government neglect of northern Ontario.

Quebec's slightly over 6 million people, 80 per cent of whom are French-speaking, must deal with economic as well as linguistic and social stresses. Canada's unemployment has centred severely in the province of Quebec. In the early 1970s Quebec had close to one-third of all Canada's jobless. Pulp and paper is probably the most important industry in Quebec. There are over fifty pulp and paper mills in the province. The province also produces nearly 14 per cent of Canada's minerals and almost all of Canada's asbestos.[14] Almost one-quarter of Quebec's employed labour force was in manufacturing in 1970, and one-quarter of these were in clothing, textile and leather industries, all of which have needed considerable tariff protection to stay alive. Quebec's agricultural sector is large, and is dominated by commercial dairy farms. (Unfortunately, milk is an over-produced commodity in Canada.) Inefficiency and over-production in agriculture are problems Quebec faces in common with other provinces in Canada. Quebec hopes to attract new industries which depend more on advanced technology and which will attract highly educated people and hire growing numbers of college graduates. If this is achieved, it will balance the weight of the primary industries and the dying traditional industries such as furniture and shoes. The tourist industry, now the third largest industry in Quebec, continues to show potential, and it is being pushed in the hope that it will become a prime revenue producer. The shipping industry has also proved to be a strong revenue producer for the province.

The Quebec social system has changed in important ways since the last century and it deserves a brief introduction. In 1900 French Canada could still be described as a rural society. The bulk of its population lived in small parish units and economic activity centred on the family farm. French Canadian beliefs were set primarily by the professions which serviced the traditional societies such as the clergy, medicine and law. There was little need for contact with English Canadians, and French Canadians could meet their needs in the French language. It was in this form that French Canada survived conquest by the British.[15]

By 1921, Quebec's population was more urban than rural and by 1971 Quebec's population was over 80 per cent urban. The remainder, living outside urban centres, continues to cling to traditional values and structures. The conflict between this rural minority and the urban majority in Quebec is quite stark. Also, the new urban industrial society is largely owned and controlled not by French Canadians but by Americans or English Canadians, who in fact carried out the industrialization of Quebec almost singlehandedly, with the tolerance of the provincial government but with little participation by French Canadians. By the late 1960s, however, an administrative elite had developed in Quebec outside the predominantly English-speaking industrial structure. This elite has been able to wrest control at the provincial level from the Church through the use of the state for such functions as hospital care, educational institutions, welfare agencies, etc. There has also been a rapid reorientation of the French Canadian educational system which has moved away from the classical training of a small traditional elite. French Canadians are now able to participate more fully in the technological society. This also heightens ethnic tensions stemming from English-speaking domination of the Quebec economy, since a number of positions of administrative and technical responsibility require French Canadians to speak English as well as French.

The impact of this reorganization in French Canadian society has affected political belief systems in Quebec in profound ways.

French Canada has been set irrevocably on the path of industrialization and technological change. The credo of the new bureaucratic elite in Quebec became one of 'rattrapage' (catching up) essentially to the North American model. 'La survivance' was replaced with a more positive 'l'épanouissement'. The mission of French Canada became a secular mission: to create a modern technological society animated by a French spirit. To some extent, implicit in such a goal is greater French Canadian control of the economy of Quebec. Working-class organizations in Quebec, however, have begun to challenge parts of this image by arguing that the overall goal of French Canada must be the redistribution of economic and social benefits in favour of the working class, and by building a truly socialist society.

Traditionally, the role of government has been small. Since in a rural agrarian society the material needs of most of the population were derived from the family farm, dependence on governmental services was minimal. On this basis, then, the government had little positive role to fulfil in this society. The main concern about government was that 'it should not take actions which might harm that society. With such little positive value attached to government, it was much easier then than now to find satisfactory terms for Quebec participation in the Canadian political system.'[16] However, with the growth of the positive state in Quebec, and the use of the state for expressing the cultural and technological needs of the province, it has been difficult to find a new *modus vivendi* for Quebec within the federation.

The state is now seen as the only agent capable of generating *rattrapage* for the French Canadian society. Yet this drift has been complicated in Quebec by conflicting notions and theories of authority. A large number of French Canadians share the popularized liberal-democratic values. A small minority believe in violence for social change. Others believe in a concerted attempt to promote the working class to a more powerful role within the society. Others, such as the Ralliement Créditiste Party and parts of the Union Nationale Party, distinguish themselves from other parties in that they support more traditional values and structures (opposing any laws on sex and divorce which might contradict the Church's position, and championing a more traditional approach to authority). This pluralization of belief systems has helped to contribute to a fragmentation of the party system in Quebec so that no provincial party was able to dominate the province. The provincial election of 1973 yielded 102 seats to the Liberals although they gained in the legislature only 54.6 per cent of the popular vote, whereas the separatist Party Québecois captured 30 per cent of the vote and only six seats in Quebec.

Given these profound strains, fragmentations and challenges within the province of Quebec, it is not surprising that French Canadians have had to look to the state at the provincial level for leadership, not only to further the aims of *rattrapage* and *l'épanouissement,* but to help the French survive within North

America. How Quebec has been politically integrated into Canada, even without having found a satisfactory *modus vivendi* with Ottawa, will occupy part of the next four chapters.

Nova Scotia (slightly over three-quarters of a million population in 1971) was one of the founding confederating provinces of the Dominion in 1867. Along with New Brunswick (639 thousand population in 1971) it has furnished Canada with many distinguished political leaders. The rich historical heritage of both provinces contributes to their unique political culture: a combination of Yankee individualism and loyalty to the British connection. New Brunswick has a large French-speaking population in Acadia, giving it the second highest proportion of French-speaking inhabitants. As Canada moves into the latter third of this century, Nova Scotia's economic prospects look somewhat brighter than New Brunswick's. New Brunswick has had problems of high unemployment, migration of the population, and high welfare costs. The province hopes to develop a multiple industry complex, based in two of its major cities, St John and Moncton. It is also giving more emphasis to the extractive industries. The provincial mineral output is not impressive but it is increasing. The fishing industry in New Brunswick and Nova Scotia does not dominate the two provinces as much as it once did, yet both remain important. Nova Scotia has attempted to improve prospects for its forest industries. It has hopes for new oil and gas refineries and for discoveries of hydrocarbons off the coast. Deep-water ports are being built in both New Brunswick and Nova Scotia, and an increasing world demand for coke and thermal coal is tempting the Cape Breton Development Corporation, originally assigned the task of finding alternative work for coal miners, to reassess sources of thermal coal in Cape Breton, Nova Scotia, and also to reassess its mandate. Both provinces exhibit intense popular allegiances to the Progressive Conservatives or the Liberals. The lack of large industrial enterprises in both provinces no doubt diminishes the opportunities for the New Democrats to build a stronger following based on large labour union support.

Canada's tranquil tiny province, Prince Edward Island (population 111 thousand), enjoys a strong tourist industry and is cautiously developing more recreational amenities and motor inns to enhance its valuable natural beauty spots. Tourism has now displaced fishing as the second major industry behind agriculture, which leans heavily on potatoes, tobacco and now beef instead of dairy farming. The provincial government is also trying to revive the idea of a causeway into the province from New Brunswick, involving foreign capital. If the causeway ever becomes a reality, this will remove Ottawa's obligation to subsidize the current ferry service to the island.

Newfoundland (slightly over 500 thousand population), with the lowest per capita income of all the provinces of Canada has traditionally relied upon its fishing industry. But under the flamboyant leadership of its Liberal Party premier, Joseph Smallwood, from 1949 to 1971, it has attempted to entice large resource-oriented developments, such as the hydro-electric power complex at Churchill Falls, the oil refinery at Come by Chance, the newsprint and liner board mill at Stephenville, and the iron ore development at Carol Lake. Now, in contrast to this emphasis, the fledgling Newfoundland Development Corporation is attempting to emphasize small to medium-size businesses, because it has been found that these large resource developments have not been as labour-intensive as originally expected.

The economic patterns of the provinces are important to the Canadian confederation for a number of reasons. A central concern of almost all the provinces is to pursue policies which increase resource development *and* development in other sectors of the economy. However, the provincial governments have to worry rather less than the Federal government about the balance between these two demands. Both in its domestic programmes (i.e. in its tax policies and in its regional economic expansion) and in its competition for foreign investment and trade priorities, the Federal government is forced to discriminate to some extent between these two provincial emphases. The Federal government is also continually faced with various international and national economic trends for which provincial governments take relatively little official responsibility. What is particularly striking about the economic ambitions of the provinces and the Federal government is the frequent lack of symmetry between their respective priorities. The Federal government may wish to cut back foreign investment and decrease the flow of capital in Canada, so as to lessen the pressure on the Canadian dollar; and it may wish to discourage certain capital-intensive projects in order to lessen inflationary effects on the Canadian economy; but none of these are concerns for which the provinces feel particularly responsible. At the very heart of the Canadian federal state, therefore, the momentum of technological and industrial growth is compounded and increased, aided and abetted through indulgence or incentives from government at both levels. Provincial competition for industry, for job creation, for tax resources, together with their general abstension from responsibility for some of the national and international repercussions of indiscriminate economic growth, can make the provinces unwitting or willing Trojan horses for the growth of some of the more unfortunate manifestations of the technological and industrial age.

(3) *The Visibility of Provincial Governments*

A singular characteristic of the heritage of all provincial communities in Canada is the apparent contrast between Canadians and Americans on the question of trust in governments. James W. Fesler suggests that 'most' of the American states

... reflect the nineteenth-century distrust of state governments generally and of each brand particularly. The result was an excess of democracy, expressed in withholding of powers from the legislature, fragmentation of executive authority, and politicalization of the judiciary. Hog-tied, drawn and quartered, many a state government was no government at all. The kingdom was but the sum of its numerous petty and often unpretty principalities. With such a heritage, state governments today find it hard to do the kind of job that will attract and hold public confidence.[17]

Such is not the case in the provinces of Canada. The British tradition of parliamentary institutions, but with executive dominance of the legislature, has greatly affected the history of Canadian provincial governments since confederation. It is true that Nova Scotia and New Brunswick remained loyal to the Yankee immigrant notion of town-meeting democracy, and both provinces witnessed a considerable degree of executive fragmentation and a near monopoly of executive functions by independent Assemblymen in the first half of the nineteenth century. Yet the general pattern of provincial government in Canada is different. Fred Schindeler's *Responsible Government in Ontario* discusses how the provinces have been characterized by strong executives and weak legislatures. For the most part, especially in this century, provincial legislatures have had somewhat weaker procedures for legislative scrutiny than the Federal Parliament; brief legislative sessions contribute to a more truncated and less penetrating legislative scrutiny of executives. If one speaks of a parliamentary 'capacity to govern', it is clear that most Canadian provincial cabinets have enjoyed considerable capacity compared to American state executives.

If the visibility of state governments in the United States is low, this is in profound contrast to Canadian provincial governments. In addition to the tradition of strong executive leadership, a number of interest groups depend upon provincial sustenance and support; this also keeps provincial governments visible. Many regional and individual grievances are channelled primarily to provincial governments and in some cases through provincial governments to the Federal government. Although there may be considerable confusion in the public mind about the functions of provincial governments compared to the Federal government many provincial functions are not so opaque as to prevent citizens from looking to their provincial governments for help and encouragement in certain time-honoured provincial areas of concern such as resources development, health, welfare, education and culture. Another reason for the high visibility of provincial governments in Canada is their intermittent tendency to become more vocal and coherent critics of the Federal Government of the day than are Federal Opposition parties in Parliament. Each year there are occasions when some provincial Governments seem to emerge more as 'the loyal opposition' to the Federal Government than do the leaders of the Federal Opposition parties, which must draw back from expressing too vocally nationwide panaceas promoted primarily by narrow regional priorities. Since the relationship between Federal and provincial parties of the same name is often kept conveniently tenuous, provincial parties are able to maintain a credible independence from their Federal counterparts. This allows for provincial Governments to be sharply critical of a Federal Government made up of the same party. Yet what is also significant, and too often forgotten, is that most of this conflict is 'loyal' in that it seldom pushes for a break-up of the federation itself.

Any measure of the actual balance of power between Federal and provincial governments would require complicated and detailed assessments beyond the scope of this chapter, yet one development is clear. There are powerful forces operating for 'province-building' powered by the provincial governments in most provinces. The growth of the state in each province is powered not only by national Federal priorities as they affect the provinces, but also by provincial Governments in their pursuit of province-building. The Canadian people have been able to turn to both provincial and Federal Governments for state action. Neither heritage nor the development of governmental structures in the provinces suggests that there is much scepticism about the use of the state *per se*. Not even in provinces such as Alberta and British Columbia, which until the early 1970s had been ruled by Social Credit governments for over two decades, and which espoused the philosophy of individualism, *laissez faire* and minimum government 'interference', was the state itself viewed controversially. The willingness of the Social Credit Party to respond to many provincial demands for economic development, welfare, social security, and so on, was almost as impressive as the willingness of other parties. Alberta's Social Credit government had produced more boards and commissions by 1964 than had been produced by either the Federal government or any other provincial government in Canada.[18] And the thinly populated weaker provinces such as Prince Edward Island, New Brunswick and Newfoundland, rather than postpone state programmes because of lack of resources have been eager to accept Ottawa's financial and technical help.

(4) *Functional Interdependence?*

What is most striking about provincial state growth, and too little noticed, is that even with these different economic, social and political characteristics of the provinces, and with articulations of conflict at high levels, Canada has continued to witness considerable integration of the state at the provincial with the Federal level, in spite of provincial misgivings.

To some extent necessity has been the mother of collaboration. British Columbia, for example, has traditionally been somewhat isolated geographically and economically from central Canada. More important, it has always felt that it has very little to gain from Canada's existing tariff structure. The way in which the Federal government deals with the principle of free trade has thus always been of considerable interest to this province (and to the west generally). Federal jurisdiction also complicates the actions of the British Columbian government in its attempts to develop (and sometimes conserve) its coastal forest and resource industries. British Columbia, jealous of its provincial rights, also finds that it has to come to terms with Ottawa. Federal authority and activity in trade and commerce, banking, control of credit, rail and ship transportation, agriculture, the criminal code, relations with foreign states, world export markets, fisheries, and the navigation authority, all add up to an unusually heavy impact on this province.

The dependence of the province of Alberta on the oil and gas industries, together with its small manufacturing sector, make it reliant upon Ottawa for vigorous export promotion schemes on behalf of these industries. In fact the premier of Alberta, in the summer of 1971, called for continual and systematic consultation with the Federal government on all energy questions when he announced the opening of a provincial office in Washington. Saskatchewan also depends on Ottawa for vigorous export programmes on behalf of grains and other products and its dependence, along with Manitoba, on Federal assistance for various welfare and regional economic expansion programmes gives these two provinces somewhat more reason to work with Ottawa.

Quebec's concern for its culture has always made it jealous of Federal invasions into what it deems to be provincial jurisdiction. This province's expanding notion of the meaning of 'culture' has led since 1960 to almost irreconcilable tests of the meaning of Canadian federalism. Quebec has not only challenged a number of Federal initiatives which appear to be an invasion of most Quebec Governments' broad definitions of provincial culture, but

49

it has been unusually imaginative in presenting counter-proposals for constitutional change. Still, the policy presence of Ottawa in what once were fields of Federal inactivity through equalization grants, regional economic expansion grants, and a host of other programmes, together with the key roles given to Quebec MPs in the federal cabinet and to French Canadians in the public service in Ottawa have helped to integrate Quebec and its state with Ottawa.

The dependence of each maritime province on the Federal government is acute. The financial dependence of the maritime provinces on the Federal government, with over one-half of provincial revenues coming from Ottawa, has been documented in a host of studies. The studies for the 1971 Deutsch Report on Maritime Union shows, for example, the dependence of maritime provinces on Federal subsidies, grants and incentives in order to promote economic expansion in these regions. This dependence turns whole departments of government in the maritimes – such as the Economic Expansion agencies in Prince Edward Island – into virtual wards of the Federal government. Although maritime premiers have always been vocal in complaints about over-all Federal policy, such as anti-inflation policies which cut back on capital investment in the provinces, they must also keep up a continuous barrage of requests for greater Federal help to ameliorate their regional economic problems. Perhaps one of the more telling comments on the relations of these provinces to the Federal government is the criticism of the Atlantic Provinces Economic Council's Fifth Annual Review of the Federal regional economic expansion programmes. It is worth quoting for the insight it gives into the dynamic of maritime provincial and Federal government relationships with one Federal department, the Department of Regional Economic Expansion.

Rather than making large staffs available for its joint planning purposes, DREE has chosen to expand its establishment into a very large bureaucracy of close to two thousand. The irony of such a situation is clearly shown in the establishment of a special section of the Federal Treasury Board to study DREE's programmes which employs more economists than does the entire New Brunswick government. . . .

Then the Council complains that, although Federal government statements about DREE programmes are couched in terms of joint planning,

What started out as a planning exercise deteriorated into a process of negotiation for available funds. Federal civil servants sat down at a table opposite provincial civil servants to debate on the allocation of a certain allotment of taxpayer's money.

What is apparently required [by the civil servants] are projects that show men and machines at work, projects on such safe things as schools, highways and sewers.

A side effect of the situation is the substantial degree to which the provinces rely on DREE for funds. Although it is difficult to document, it may be assumed that provinces which strongly criticize DREE do so at their peril. There is nothing in the legislation that says how DREE shall mete out its favours, consequently a province is left to its own devices in getting its share of the pie. The general state of the 'special areas activities' offers considerable scope for politically motivated agreements on the part of both the Federal and provincial governments.

To point to the forces producing this considerable interdependence between the federal and provincial governments is not to argue that the Federal government's use of its power has subordinated all of the provinces to the same degree as has occurred on issues of economic development with the maritime provinces. Until the Trudeau Government came into power, Canadian experience gave little support to the belief that federalism was a transitional stage on the road to a unitary state.[19] When, in the 1930s, Canada needed vigorous Federal action to help lift the country out of its economic depression, the Judicial Committee of the Privy Council concentrated on delineating jurisdictional boundaries at the very time when the public interest seemed to require blurring of the boundaries. Immediately after the Second World War, Federal politicians were loath to give up the centralized power they had enjoyed during the war. Postwar Federal Governments were able to continue their overall dominance in the taxation field in an effort to orient Canadian confederation towards more centralist priorities.

A host of committees brought specialist civil servants together to develop and administer intergovernmental agreements and to discuss extensions of joint endeavours to solve problems outside any single jurisdiction. By these mechanisms, views were exchanged, tensions eased and some flexibility introduced into the Federal system, by *ad hoc* agreements, capable of change as circumstances required. In short, the practical workings of the federal system in the postwar decade came to be decided more and more by politicians and administrators who shared a common interest in making the system work rather than in determining its internal dividing line. The result was an intertwining of the activities of ten (later eleven) governments through cooperative arrangements which made the British North America Act a less and less accurate guide for determination of which government provided which service.[20]

This development led to what has been called a fused federalism, but has also led to considerable interdependence. The Federal government expanded into provincial jurisdiction by the use of conditional grants even though it may have lacked a consistent rationale of the national interest to justify such extensions. Most observers agree that by the mid-1960s a swing had begun against this centralization and the provinces began to regain their influence in the Canadian condominium as provincial cabinets and bureaucracies began to improve in competence and confidence.

Since the Trudeau Government of 1968, Federal-provincial relations have had to cope with a number of Federal initiatives, and the balance of the Canadian federal system is now more difficult to assess. Mr Trudeau's use of the criminal law and the Federal spending power is perhaps slightly greater than that of his predecessors but his real distinction lies in his attempt to make Ottawa not only a source of funds but a centre of expertise and technical resources which can be offered to the provinces when Ottawa wants to have influence in what is predominantly provincial jurisdiction. It is probably fair to say that the powers of some provincial governments (especially the richer provinces) and the influence of the Federal government have grown, depending on the field, while the powers of the weaker provinces have declined since the early 1960s.

Much of the provinces' regulatory responsibilities has not diminished. This therefore continues to give them leverage with Ottawa. Yet Ottawa's expanding use of the criminal code, its technical expertise and above all its allocative 'spending' power have given it continual leverage. In fact the fiscal history of Canada falls into three distinct periods, culminating in a situation in which the spending power of the Federal government is clearly constitutionally, if not politically, impossible to resist. The first period, 1867 to 1912, in which statutory subsidies of the type envisaged by the British North America Act constituted the sole contribution of the Federal government to the provinces; the second, 1912 to 1944, in which, in addition to constitutionally required or politically advantageous direct subsidies to the provinces, the Federal government, in a somewhat episodic and *ad hoc* manner, began to intrude upon the provincial domain through the use of conditional subsidies or 'grants-in-aid'; third, 1945 to 1975, in which the Federal government, continuing its wide uses of power assumed during the Second World War for purposes of national defence, has attempted to initiate and co-ordinate universal social and economic programmes once seen as exclusively within the provincial domain, rather than to reduce the incidence of Federal taxation to allow each provincial jurisdiction the economic ability to produce its own programmes.

It is true that major new Federal programmes, such as the Canada Pension Plan and Medicare, have resulted in a shifting of provincial expenditure and have to some degree forced Federal priorities on the provinces. Yet other Federal programmes, such as Regional Expansion Grants, the Local Initiative Programme grants, complicate any assessment of the federal-provincial power balance. The difficulty lies in unravelling what federal-provincial 'coordination or consultation' means. Many of the new initiatives from the Federal level have involved considerable consultation and coordination with the provinces. To some extent this 'coordination and consultation' has meant that Ottawa ends up doing little more than providing funds for provincial and municipal projects which are already planned and decided at these levels but which needed Federal funding to become reality because of depleted provincial treasuries. A number of Federal programmes therefore have simply resulted in the funding of proposals already put together by the provinces or the municipalities or other local groups. Garth Jones has suggested, in his synopsis of various case studies of organizational change in central and local government in Great Britain, that in intergovernmental relations over time, the 'change agent' (for example in Canada the Federal government's regional expansion grants programme) eventually loses practical control to the 'client system' (e.g. the provincial or

Table 2
*Estimated Federal Payments to Provinces and Municipalities *1975-6*

	(in millions of dollars)		
	Nfld	*PEI*	*NS*
Statutory subsidies – BNA Act	9.7	0.7	2.2
Equalization	203.4	48.7	243.2
a. adjustments for prior years†	—	—	—
Revenue guarantee†	—	—	—
Part V payment – undistributed income on hand	0.3	—	0.3
Public utilities income tax transfer	2.1	0.5	—
Total unconditional payments	*215.5*	*49.9*	*245.7*
Hospital insurance‡	47.4	9.4	78.6
Medicare	20.6	4.4	30.6
Professional training	0.1	—	0.1
Health Resources Fund	4.7	0.2	3.2
Canada Assistance Plan‡	36.9	6.8	31.5
Total health and welfare	*109.7*	*20.8*	*144.0*
Post-secondary education § – cash transfer	7.1	1.6	21.4
– income tax offset¶	9.5	1.9	18.9
– total	16.6	3.5	40.3
Municipal grants in lieu of taxes	0.5	0.1	6.2
Economic development – general	32.7	—	23.5
– other**	13.0	28.0	21.2
Bilingualism development	0.2	0.2	1.0
Total other – excluding income tax offset	*53.5*	*29.9*	*73.3*
– including income tax offset	*63.0*	*31.8*	*92.2*
Total payments to provinces (excluding income tax offset)	*378.7*	*100.6*	*463.0*
Equalization payments – dollars per capita	372	409	296

* Total may not agree with Main Estimates because of transfers to the Yukon and Northwest Territories, because of inclusion where applicable of tax abatements to Quebec and because of rounding.

† The distribution of the prior year equalization adjustment and revenue guarantee payments are not available by province.

‡ Payments to Quebec for hospital insurance and Canada Assistance Plan include the value of an individual income tax abatement of 16 points and 5 points valued at $619.7 million and $183.6 million respectively.

¶ *Value of income tax offset associated with post-secondary education program*
(a) individual 4.357 points		8.0	1.6	16.2
(b) corporation 1 point		1.5	0.3	2.7

** Includes grants paid under A.R.D.A., special areas, and FRED programs.

Source: *How Your Tax Dollar is Spent 1975-6*. (Information Canada, Ottawa, 1975).

NB	Que	Ont	Man	Sask	Alta	BC	Total
1.8	4.5	5.5	2.1	2.1	3.1	2.1	33.8
217.1	1,033.4	—	124.4	115.4	—	—	1,985.6
—	—	—	—	—	—	—	60.0
—	—	—	—	—	—	—	340.0
0.3	3.3	5.9	0.7	0.2	1.1	1.9	14.0
—	3.7	14.4	0.5	—	12.2	1.8	35.2
219.2	*1,044.9*	*25.8*	*127.7*	*117.7*	*16.4*	*5.8*	*2,468.6*
61.8	602.7	747.3	104.6	88.4	178.2	225.5	2,143.9
25.4	233.3	311.0	39.5	34.5	67.6	93.3	860.2
0.1	0.6	0.8	0.1	0.1	0.2	0.2	2.3
1.0	14.3	4.2	3.0	2.0	1.0	3.4	37.0
37.9	461.4	295.8	46.1	42.3	79.7	118.6	1,157.0
126.2	*1,312.3*	*1,359.1*	*193.3*	*167.3*	*326.7*	*441.0*	*4,200.4*
8.8	216.8	148.2	17.6	15.5	55.4	18.6	511.0
13.5	191.7	360.4	29.6	24.8	79.4	104.5	834.2
22.3	408.5	508.6	47.2	40.3	134.8	123.1	1,345.2
0.8	17.4	33.0	5.3	2.0	4.3	6.0	75.6
29.1	50.1	22.2	11.8	10.8	4.9	0.9	186.0
14.3	48.6	3.6	15.1	23.3	15.4	7.0	189.5
7.8	62.1	27.6	2.4	0.7	1.1	1.2	104.3
60.8	*395.0*	*234.6*	*52.2*	*52.3*	*81.1*	*33.7*	*1,066.4*
74.3	*586.7*	*595.0*	*81.8*	*77.1*	*160.5*	*138.2*	*1,900.6*
406.2	*2,752.2*	*1,619.5*	*373.2*	*337.3*	*424.2*	*480.5*	*7,735.4*
322	167	—	124	127	—	—	—

§ The Federal government has undertaken to bear 50 per cent of the eligible costs of post-secondary education in each province. The contribution takes the form of (a) a Federal individual income tax abatement of 4.357 points and a Federal corporation income tax of 1 point, (b) where applicable the equalization arising from those tax points, and (c) a cash transfer equivalent to the eligible contributions less the value of the tax points abated and the associated equalization. The Federal contribution for a fiscal year for all provinces may not exceed 115 per cent of the Federal contribution to all provinces in the immediately preceding year.

NB	Que	Ont	Man	Sask	Alta	BC	Total
11.2	160.0	293.7	24.3	19.2	49.4	85.0	668.6
2.3	31.7	66.7	5.3	5.6	30.0	19.5	165.6

municipal government) if the client system is closer to the policy objects in terms of research, communication, day-to-day contact and supervision.[21] If Jones's insight is at all accurate, this raises some profound questions about the long-term effect of a number of federal-provincial programmes, in which it may appear that the Federal government is acting as the 'change agent', but in the long run may end up subservient to the client system because of the latter's effective contact and communication with the group being served. In fact, this unease is evident in the Federal government's complaints about the high level of provincial funding of hospital construction and the concomitant need for the Federal government to match provincial expenditure under the requirements of the shared cost programme with the provinces.

This development then may be leading to more practical provincial influence in joint programmes. Also the complex nature of some interprovincial policy collaboration may leave Ottawa with no constructive role but to accept what the provinces can agree to. This development deserves a somewhat extended assessment here because its implications, though profound, are by no means obvious.

It is widely believed that successful Federal-provincial interaction in joint decision making from 1945 to 1960 was the result of the participation of highly specialized bureaucrats. Programme specialists were successful in reaching agreement if the issues considered did not involve general objectives and if the specialists were able to act relatively independently from both generalist bureaucrats and the politicians. Therefore the dominance of highly particularistic considerations in Federal-provincial relations may explain 'the joint federalism' of the 1945–60 period in Canada. Attitudes, procedures and values common to particular groups of programme specialists provided common standards to which officials from Federal and provincial levels could defer. What is more, it is said programme specialists acted to remove certain types of decision-making from the more general policy-making arena where politicians and higher civil servants could interfere. Accordingly they settled disputes internally to prevent any interference. This general argument concludes that there has been much more effective collaboration in the functional programmes of government because of the importance of technical considerations for these programmes.[22] While this insight may be generally valid, it can be misleading if two aspects are not closely examined: first, the organizational context in which the technical decisions take place; and secondly, the nature of the technical issue under consideration.

With respect to the organizational context, there appears to be several variables that are of relevance to the nature of the consultations even on technical matters. The first variable concerns the personnel involved. The issue is a classical one in the study of bureaucracies. Are the participants line or staff personnel? If line personnel are involved then there may be potentially greater opportunities for effective collaboration. However, if staff personnel are also involved, then it appears that factors other than simply technical considerations can be introduced. One study of wildlife policy for the 1959 'Resources for Tomorrow' Conference in Ottawa suggests that this is an important factor. It compares the British Columbia Game Branch, which is a line organization controlled by a central office charged only with fish and game administration, to the Department of Lands and Forests in Ontario in which field officers perform a variety of functions related to resources, of which fish and game is only one; and the senior game officials serve in effect as staff officers at the central office. A related problem is the locus of control for making decisions and the degree and extent to which control is defined. This influences the nature of interaction. Compare the Alberta Act, in which there are specific outlines of the powers vested in the governor-in-council, the minister, and the game director, to the situation in Nova Scotia and Quebec where the Acts themselves contain specific provisions respecting hunting seasons and bag limits. In those provinces the legislatures reserved considerable authority to themselves. Taking the organizational context further, another study for the conference introduces into its discussion of water management in Canada the question of participation by individuals other than provincial and Federal technical personnel. In some cases there is an inclusion of local community representatives as part of a 'grass roots approach' to water management. Another study of agriculture refers to the importance to policy-makers of a firm foundation close to the people concerned with the particular resource areas of the public agencies involved. In this situation the result may be that some key personnel in government agencies will be at least partly

57

responsible to local organization. Accordingly, this is a factor which might be an important influence to add to the influence of technical competence and collaboration. Or, take the example of the power of certain economic interests which act as barriers to effective water management, there has been conflict between log-driving interests and power interests in Quebec and Nova Scotia for example. Another study has pointed to the conflict between recreation interests and preservation of fishery resources in New Brunswick. A potential clash of interests is evident then in technical discussions between multi-resource departments. For example, the primary disadvantage of multi-resource departments, from the fish and game viewpoint, is that some appear to be dominated by another resource of predominant importance from the economic point of view. As a result, the interests of wildlife and recreation may not be represented with sufficient force at the policy-making level. It is worthwhile, therefore, to recognize that the usual distinctions between technical versus political or functional versus general can be potentially misleading in that factors usually associated with politics can also be of consequence in the technical and functional issue areas.

However, for an indication not of relative power between Federal and provincial officials but of the growth and inter-relationship of the state at either level, all the momentum in the foregoing is instructive. Regardless of the interest groups promoted, or the amount of dominance by specialists, or the 'politicizing' of issues, the fact that provincial and Federal governments are promoting their concerns through an increasingly complex set of meetings and negotiations with each other, helps to show how society is becoming increasingly tied to government action at a number of levels. Provincial governments, with their ever-increasing responsibilities, have found it necessary to enlist Federal cooperation, expertise and funds for a host of projects. This has had the effect of tying both levels of government to each other and of promoting integration of the overall state apparatus (Federal, provincial and municipal) in Canada.

Let us list some examples of this increasingly wide network of collaboration. Not only does the cabinet's staff arm, the Privy Council Office, now have a Federal Provincial Affairs Division, but ministers and deputy ministers are increasingly involved in Federal-provincial meetings. In June 1970 there were 57 formal

Federal-provincial committees at this level, 260 multilateral committees and subcommittees and 150 bilateral committees of the same type.[23]

Here are some examples of what is done in some departments. There is a mass of detailed research and consultation with the provinces through the Department of Agriculture, including such diverse activities as consultation with provincial departments of agriculture on the use of insecticides, control of cattle grubs, promotion and production of pedigree seed in agricultural production, studies of agricultural land utilization, participation in provincial outlook meetings for agricultural exports, and monitoring of the powers of provincial marketing boards. The Department of Transport consults closely with provincial governments on many of its activities, ranging from the site of Federal airports, railway facilities and marine ports, to the study of recreational resources in the Rideau and Trent-Severn Canal System. The Department of Fisheries and Forestry is in continuing consultation with provincial governments, ranging from such detailed work as exploring for shellfish, seaweed, and molluscs; assisting swordfishermen; drawing up proposals to reduce pollution in the pulp and paper industry; revising migratory bird regulations; negotiating Federal participation in water projects; investigating and regulating water resources; and designing and demonstrating improved fishing vessels equipment. The Department of Manpower and Immigration cooperates with the provinces in assessing training requirements; standardizing tradesmen qualifications; building and equipping occupational training facilities; administering, with nine provinces, the Vocational Rehabilitation of Disabled Persons Act.

The financial relationship between the Department of National Health and Welfare and the provinces is, as already mentioned, enormous. Most of these transfers of funds to the provinces for Medicare, hospital construction, the Canada Assistance Plan, etc. may not involve as much liaison as the large amount of funds implies. However, Federal departmental officials take part in technical meetings on medical care to consider extensions of the benefit coverage, eligibility, portability, diagnostic coding of services, professional earnings and provincial fee schedule comparisons.

Perhaps the one Federal department which spends most of its time in day-to-day contact with the provinces, is Regional

Economic Expansion. In fact it was established in 1969 to do most of its work 'in cooperation with the provinces', to quote from its *Annual Report 1970–71*. Planning for most of its strategies to reduce regional disparities and the implementation of most of its plans and programmes are all done in collaboration with provincial authorities.

Nor are Federal-provincial relations made up solely of these hundreds of meetings on detailed programmes. The Federal Department of Finance now meets and consults continually, through its division on Federal-provincial relations, on major questions of fiscal policy. This is often supplemented by help from the Privy Council Office on a host of major policy questions. Efforts to break through to new levels of consensus on broad policy are also conducted in meetings of the heads of governments, which for the last fifteen years have occurred annually or even more often.

The well-publicized criticisms of the Federal government made by provincial premiers and their ministers and disputes at the ministerial level in Federal-provincial meetings attract considerable public attention. All this can mystify. The differences at this level are real, as are the differences at the more bureaucratic and technical levels. Yet the publicity given to conflict obscures what is probably more important: the vast amount of agreements to cooperate, to define common standards, to do joint studies, to integrate programmes, to indulge in mutual assistance, and to improve and amplify existing programmes with each other's help, within joint programmes or not. The shuttling back and forth to meetings in Ottawa and to provincial capitals of officials from both levels of government has almost reached a state of congestion. The provinces' pursuit of Federal funds and of a share in Federal planning on problems that concern them force them into dialogue with the Federal government. The Federal government, with its own motives for more integrated and efficient programmes and for more influence in areas that concern it, responds and initiates. The highly publicized conflicts, especially in provincial speech-making at heads of government conferences, serve in fact to hide the great and growing structure of collaboration and coordination that is developing at the level of the state to promote both province building and nation building.

Another significant development which has increased Federal-provincial contacts is the tendency since the 1960s for the Federal government's cabinet committees and the Federal public service to *plan* policy on the basis of broad national problem areas. Ottawa now goes ahead to integrate its own activities and to concentrate on the supra-regional necessities for policy instead of postponing planning because of partial or concurrent provincial jurisdiction over various public policy areas. The Trudeau Government has intensified this trend to supra-regional planning through its programme budgeting techniques, through cabinet reorganization by function and broad issue area, and by the perspective and attitude of the planning and priorities network of the Privy Council Office and the Treasury Board. Although there has been little explicit comment from the provinces on this informal structuring in Ottawa, the reservations of Quebec's former deputy minister of intergovernmental affairs about this process of 'side-door federalism' not only describes its impact but points to one source of Quebec's concern about Canadian federalism.

The forces of the centralism of the federal government since 1968 are much more subtle now. Ottawa doesn't attack frontally, but from the side. They won't create a Municipal Affairs Department but they do set up a Secretariat of Urban Affairs. Then a couple of years later it becomes a department – same thing in the environment field. They invade areas by osmosis, through their financial and structural powers. It's not the same type of centralism. It puts the emphasis on the problem areas of the future. But the results are the same.[24]

Surely almost all of the major Federal government initiatives since 1968 could elicit such a complaint. Federal programmes for such Federal purposes as regional economic expansion, urban affairs, local initiatives, opportunities for youth, environmental protection, could be interpreted as partial invasions of provincial policy areas by use of the Federal spending power. It is notable that in November 1972, the first ever tri-level (Federal, provincial, and municipal) meeting to discuss urban policy was held. This assembly agreed to meet again in the future. The forum was Federally initiated. The provinces, with their control over municipalities, reluctantly agreed, in the hope perhaps of prying some funds from Ottawa for urban development. Also the first exclusive conference ever held of Western provincial premiers with the Prime Minister, to discuss 'Western Economic Opportunities' in July 1973 was notable for the way in which 'constitutional jurisdictions' were overlooked as the premiers pleaded for financial help to solve various problems of provincial jurisdiction.

In sum, then, it is no easy matter to identify the precise balance between the Federal and provincial governments in Canada. The tendency of the Federal government to use its powers vigorously, and to devise national policies which involve participation in what a province such as Quebec might define as provincial jurisdiction, raises the spectre of Federal 'imperialism'. Yet the growing competence of provincial governments, their essential vitality springing from their close contact with various local clienteles through their administration of Federal-provincial programmes, and their own vastly increased efforts at basic planning suggest that the usual locus of affective allegiance and of policy intelligence may be more provincial than Federal in many vital policy areas.

For an understanding of Canada's political and social integration, it may, in the last analysis, be less useful to measure with precision the Canadian federal balance or to concentrate on the highly publicized conflicts than to recognize the great coral reef of joint meetings, structures, and agreements, written and unwritten, between both levels of government. The patterns of mutual non-interference and interference between Ottawa and the provinces have led to a growing context of collaboration and coexistence between the provincial and Federal levels of the state.

It is true that on some issues – the highly publicized conflicts between heads of government – much competition and lack of cooperation occurs. Richard Simeon's study of the Federal-provincial conferences and bargaining surrounding the Canada and Quebec pension plans, tax agreements for 1967 to 1972, and the review of the British North America Act beginning in 1967, found considerable executive dominance and conflict among heads of government.[25] This is not surprising since these are issues of the utmost importance to the image of Governments in Canada. He goes on to assert that in these grand issues Federal-provincial disagreements are 'as much, if not more' differences between Governments than between regions. 'The Federal and provincial governments compete to gain credit, status and importance and to avoid discredit and blame.' For major redistributive issues such as these, these motivations were, no doubt, important. Yet for a host of distributive, positional, incremental, technical, and research-oriented policies and issues, the situation is perhaps more complex. Executive dominance may be far less for these issues. Highly visible political conflict occurs less frequently on these issues. Hence the network of quiet collaboration at departmental and inter-departmental bureaucratic levels becomes influential once again.

The context of increasing functional interdependence of the state, together with the state's increased penetration of society, helps us to understand how Canada is growing increasingly integrated at the state level, if somewhat more slowly at the societal level. Yet – as the Quebec nationalist has always seen – if the state appropriates more and more of society, societal fragmentation may lose its potency as a restraint to schemes of political integration. Perhaps this has already occurred to a considerable degree. Let us now examine the growth of the state in Canada to grasp this more fully.

3 The Growth of Government in Canada

(1) Some Causes

We have already noted that the activities of government in Canada have grown considerably since confederation. Even though the sweep and complexity of societal patterns and of private economic activity have widened, the insinuation of government into these activities is probably more than keeping pace. Private enterprise and autonomous social patterns are now far less private and autonomous than they seem.

Because Canada is not ruled by a totalitarian system of government, and because it is not a nation which cultivates the ethos of public officialdom evident in a country such as France, the role of the state in defining the nature of Canadian society is often overlooked. Even more perplexing has been the steady growth of government in Canada, even though the country is in many ways profoundly conservative. The unwillingness to break with Britain, the retention of monarchial forms, the caution even of 'reform' parties in power, the weakness of the socialist movement at the Federal level, the muted nationalism, the fidelity to 'peace and order', are the well-known examples of Canadian conservatism.

Why then this growth of the state in Canada? Richard M. Bird's *The Growth of Government Spending in Canada* suggests that government expenditure grows because the relative importance of public sectors always increases with rising per capita income. He also suggests that government revenues seem always to be sufficiently forthcoming to meet required levels of expenditures, rather than vice versa. If so, perhaps the growth of government in Canada, as in other industrialized countries since the Second World War, is another example of the liberal technological state being forced to expand to correct and forestall the abuses, sufferings and uncertainty wrought by the technological juggernaut. Many of the prescriptions for the American public sector by a Heilbronner or a Galbraith are almost descriptions of some actions in the Canadian public sector. Yet something more can be said about Canadian public policy at the Federal level. The growth of government activity had been greatly facilitated by the far from impotent and far from static nature of the Canadian conservative approach to political and economic development. It is generally assumed by theorists of political development that development comes only if local particularisms are broken down. It is also assumed that national integration is facilitated if governing parties are internally created (i.e. within legislatures), rather than externally (i.e. based on societal divisions). In fact the conservatism of Upper Canada unleashed drives which powered the movement towards the national integration of Canada even though the political parties in Upper Canada arose from divisions in society. Nova Scotia's and New Brunswick's parties were more 'internally' created than Upper Canada's, yet they did not attempt to break down the local particularisms in these colonies since the early nineteenth century. It might be suggested therefore that the state in Canada has developed in two different ways and both have been powered by what can loosely be called a conservative belief system. First, the thrust to national integration has been powered by Upper Canadian conservatism. Second, the drift to a host of distributive regionally sensitive, state-promoted programmes has been propelled by maritime and Lower Canadian particularism and the unique nature of the conservatism which fosters this.

The use of state power to foster particularisms (or at least to allow them to persist), and to promote at the same time projects which help to develop ties to hold the nation together, have been characteristic of much Liberal and Conservative party public policy at the Federal level since confederation. These two approaches are conservative in two senses. The liberal faith in the iron discipline of the market (regional, national and international) has not been allowed to dominate Canadian development completely. Nor can these approaches be called quasi-socialist because, in the pursuit of more regional vitality, they did not aim primarily, if at all, to transform the power structure inherent in the particularisms or in schemes of transcontinental cohesion.

The Canadian belief system has been conservative for a long time. These attitudes perhaps emerged most clearly during the war of 1812 and have persisted ever since. S. F. Wise has provided a vivid summary description of this emergence.[1]

Broad loyalties did exist in the British America of 1812, but they were markedly colonial in character. The elites were deeply committed to the Crown, to the values of British civilization, and to a conception of their destinies within the British imperium. Their sentiments were shared by part of the colonial population, but in each province there were groups to whom such notions were meaningless ... each colony was a welter of parochialisms, of disparate groups cut off from one another by differences of origin, religion and language, and by poor communications. Among many groups, self-justifying and self-sustaining myths had already been generated; the crucial task for the conservative elites, and one for which they were singularly ill-fitted, was somehow to break down such nascent petty separatisms and instead to inculcate higher loyalties, whether to the province or to the idea of a British America.

The attitudes to the war of 1812 in the colonies illustrate the different intensities with which conservative beliefs were held in the Canadas compared to the other provinces.

Generally speaking, political leadership in Nova Scotia and New Brunswick was more open in its attitudes and more pragmatic in its methods than that of the two Canadas. Maritimers, both well-placed and simple, saw the war of 1812 not as a deadly conflict between absolutely opposed political systems but as a splendid opportunity to profit from the shortsighted trade policy of the Madison administration, and so, on 'the Lines' between New Brunswick and Maine, a truce was declared for the duration, and American citizens and British subjects fraternized freely to their mutual benefit. To Canadians of both languages, however, the war was one for survival; the French-speaking elite depicted Americans as Goths and Vandals bearing the new barbarism, and the Upper Canadian propagandists saw them as hypocrites with liberty on their lips and conquest in their hearts. Though Nova Scotians and New Brunswickers were active as privateers during the war (for some, a most lucrative occupation) and maritimers took part in some of the Canadian campaigns, there was no siege mentality in either province, nor any reason why there should have been. ... For the Upper Canadian conservative, the war was an opportunity to cleanse a society that had been in mortal danger from internal rot. Thousands of acres of land belonging to men of dubious loyalty were confiscated; a network of informers ferreted out those suspected of harbouring American sympathies, and loyalty oaths were imposed wholesale. 'Loyalty' itself came to mean not simply the traditional allegiance to the British Crown, but also adherence to the social, political, religious, and cultural values essential, in Tory eyes, to the preservation of the province. The Loyal and Patriotic Society, formed during the war, symbolized the coming of a fully conscious conservatism seeking to monitor all conduct.

Life in British North America soon quietened down after the war, but the belief system persisted and affected government. The growth of government in Canada was fostered first by the governors together with their more or less conservative councils. Until 1831, when governors lost most of their financial powers to assemblies, most governors participated quite extensively (and often arbitrarily) in the colonial affairs of British North America. In the Canadas the governors' opponents condemned not the phenomenon of state action as such but the composition of the tenants of the state such as the 'cliques' and 'family compacts' (the so-called closed elites in each province). In fact, the retreat of the state from the over-all direction of human affairs was really a brief interlude occurring primarily in Britain in the first half of the nineteenth century but not in British North America. In British North America and on the continent of Europe state activity was not so quiescent. It does not appear that the growth in the activities of government in Canada has required a profound ideological shift in the minds of most Canadians about the importance of government. In fact the dual conservative traditions in Canada have been congenial to this growth.

(2) *The Development of Some Major Government Activities*

In 1867 almost all of the three and a half million population of New Brunswick, Nova Scotia and Canada lived along the river valleys east of the Great Lakes or along the coasts of the maritime provinces, in the valley of the St Lawrence and in the southwestern peninsula between Lake Ontario and Lake Huron. Montreal was the largest town, with a population slightly in excess of one hundred thousand. Eight other towns had a population of over ten thousand. Most Canadians lived on farms or in villages or in lumber camps. Because the industrial revolution had by then taken hold in Europe, considerable demand for the importation of food and of raw materials from countries such as Canada helped to build up an important export trade for timber, fish and agriculture. Those who did not work at such extractive industries were usually engaged in pioneer agriculture.

In most agricultural communities, families were still compelled by force of circumstance to be self-reliant, roads were poor or nonexistent and the railway expansion, which was greatly to alter this isolated farming way of life, did not begin in earnest until a decade before confederation. The principal problems of the day were not the difficulties of social adjustment in the complex urban society, but the task of 'organizing a concerted attack upon nature'. The author of *The Growth of Government Activities Since Confederation* for the Royal Commission on Dominion-Provincial Relations in 1939 could write

It is enough to say that we have made a pretty convincing conquest of nature. In a comparatively few years of rapid industrial growth, we have managed to precipitate on ourselves most of the problems of urban industrialism. By moving eagerly into the full current of the industrial revolution, we have forsaken our pioneer self-sufficiency for economic interdependence. We have not only become interdependent among ourselves on a national scale; few countries are more deeply committed to the international division of labour. . . .[2]

The so-called 'free-economy' which brought about this rapid development was self-adjusting in a narrow sense. But, as Professor Corry noted in this report, it 'made no provision for the social adjustments which had to follow what appeared to the sufferers as its capricious action. The sufferers were many and when they secured the franchise, they laid those problems of social adjustment on the door step of the political authority. . . .'[3]

These pressures on political authorities for increased state responsibility for social welfare and for greater state responsibility for economic development are common to all Western countries, but it important to note that they have not always followed the same pattern of development in each. The dual conservative strategy allowed Canada, which had got off to a slow start in the race of industrial expansion, to put its early emphasis on state assistance to various forms of economic activity rather than on extensive regulation. It is easy to understand why Canadians have not had any great fear or prejudice against state action as such. As Corry noted, 'an authority which gives away homesteads and timberlands is not likely to arouse contempt while its benevolence is worth cultivating.'[4]

The Upper Canadian conservative mind saw that the opening of a huge new sparsely populated country required more than individual initiative. It required organized and concerted efforts to overcome natural obstacles. It has not been difficult, therefore, to get elite and popular agreement in Canada on a wide range of state action on behalf of schemes of economic development. This has led not only to Canada's impressive national railway network, much of it built in the last century, but it has been consistent with more distributive types of conservative policy in that it has been natural for an industry to secure government aid if the key political unit making up the regional political community is dominated by a single industry. The influence of manufacturing interests in central Canada has contributed in part to Canada's tariff structure. The power of the oil, mining and gas industries in various provinces has led in part to generous tax provisions for these industries. (Perhaps the most substantial allocation to these industries came in the Federal government budget of 15 April 1955, when the minister of finance announced that the experience with 'special tax provisions' for the oil, mining and gas industries had 'clearly established their value in promoting expansion. . . . I now propose to make them a permanent part of our law.' A further series of tax concessions were made to the oil, gas and mining industries by the Federal government in the budget which it introduced in April 1962.) Railway subsidies, and other forms of regional economic development assistance, have been pursued with ever-increasing expenditure in certain portions of

Quebec and the maritimes and have been ardently sought by these political units.

The power of the grain industry in the prairies has led to a host of plans which lend money to farmers, subsidize their schemes of cooperation, guarantee loans to wheat pools, and establish support prices. The role of agriculture, not only in the Canadian economy but in government, has always been important thanks in part to over-representation of rural constituencies in both provincial and Federal legislatures. At first the Federal government made annual grants in aid of agricultural instruction in the provinces in 1913. But it has gone far beyond that since then. For example, of the estimates of $325 million for the Federal Department of Agriculture in 1970, major assistance programmes accounted for $214 million. And the agriculture prices support board, established in 1944 to maintain agricultural prices by purchasing farm products when supplies exceeded demand, and storing them if necessary to remarket later, ended up running a net loss on butter and butter fat of $134 million in 1969. Freight storage assistance for western feed grains, also are considerable.

Although they often become mixed and interdependent, contemporary descendants of the two original conservative attitudes to the state are not difficult to find in all Canadian political parties. What might be called 'distributive conservatism', which fosters programmes of state aid, not to dissolve but (with some exceptions) to sustain and enhance various parochialisms, patterns and interests already in place is evident not only in provincial government activity in the maritimes but in Federal policy there and elsewhere. In this sense the maritime brand of conservatism is akin to Quebec, prairie and rural Ontario conservatism. Subsidies, assistance, and so on, for fisheries, agriculture, and transportation are relevant not only to the maritimes. The Upper Canadian brand of conservatism, which one might call 'developmental conservatism', with its ambitions for broad nationwide schemes of integration and development, spurred by the interests of central Canada, has never been able completely to subjugate the distributive strategy. It has not been able to carry all before it because of the continual vigilance of all regions against the central Canadian 'neo-imperium', and because central Canada has itself succumbed in part to distributive conservatism. Internal dependence on tariffs, subsidies and on various types of state assistance are no less real because central Canadians prefer to describe such indulgences as part of a larger, more nationally integrative, scheme of development. The Upper Canadian world of central Canadian-dominated powerful monetary institutions, aid to secondary industry, high tariffs, state assistance for research, technological development, nationwide travel and communication assistance, depends upon the state's indulgence. In spite of various parochialisms in society, developmental conservatism may have helped to enhance the power of many central Canadian interests, yet – most important – it may have helped to lead to the state's penetration of society in ways vastly more nationally integrative in effect than the distributive brand of conservatism. On the other hand the distributive approach has been of substantial importance in helping regions and provinces to maintain their personality and identity. Thanks to the vigilence and grip of this part of the conservative tradition, the homogeneity implied by developmental conservatism has not been allowed to prevail completely even in the technological age. The distributive approach is so attractive that all parties, NDP, Conservative, Liberal and Créditiste, believe in maintaining for example the family farm and in saving local industry. This approach may have enabled Canada as a whole to maintain, to some degree, a distinct personality.

Each wing of this conservative tradition has well-known academic defenders. Although he does not write with economic parameters foremost in mind, the philosopher George Grant, in his attacks on American technological and cultural homogeneity, in his defence of the un-American temper of English Canadians, is in the 'distributive particularism' tradition.[5] Donald Creighton, one of Canada's foremost historians has, in large measure, defended the nationally integrative view. His insistence is that Canada's manifest destiny was to exploit the St Lawrence river as the conduit with which to develop west of the river, to build a vast 'Empire of the St Lawrence' within the British, not the American orbit. This is a good example of the Upper Canadian conservative view.[6]

Up to the First World War, Canada developed by using both these conservative strategies. Even though the excesses implicit in John A. Macdonald's protectionist policies were criticized in the Liberal party's flirtation with free trade and with reciprocity with the United States, the main lines of this tradition were maintained by the Liberal prime minister Sir Wilfrid Laurier. It was not until the premiership of the Liberal leader William Lyon Mackenzie King from 1921 to 1930 (with a brief interruption in 1926), and from 1935 to 1948, and under later Liberal leaders, that this tradition became weakened by the Liberal party's open invitation to American capital to 'develop' Canada. This invitation began to be accepted in earnest in the 1920s. By 1930 American investment in Canada had exceeded the British. After the Second World War the pace of American investment in Canada quickened again so that by 1975 most of Canada's oil and gas, and almost half of its manufacturing sector, is American-owned. The 'development' of Canada into a pattern set by the United States is in fact the ultimate contradiction to the spirit which animated the original conservative tradition. If the Conservative party leadership had not fostered various nation-building state enterprises under Macdonald, Borden and Bennett, and had not rehabilitated the influence of the west and the maritimes under the Conservative prime minister John Diefenbaker from 1957 to 1962, the lineaments of a nation-state distinguishable from the American would be more difficult to find in Canada today.

Yet the Liberal party did move somewhat closer to the conservative traditional belief in strong state leadership after the depression of the 1930s. For example, compared to the United States, Canadian experience with the use of the public corporation is in striking contrast. Not only has public ownership been more widely extended in Canada at the Federal and provincial levels but it has been extended by both Conservative and Liberal Governments at the Federal level and by all parties in the provinces. This extension has taken place in the absence of any acute public controversy over the role of the state in the economy. From the beginning, telephone and electricity supply systems have been more or less publicly owned by the provinces. At the Federal level the Conservative-Unionist Government took over the Canadian National Railway in 1917. There was little public controversy. In fact, A. W. Curry in his *Canadian Transportation Economics* suggests that 'the Canadian public slid into government ownership'.[7] Nor was there much debate over the principle of public ownership in the field of broadcasting. Both the Liberals and the

Conservatives actively supported the recommendation by a parliamentary committee in the early 1930s to establish the Canadian Radio Broadcasting Committee. This was the precursor of the Canadian Broadcasting Corporation. The Conservative Government established a central bank in 1935. Both the Liberals and the Conservatives supported the principle of state ownership of Trans Canada Airlines, now Air Canada, in 1937. The experience of TCA is not unlike the experience of the Canadian Development Corporation (a public corporation to direct more Canadian capital to buy into key industries in Canada) established in 1971. On both occasions the minister introducing the bill indicated that he hoped that private individuals or companies would buy stock in the Corporation, amidst considerable doubts, expressed on both sides of the House, about whether any private buyers would in fact come forward. In fact, the former Conservative prime minister R. B. Bennett argued that if the Federal government allowed private share holders to buy into TCA 'we shall be going in the wrong direction'.

Because of the late arrival of the industrial revolution in Canada the history of state activity in the social services in Canada is somewhat different from the early and direct role of the state in economic development. Here the Canadian conservative tradition until 1945 appears almost reactionary to modern observers. Retarding state penetration of society for social services, especially at the Federal level, has been the special nature of the original rather conservative ideas of individualism in Canada. The original experience of 'individualism' in Canada is not so much atomistic as based on the solidarity of the family. It was essentially the experience of individuals, together with the support of their family, prevailing against the harsh natural environment of Canada. A conviction about the value of this way of life, and the later arrival of the industrial revolution, may have helped to sustain a belief in this type of self-reliant individualism. It was strong enough to postpone any serious attempts to develop state-run social services, other than education, until after the First World War. While Canada has always been much bolder than Britain in its use of state assistance to industry, Britain went much further much earlier than Canada in providing social services, particularly through municipal agencies. Another factor was the division of constitutional authority set down by the British North

America Act. Yet, by the middle of this century, the decline of the social solidarity which supported the family, and the particularly harsh sectoral and cyclical economic fluctuations caused by the climate and by international markets, combined to make demands for more social and welfare services irresistible. It was not until 1930, however, that the Federal government acknowledged a *de facto* responsibility for providing financial assistance for the unemployed and for the victims of drought (when these were of unusual severity). In 1935 the Federal government enacted a measure designed to establish a national system of unemployment insurance, although this was declared unconstitutional by the Judicial Committee of the Privy Council in 1937. After this the Federal government requested the provinces to give their consent to an enabling amendment to the British North America Act to allow a Federal unemployment insurance programme. The provinces agreed in 1941.

Until the Federal government's grant for old age pensions was established in 1927, the care of the aged who were in want was left to private charity and to the municipalities. (In most of the provinces, the municipalities maintained 'houses of refuge' for destitute aged persons.) When the Federal government agreed to pay 50 per cent of the cost of old age pension schemes in 1927, the western provinces and then Ontario rapidly took advantage of this legislation, and the maritimes followed when the Federal government raised its contribution to 75 per cent. Quebec adopted the scheme in 1936. The prairie provinces have acted with the greatest alacrity in extending social services in Canada. The isolation of the prairie farm has no doubt been a factor. For example, the prairies were the first areas of Canada to institute mothers' allowances on the death or disablement of the father. Manitoba made provision for such allowances in 1916, Saskatchewan and Alberta followed in 1917, Ontario and British Columbia in 1920, Nova Scotia in 1930.

Government intervention for the protection of public health has been a fact of life in Canada since 1794, when Lower Canada (now Quebec) passed a Quarantine Act requiring incoming vessels to submit to quarantine, in order to prevent the introduction of pesticidal diseases from abroad. Local boards of health were provided with compulsory powers for inspection of and cleaning of premises in Upper Canada (now Ontario) in 1833, following an outbreak of cholera.[8] Yet at the time of confederation health was generally considered to be a local problem. In Corry's words it did not 'engage the attention of the framers of the British North America Act'. As a result, Federal power in this field remains very limited and Federal financial contributions in this field were not stepped up to any great extent until after the Second World War. A Federal Department of Health was not established until 1919; it was charged primarily with conducting research and promoting public education on health matters, and with cooperating with the provinces in coordinating public health work throughout the country as a whole. The provinces have been more deeply engaged in health work and health services since the latter part of the nineteenth century. In the welfare field, the 1940s witnessed the introduction of several new measures by the Federal government. The Unemployment Insurance Act of 1941 providing unemployment benefits has already been mentioned. The Family Allowance Act of 1944 initiated a programme of allowance for children under the age of sixteen. A national Health Grant Programme was begun in 1948 and broadened in 1953. These grants are to help to rectify deficiencies in the public health services provided by the provinces, such as the four special grants for hospital construction, general public health, mental health and public health research.

Federal expenditure on health and welfare now consumes a large part of the Federal budget. Preliminary estimates for this expenditure at the Federal level amounted to over one-quarter of all the expenditures of the Federal government – $7.8 billion for the fiscal year 1975–6. Of this, family and youth allowances totalled $2 billion. Federal 'Canada Assistance Plan' expenditures were $766 million. (Payments under the Canada Assistance Act are for sharing the costs of assistance and welfare services provided by the provinces to persons in need, including the costs of food, shelter, clothing, utilities, and essential household supplies, funerals, health care services, etc.) The Federal government estimated that it would contribute $1.5 billion to the provinces under the Hospital Insurance and Diagnostic Services Act. Federal contributions to the provinces under the Medical Care Act were estimated at $862 million.

The role of the Federal government in Canada in providing education developed rather later, mainly because of the constitu-

75

tional jurisdiction given to the provinces over education. At the time of confederation, free elementary schools financed by municipalities were made compulsory in most provinces. The provincial governments made grants to local authorities for schools before 1867, and these grants were rapidly followed by central provincial supervision of education. By 1876 Ontario, for example, had a Department of Education with a staff of experts and a responsible minister at its head. The early secondary schools were religious or private institutions. Free secondary education with provincial assistance and supervision did not come until after 1870.[9] Since the early colleges devoted to higher education were founded by religious denominations, they were comparatively free of public control. Now, universities, although receiving most of their grants from provincial governments, maintain considerable independence in their operation. In western Canada there was a desire to avoid dissension between religious denominations. Thus university education was placed under the control of provincial institutions, almost entirely supported by public funds. Because of this clear jurisdictional power of the provinces over education, the Federal government has been careful not to offend the sensitivities, primarily of Quebec, in granting educational funds to the provinces. In 1960 for example, the Federal government's expenditure on education was confined primarily to its jurisdiction within the northwest territories and a small contribution to post-secondary education, allowing Quebec an extra percentage of the Federal government's tax receipts compared to other provinces in the place of direct grants for secondary education. By 1975–6, however, estimated Federal expenditures on 'education' comprised 2.5 per cent of its budget, most of which was the $512 million for post-secondary school adjustment payments to the provinces through the Secretary of State, $89 million through the Federal government's programme to extend bilingualism and biculturalism, and $53 million for the student loan programme.[10] Also $100 million was to be spent on the education of Indian and Eskimo children in the northwest territories. Since 1919 the Federal government has shared wth the provinces the costs of various programmes for the retraining of adults for employment. Beginning in 1919, provincial governments offered a number of adult training programmes and were reimbursed in part by the Federal government. These expenditures were estimated at $688 million for 1975–6.[11]

Most of the provinces spend close to one-half of their budgets on education. This has led to increasing demands for Ottawa's help, however indirect. The most lucrative indirect solution has been the provision of funds not for 'education' but for 'technical and vocational training'. Since 1961, under a formula for the distribution among the provinces of Federal contributions under the Technical and Vocational Training Assistance Act (for financial assistance to the capital cost of training facilities) Ottawa has spent a considerable amount of money (over 2 billion dollars). The Assistance Programme was begun in 1961 under this Act. It continued under the Adult Occupational Training Act in 1967 which set a limit on the total amount payable to each province. In 1971–2, for example, the forecasted expenditure was $337 million for occupational training for adults and $76 million for assistance to the provinces for technical and vocational schools. Not until the late 1960s, however, did Canada begin to approach the per capita expenditures on higher education in, for example, the United States and West Germany. In the mid–1960s the number of students in higher education per 100,000 of population was, in the United States 1,738, in West Germany 1,010, in Canada 619, in France 409, and in Britain 256.[12]

If housing is also looked upon as a social service, it is important to note that from the end of the 1950s to the beginning of the 1970s 40 per cent of the 1.8 million new houses started in Canada were aided one way or another by Federal loans, grants, subsidies or equity participation. Only recently, however, has provision of public housing in Canada begun to reach significant proportions. Since 1960 Federal loans have also been available for providing student accommodation. In contrast to Britain, France and Germany, however, state activity in the housing market in Canada has been largely confined to making it easier for private individuals to secure mortgage loans. In France there has been a policy not only to sponsor the private mortgage market but to build houses directly. West German policy has emphasized the provision of interest-free loans to local authorities, public and private housing associations and to private builders, who in turn agree to keep rents low and to house only the relatively low paid.

77

(3) *The State, the Business Community and Other Interests*

A concomitant of the role of the state in the distributive and developmental history of Canadian economic growth is the dependence of parts of the business community on state initiatives. In 1879 the protective tariff, which had been established by previous governments, was broadened by the Macdonald administration into an integrating 'national policy' by the addition of a railway to the west. Since 1879 the protectionist policies of Macdonald have been followed consistently by all Federal Governments (accompanied by expressions of hope that better conditions for free trade will somehow emerge). This policy – especially the protectionist part of it – has provided some important patronage discretion to the Federal Government. Yet it has also allowed the state to grow, through the tradition of state encouragement of national development and the tradition of distributive particularism.

At the beginning this patronage was less obvious, since the establishment of the Board of Customs in 1888 and the extension of its power in 1904 did not noticeably qualify the requirement of the Federal government to enforce unequivocally those tariffs established in the various statutes. Yet in fact the Board of Customs was given no more than a quasi-judicial power to interpret tariff legislation in order to ensure that some informal adjudication of disputes (with occasional government influence) between importers and custom officials could be made. Not long after the turn of this century a steady increase in executive discretion in tariff-making became evident, and the executive began to be authorized in certain special circumstances to give protection on a day-to-day basis. This gave the executive unusual power to insulate certain businesses against foreign competition as well as to build political alliances with such groups. In the 1920s both the Liberals and the Conservatives condemned this discretionary use of executive power, but neither made any substantial renunciation of these powers once in office. After the Second World War and Canada's acceptance of the General Agreement on Tariffs and Trade, the Canadian tariff structure became more settled. Although considerable discretion can still be exercised by the Government of the day in interpreting various Tariff Acts, executive discretion does not appear to have returned to the same mercurial extent as in the early part of this century.

Not unexpectedly, after the adoption of the National Policy in 1879, it soon became necessary to pass legislative measures to prevent the fostering of monopoly practices, either through unification of financial control of whole industries or through combinations of independent producers dividing the market, limiting output and maintaining prices. A bill introduced in 1889 attempted to attach criminal consequences to certain agreements in restraint of trade. Yet opposition to the measure allowed it to become so watered down that it had little practical effect. Not until 1900 was an amendment passed to make certain combinations to limit supply and to maintain a range of prices a criminal offence punishable with a fine and imprisonment. Also in 1897 an amendment to the Customs Tariff Act provided that, on the initiative of the governor in council (in effect the cabinet), a judicial investigation could be made into allegations that an injurious combine existed. If such a combine was found to exist the governor in council, if satisfied that the injurious operation had been facilitated by a tariff, could reduce or remove the tariff on the articles in question. Again, in 1904 an amendment was made to the Excise Act providing that licencees under the Act who indulged in unreasonable restraints of trade would have to forfeit their licences. Apparently these devices were not very effective. Nor was the Combinations Investigations Act of 1910 which set up an administrative board appointed by the minister of labour to look into combines, since the launching of an investigation was retarded by complicated preliminary steps which were left entirely in the hands of private individuals. Then the Combines Investigation Act of 1923 charged a permanent official, a registrar, with the administration of the Act and it provided that he, or *ad hoc* commissioners, investigate all alleged combines. He could do so on his own initiative or at the request of a minister. Yet the power of the registrar was limited to making investigations. Penalties could only be imposed by taking criminal proceedings in court.[13] In essence, it has been the threat of an investigation, not prosecution in the courts, that has usually deterred some restrictive trade practices. Section 411 of the Criminal Code (formerly 498, passed in 1900) has proved to be the most workable basis for controlling combines, in spite of the rigidity of court interpretation of this provision.

In fact the three major political parties are not against all oligopolies or monopolies. Although the New Democrats, Canada's major Socialist or near-Socialist Party, would choose certain industrial sectors for state ownership, even the two major Federal political parties in Canada believe in 'freeing the market' only within limits. All parties agree in part on the need for more Canadian ownership of Canadian industry and for more labour-intensive industry in Canada, and these are in fact two examples of limits to be put on a free market. Yet the free market itself is flawed in Canada by oligopolies and interlocking interests. To some extent extraordinary examples of unfreedom persist. In Canada, as in Britain but unlike the United States, effective restraint of trade through diffused shareholding in competitive firms, or through interlocking but crossing directorships, is not by itself considered against 'the public interest'. Nor, of course, is the monopoly effect of patents considered against the public interest. There are quasi-monopolistic privileges given through statutory exceptions for large export industries (in the case of the 1960 Combines Bill) and for other industrial formations deemed vital to Canadian national development and marketing coherence (such as the implications in the 1971–2 Farm Market Products Act and the oligopoly and monopoly powers enjoyed by various Crown corporations).

It has also been difficult in Canada for the corporation disclosure provisions in the Federal Corporation Acts to be made nationally applicable because a number of major companies are provincially (not Federally) incorporated. Quebec and Ontario, for example, have more lenient laws of corporate disclosure than Ottawa. This explains in part why little progress has been made at the Federal level in the field of corporate disclosure. In fact not until 1970 did changes come to the Corporation Act, prescribing disclosure of financial statements of businesses with profits over $250,000. This Act had not been altered since 1934. Because of abuses by manufacturers, retailers, advertisers and others the Federal government is moving to other fields hitherto untouched by the state, such as truthful advertising and other pieces of consumer legislation. Because of their very recent passage, these efforts have not been in existence long enough to permit a reliable assessment of their overall impact on the business community.

Another reality flaws the notion of a perfectly free economy in Canada. Since the massive penetration of American influence in the economy – especially since the Second World War – some parts of the Canadian business community may have become more attached to American parental needs than to either government incentives or to the natural character of the Canadian marketplace. Some observers go so far as to describe parts of the Canadian business elite since the Second World War as a 'secondary elite' to the primary business elite in North America which is American. Certainly the growth of multi-national (mostly American) companies in Canada has played a large part in the life of the Canadian business community. Therefore Canadian financial institutions, even if largely Canadian owned, and the Canadian-owned companies which supply the multi-nationals with goods and services, are in fact dependent in part on decisions made outside of Canada (i.e. in corporate head offices and in Washington). The extent to which this is true is the extent to which the business class of Canada may not be a powerful enough force to engineer an independent Canadian course in North America without the pressure of state controls or without the help of continual government incentives and encouragement to develop in directions more congenial to long-term Canadian national interests. It is notable that even with help the community has not exhibited great vigour in pushing independent research and development. For example, in a speech on 26 March 1972 the Canadian senator Maurice Lamontagne was moved to complain of the 'lack of enthusiasm', 'the apathy', 'the passive' stance Canadian industry exhibited after the Federal government called for industry reaction to the Second Canadian Senate Report on Science which opened the way for more government research and development incentives to private industry in Canada. This passivity may be a logical result of the fact that some of the business sector looks beyond its borders for decisions on such matters.

Provincial governments, in pursuit of industrial development, employment-creating activity and broader sources for taxes have encouraged foreign investment. The Federal government has encouraged foreign investment in countless ways but especially in secondary manufacturing through the tariff and in primary industry through tax provisions. Foreign ownership dominates most of the extractive industries, such as the mining and petroleum industries. The Federal tax system has clearly invited not only this but the concentration of foreign owners. To quote Eric Kierans in his paper 'Contribution of the Tax System to Canada's Unemployment and Ownership Problems', delivered to the annual meeting of the Canadian Economics Association, 3 June 1971:

We have not only extended a warm invitation to foreign capital but we have told it where to go. If you invest in the service industries we say you will have to pay taxes on 87 per cent or 90 per cent of your profit. On the other hand, in metal mining, you will only have to pay on 13 per cent, and on petroleum on 5.7 per cent of your profit. The invitation says in effect 'Come and gut us.'

The effects of tax policy varies not only from industry to industry but also varies from the size of the firms within industries. Within each industry the larger the firm, the smaller is the percentage of your book profits that are taxed. For small firms, the typical Canadian case, capital is a scarce factor. ... If the small firm uses capital sparingly it is economically less able to take advantage of the tax subsidies that go to larger competitors.

The strongest investment boom in Canada's history occurred between 1954 and 1957 when investment rose from $5.8 billion to $8.8 billion. This boom was stimulated in part by the special tax provisions for the extractive industries in the Federal government budget of 1955.

Government policy at both the Federal and provincial levels has also failed to encourage much Canadian-produced and Canadian-owned innovative secondary manufacturing activity. Although almost one-fifth of Canada's GNP is exported, Canadian policy has to a large extent relied primarily upon large exports from the extractive industries but it has encouraged high foreign investment in these sectors as well. Canadian exports are heavily concentrated in wheat, iron and other metal ores, petroleum, natural gas, wood pulp, newsprint, lumber, flour, aluminum, coal, and primary iron and steel products. Whereas in most industralized Western countries end-products account for over half of exports, they account for far less in Canada. Nor have governments in Canada been particularly vigorous in forcing the manufacturing sector of the economy to be other than a minia-ture replica of foreign companies. Maintaining the tariff and providing some tax breaks dominated Canadian public policy in this sector until the 1960s. (Under the Diefenbaker government, some steps were taken to improve the plight of small business in Canada through the establishment of the Industrial Development Bank to grant loans to fledgling Canadian companies and a lower tax rate for corporations that made profits of less than $25,000 a year.)

Government policy toward business is reflected not only in tariff, competition, and tax policies but through a myriad of other outputs too numerous to outline here. Yet one significant Canadian development, greatly accelerated since the end of the Second World War, is the practice of providing grants (some tax free), subsidies and other incentives to businesses in the course of government attempts to accomplish other general policy objec-tives such as 'regional economic expansion', or 'employment' or 'export incentives' or 'industrial rationalization'. Here it is not necessary to disentangle the extent to which these indulgences may be more effective as political patronage than as efficient levers for accomplishing the policy objectives mentioned above. (The Quebec Federation of Labour issued a report in the autumn of 1971 condemning the Federal government's regional economic expansion grants and some provincial government programmes as of little value other than as a source of patronage.) But what is notable about this growing list of indulgences is that a reliance on the state not just for non-interference, but also for subsidies and grants, has been as heavy (if not heavier) among large industries as among small. The Federal government's host of industrial aid programmes include: PAIT (Programs for the Advancement of Industrial Technology), IRDIA (Industrial Research and Development Incentives Act), PEP (Programme to Enhance Productivity) and DIP (Defence Industry Productivity Programme). For example, the Federal Department of Regional Economic Expansion planned expenditures of $114.7 million for 'industrial incentives' for 1971–2 (as well as an additional $87.6 for 'infrastructure assistance').[14] The Federal Department of Industry, Trade and Commerce estimated expenditures of $25 million to 'advance the technological capability' of the Canadian manufacturing (non-defence) industry and another $42.3

million for the defence industry for 1971–2; $31 million for 'general incentives to industry for the expansion of scientific research and development in Canada', and $20.5 million to 'construct fishing vessels' and 'to provide assistance to the shipbuilding industry'.[15] The cumulative total of aid to industry simply for export assistance from 1961 to 1971 reached $819 million. (It is notable that small business does not greatly benefit here. Most of the heavily assisted industries have been dominated by large corporations, e.g. telecommunications, ships, locomotives and power generation.[16] However in 1973 the Federal government proposed more government help to supply venture capital for small businesses.)

The Federal government has also been quick to cushion business when faced with a general economic crisis. In the wake of the American surtax on selected Canadian exports instituted on 15 August 1971, the Federal government earmarked $80 million for a programme of assistance to help industries that would be affected. Another $156 million was set aside to help Canadian manufacturing and processing firms 'affected by the imposition of foreign import surtaxes or other actions of a like effect'.

What is significant about the growing amount of state aid to private (and public) industry in Canada is not so much that it occurs – Canada would indeed be unique if it did not – but that unlike the United States, where some ideologically consistent free enterprizers argue against government subsidies to private industry unless tied clearly to 'national security' needs, there has been no audible or visible ideological tension in Canada about this practice. Neither the Chamber of Commerce nor the Canadian Manufacturers Association have expressed any reservations about this 'interference' with private enterprise.

In fact the growth of the state raises profound reservations about the autonomy and independence of interest groups in general including business. As J. P. Nettl once suggested for interest groups in Britain, pressure-group politics are less 'real' than they seem. 'The power of the state, like a magnet, sucks in many interest groups from the periphery, away from their own self-interested groupings, thus gradually emasculating many groups while preserving their outward shell of autonomy and independence.'[17] This process is obvious in the case of a number of important so-called independent interests and their associations ranging from Indian Bands and the Canadian Federation of Agriculture to an endless array of business and other associations.

Perhaps the citadel of power in the private sector can be found at King and Bay streets in Toronto, the head offices of most of Canada's mammoth chartered banks. Yet the concentration and significance of this financial colossus – for all the other difficulties it may create for equitable Canadian development – does have the paradoxical value of giving Ottawa direct and effective agents for its policy shifts on levels of credit, liquidity and interest rates. Ottawa can work immediately through these banks, and do much to set the contours of the so-called 'free economy'. Since it is not difficult to document business dominance of the funding of the Liberal and Conservative Parties, it is assumed that the dynamic of pressure is one way: the business community on government. Yet further reflection suggests that the cost to many business and other interests of its symbiosis with the state could be the erosion of some of its essential autonomy. Therefore free enterprise in Canada can become flawed not only through the gradual elimination of the small private entrepreneur by the growth of large oligopolies, or by the strait-jacket knitted by foreign ownership, but also by the largely unnoticed (since no one has a vested interest in noticing it) phenomenon of government-sponsored, government-encouraged, patterning of business activity.

The image of the rugged entrepreneur persists (even if the reality is becoming increasingly rare) because in Canada he is, as J. P. Nettl once suggested for Britain, 'the only example of a specific business identity that we have'.[18] Economists need this model in order to theorize, project and prescribe. Ministers of Industry, Trade and Commerce, for their own reasons, keep this image illuminated in speeches calling on businesses to export more, to innovate more, and to take more chances more often. Yet many Canadian businessmen are to be forgiven if they find such ministerial exhortations naive: exporters feel they need government help, not exhortations; the managers of foreign-owned businesses know that innovation, risk-taking and exporting are to be done from the home country not from the hinterland. The history of established Canadian firms confirms the success of qualities other than dangerous risk-taking. Yet business retains the image of the rugged entrepreneur, not because it fully

85

accepts it but because it has not as yet found an image with which to replace it.

The necessity for government to consult with interest groups may also force an associational pattern of such groups which in many cases can deflect and distort their natural economic tendencies. Business needs to organize its associations in a way that will allow it to communicate with the Federal government. Although Canada has a number of businesses with firm regional roots, the need for an associational connection with the Federal government forces business associations to follow not a regional pattern but a Federal or national pattern. Let us take one small example. This necessity unites in many cases what, if it were not for the Federal government's needs, it would be essentially unnecessary to unite. From countless points of view Canadian-owned enterprise and foreign-owned enterprise should be profound adversaries; but the need for nationwide farm, business, labour and other associations to meet the Federal government's obligation to consult with nationally representative associations forces them into Federal and national associations. Yet both these distortions – the blurring of regional interests and the blurring of domestic and foreign-owned interests – can tend to work against smaller firms and obscure reality still further. Large Canadian and foreign firms do not like to give the impression of dominating associations, and they therefore help to supply services and personnel for associations, while leaving the combat responsibilities of the association with government to representatives from smaller firms. Yet while the larger firms maintain their influence in the association, vital interests of large domestic and foreign-owned firms, such as pulp and paper companies, oil and gas companies, and automobile companies, are also promoted unilaterally. Therefore the private sector's interaction with government in Canada is somewhat similar to that in Britain. There are two constellations: one made up of firms powerful enough to deal directly and regularly with government; and another, a more atomized world, which must articulate primarily through an association. Dealing with government departments has become a professional business, ever more institutionalized; medium to small-sized business representatives lack status and privilege. Associations and large firms lack neither and enjoy almost institutionalized contacts with government. What often results is that associations help to do the government's work by summarizing the representations of the atomized world of small and medium business, while allowing large firms to listen in. The costs of this relationship for small to medium-sized business, where in fact most of the rugged entrepreneurs may still be found, has seldom been noted in Canada. The role of government in structuring this relationship and hence flawing the image of political scientists of a 'fluid pluralism of groups and interests pressuring government' have gone largely unnoticed in Canada.

In his *Elite Accommodation in Canadian Politics* Robert Presthus finds considerable cohesion, reinforced by shared interaction, political roles and socio-economic properties, among the Canadian political elite (which he defines as including directors of interest groups, cabinet members, MPs, public servants). He finds significant correlations between group interactions with government and their political effectiveness. One-fifth of his sample of Federal public servants who responded even admitted that 'mutual dependence' between 'interest groups and ourselves' was the source of interest group influence. Two-fifths of his entire Canadian sample (which included 451 bureaucrats and legislators from three provinces and Ottawa) admitted that they have been influenced at one time or another to the extent of 'coming to agree' with a position advanced by a lobbyist. Yet also significant is the degree to which the government members of the political elite (MPs, bureaucrats and ministers) perceive themselves as somewhat independent of group pressures. His Table 11-10 shows that only one-fifth of the Ottawa portion of this elite would even agree that 'the information and services' provided by interest groups are 'a necessary part of government policymaking' or that such services 'are necessary to make government aware of the needs of all citizens'. Worth noticing too is the revelation that his sample of Ottawa bureaucrats ranked (in his Table 8-3) the 'public interest' as the major locus of government responsibility, with the 'Government's expectations' second, 'interest group' needs third and 'party policy' fourth. Presthus surmises that given 'the ubiquity of departmental-clientele relationships' it may be that 'this expressed sensitivity to the public interest is mainly honourific' yet there is much evidence in his own study and others to indicate that the bureaucracy's sense of competition with interest groups as sources of information to ministers and the varied tasks of political leaders make both something more than mere registrars of the pressures of the most politically active interest groups.

Perhaps the ultimate irony here is that some government activity not only flaws the model of government responding to the private sector but in fact reverses the model. We see this especially in the brave new world of the public servant acting as entrepreneur and of the businessman acting as public servant. At the Federal and in many instances at provincial levels, government often tries to promote certain efforts to improve the private sector and private enterprise ends up serving. Governments arrange, finance and publicize trade missions, trips to trade fairs, technological innovation and incentive programmes. The Federal Department of Industry encourages improved styling and design, finds new technologies, stores data for the construction industry, subsidizes ship-building, and does major surveys on markets for such products as power generators, aircraft equipment and hardwood furniture. The Federal government is now supplying funds for precontractual work for export firms, defraying costs of infrastructure, and so on. Business and its associations are expected to respond.

The Canadian labour movement too is affected by the state. Not only are many well known rights of union organizations guaranteed, but other day-to-day activities of labour unions are often affected by the state. The power of the Canadian labour movement may be weakened somewhat by the fact that it has not been able to centralize its national organization to the same extent as in Australia and New Zealand, for example. It is fragmented by divisions into English-speaking and French-speaking groups and into unions that are affiliated with the United States and those that are not. Yet even with this fragmentation, and with considerable provincial legislative power because of their control over 'property and civil rights', a Canadian labour code has been fashioned in large measure out of provincial codes. The Canadian Association of Administrators of Labour Legislation, a body made up of the deputy ministers and senior officials of the provincial and Federal labour departments, has helped to develop and maintain a somewhat similar basic policy on labour relations across the country. Although constitutional interpretations have given the major role in labour relations to the provinces (in times other than world wars), the Federal government is quite active not only in administering its labour standards and safety codes but also in conciliation under the Industrial Relations and Disputes Investigation Act. From its inception in 1948, conciliation proceedings under the IRDI Act up to 31 March 1971 saw 1,775 disputes referred to conciliation officers, 1,159 settled by conciliation officers, 549 referred to conciliation boards and 403 settled by them.[19]

Also instructive is Canadian legislative policy in labour relations. Policy has clearly been much more preoccupied with the prevention and settlement of industrial conflict than has been the case in the United States, for example. The preoccupation is understandable. Canada has been the scene of large and frequent industrial conflicts. Conflict can be traced in large measure to the stresses caused by cycles of economic expansion and contraction and by the threats to labour caused by the pace of technological change. Yet these conflicts have been exacerbated by the deep-seated gulf between rhetoric and reality. In Canada both employer and union spokesmen proclaim the ideology of maximum freedom of 'free enterprise', 'free unions', and 'free collective bargaining'. Yet in the words of one prominent scholar of the subject:

> They depend upon a highly complex and somewhat rigid system of laws and administrative procedures with one another ... employers ... depend increasingly on government to enact and enforce laws that will protect them against strikes or other activities of organized labour that would interrupt production or infringe unduly upon management prerogatives.
>
> Union spokesmen, for their part, uphold the ideals of workers' freedom to organize into unions and freedom to strike, picket, and boycott. To achieve such freedoms has likewise led the trade union movement in Canada to depend upon governments to enact and enforce laws that will protect them against various anti-union policies and practices of employers. But such protection has been achieved only at the cost of laws on behalf of employers that put sharp restrictions on unions' freedom of action.[20]

What has developed therefore in the opinion of the author quoted above is excessive dependence upon legal prescriptions and procedures, despite union and employer ideologies that profess to uphold freedom from government control.

The influence of these and provincial efforts of conciliation on the labour and business communities may be greater in Canada than in the United Kingdom and the United States because in Canada there is provision for compulsory conciliation and arbitration. This compulsion may enable the Labour-Management Consultation Branch of the Federal Department of Labour to boast that its nationwide programme of 'joint consultation' creates better understanding between the two parties, reduces the number of normal grievances, and accelerates the settlement of collective agreements. Its statistics on the extent of this programme also reveal that the state is deeply involved in such efforts.

At 31 March 1971, there were 782,919 participants in joint consultations. Of these, 148,623 represented 460 labour-management committees . . . in companies under Federal jurisdiction and 634,296 represented by 2,276 committees in companies under provincial jurisdiction. More than 10,000 meetings were held with management, union, Federal, provincial, and civic representatives to service existing committees or to promote the joint consultation philosophy. There was 1,957 contacts with individual organizations under federal jurisdiction and 4,706 under provincial jurisdiction.[21]

Nor are business and labour unique in their ever-widening relationship with the state. The relationship of interdependence between farm groups and Federal and provincial governments ranges from contacts on departmental advisory councils, boards and commissions to lobbying for research grants or for increased price supports. Given the failure of the private sector to sustain them, other groups and associations, which were considerably independent twenty years ago, now find themselves in a position of financial dependence on, even if not as yet detailed control by, the state. For example, the Federal government in 1971-2 produced programmes of assistance to countless numbers of groups and associations through the Federal government's Opportunities for Youth grants and its Local Initiatives Programme. Over $100 million was allocated for 1972 for each of these two programmes. The Federal government had received, by the beginning of 1972, 3,722 project applications from private community organizations and 1,233 from municipalities.[22] In the field of culture, Federal grant recipients include the National Film Board; the Canadian Film Development Corporation; 'youth groups defining and solving problems related to transient youth, unemployed youth, etc'; native groups; citizens groups; welfare organizations; fitness and amateur sport; consumer organizations; bilingualism development in the non-government sector; and the Canada Council (which supports independent research in the social sciences and the humanities, the arts, gives grants to book publishers, etc.). Farm, professional, labour, trade and community groups, by taking seats on departmental advisory councils or by establishing an informal right to be consulted, may bring themselves influence but they can also diminish their independence by integrating themselves with the state.

(4) *The State's Identification With Society*

The state has advanced in its relation to society so that it now enjoys an important role in setting not only the contours of economic, social and associational life but also the nature of Canada's federal society. As we have seen, the agreements on confederation from 1864 to 1866 were profoundly centralist, barely confederal, giving the Federal government statutory preeminence over the provinces in a number of vital policy fields. After a resurgence of provincial influence in the first half of this century, Ottawa's concern for the development of programmes that deal, in its words, with 'broad national problems' such as 'community development', 'training', 'regional development' and 'urban policy' has been carefully phrased so as not to appear to be an invasion of provincial jurisdiction over such matters as 'culture' or 'education' or 'municipalities'. This Federal instinct when combined with the Federal government's unfettered spending and taxing power, is able in effect to force provinces to accept Federal initiatives in those areas of policy in which pressure on provincial treasuries is heavy and continuing. Yet in one sense it matters not where the initiatives or ultimate leverage lie. The growth of the state apparatus – Federal, provincial and local – continues, thanks to the momentum afforded by the not infrequent possibility of substitution by Federal for provincial activity if the provincial governments find themselves unable or unwilling to increase their activity.

The role of the state in early Canadian economic development was of utmost importance in the last century. The 'state' was not, of course, single or constant. For example, financial assistance for the construction of railroads was provided by municipal, provincial, Federal and imperial governments. And provincial, Federal, even municipal governments all continue to play a role in economic development today. Yet what is important to note for our purposes is the readiness of these governments to plan and encourage economic activity. Lord Durham noted in 1839 the contrast between the proclivity of governments in the 'old world' to spend vast sums on defence and the proclivity of governments in the 'new world' to spend vast sums on 'their war with the wilderness'. Durham may have been thinking of the United States but certainly his words apply to what is now Canada. The governments of Nova Scotia, Upper and Lower Canada had spent much on canals and railways. Soon after confederation the Federal government put great efforts into organizing and planning the settlement and agricultural development of western Canada, to settling the economic conditions for heavy industry in Ontario and light industry in Quebec and to attempting to abate the decline in the maritime economy.

In this century too the state has been active. The west coast pulp and paper industry has been encouraged. Improved canal and railway systems culminating in the St Lawrence Seaway have been pushed. These eventually led to an emphasis not solely on transport improvement but on the construction of hydro-electric power developments on the St Lawrence and at Niagara Falls. After the Second World War, the Federal government, thanks to tax increases, encouraged the exploitation of new resources of crude oil, especially in Alberta, and even allowed the eastern line of one pipeline to terminate in the United States for refining there. (The Federal government, however, has been more restrictive over exports of natural gas and hydro-electric power.) The state, therefore, has a tradition of planning, financing, and encouraging certain key areas of economic life.

After the Second World War, however, it is safe to say that the state missed a major opportunity to co-ordinate economic development with national independence. A great opportunity was missed to motivate Canadian industrialization. The war effort accelerated Canada's industrialization, giving Canadian businessmen and labour considerable experience in the techniques and discipline of large-scale production. For example, Canada had all the elements needed for an indigenous automotive industry. No massive investments were needed to make Canada a nation of heavy industry. Canada was a capital exporter. Instead the Liberal Federal Government in effect rejected this new indigenous pattern and converted itself to a belief in the efficacy of 'free' international capital movements. Amidst some Conservative and CCF complaints, it allowed American capital to shift Canada back to a concentration on the extraction of natural resources, hence squandering much of Canada's industrial capital accumulation.

This submission to continental market forces was a break from the original Conservative strategy for economic and political development. Federal leadership under Macdonald emphasized mobilization of debt capital for its all-railway route to the west and its 'national policy' of protection. It may be that the German experience at the time in using more state-owned enterprises might have been equally effective; but the capital might not have been sufficient to the task. It can be said that without both these initiatives the Macdonald and Upper Canadian conservative conception of the transcontinental nation would not have been possible. It might be added that these initiatives also allowed for the indispensable presence of the state in the 'new Canada' west of Lake Superior. Federal government support for a railway to the west coast helped the Federal part of the state to manage British Columbia's entry into confederation. State management of the settlement of the prairies also helped to build not only a transcontinental nation but a transcontinental state as well. In fact the role of the state in the first twenty years after confederation in developing the Canadian nation was so pervasive that it is difficult to separate empirically the will of the state from the attributes of the nation. What was constructed was a nation/state or state/nation. The experience of the last third of the nineteenth century shows that the state (primarily the Federal part of it) was the main element in developing the nation and the society.

(5) *The State and Canadian Society: A Summary*

To comprehend the state's relation to society, especially in the development of Canada, one must question a well-known Marxist assumption about the nature of states. Marx unquestionably regarded the state as a mere superstructure, a sort of subsidiary organism or 'shell', which gained its character solely through the way its inhabitants used it. Marx could see without much difficulty that the bourgeoisie, more or less, were the tenants of the state apparatus of Europe. In Canada Marx's definition of bourgeoisie probably describes the tenants of the Canadian state apparatus, at least since responsible government in 1848, if not before. Marx noted, too, as Stanley Ryerson[23] and others have noted in the case of Canada, that the state was frequently used to repress rebellions and to maintain order. From this coincidence of events with action, Marx made the simple conclusion that the state was nothing except a protagonist in the class struggle. However, this interpretation is partial and therefore deficient. It ignores, in the Canadian and probably in most national, contexts, the singular character, the specificity, of state power which distinguishes its power from mere partisan class political power. Jacques Ellul perhaps overstates but he helps us to see this in *Autopsy of Revolution,* where he argues that the character of the state has to be explained not solely in terms of the class exercising state power but in terms of the structure of that power.

The state, in relation to the economic and social system is super order, an active organizer, and not a machine . . . It appears that the state's role is primary, not secondary. Totally creative, and not merely the instrument of the class struggle, it manifests the profound essence of society and makes us realize that . . . what is at stake is not the relationship between two classes within . . . society, but the relationship of that society to the state. Only within such a conceptual framework can the essence and relative value of the class struggle be seen and the state's sociological role in the emergence of classes be understood. The class struggle does not explain the state, for it is ultimately subordinate to the state. [The class struggle] is not the motion of history, the real issue is the new structure of that power: the invasion of society by the state . . . the growth of the state, its superordination in relation to everything around it and its crucial nature, is not confined solely to authoritarian states or dictatorships. Neither its constitutional form nor its system of operation is of prime significance.[24]

Thanks to its growth in Canada, and its ability to identify itself with national development and local particularisms, the state took on a life of its own. Its essence is far more complex than Marx suggests. It created political units at confederation, it created, fostered and protected certain cultural and economic attributes, and it created and sustained certain demands and elites which are far more complex than are those of the bourgeoisie. From the nation-building exertions of the first fifty years to the distributive and foreign investment incentives of the last fifty, the creations of the state were the results in part of the partisan use of the state by its tenants; but they were more than this. The state gradually began to assume responsibility for more and more activities because no agency existed in the society as a whole capable of doing what had to be done. As we have seen, railways were financed and then finally bought by the state. Health, education and care of the destitute became less private concerns of the family and the Church and more state concerns. In the 1970s one also finds that one common denominator of most of the problems created by the technological age, such as pollution, drugs and traffic jams, is that they require government help (often Federal government help) to correct and forestall. Soon the articulations of all political parties and demand groups in society, whether bourgeois or not, if unhappy with specific acts or inactions of the state, increasingly begin to place their emphasis on the state for ameliorative action. What is more, the needs of individuals and of society in Canada increasingly began to be packaged and articulated not simply from individuals and sub-units of society to the state but increasingly from one part of the state to another part of the state through the dialogue of federal-provincial relations or through bureaucratic channels and bureaucratic internal interaction. The state hence becomes increasingly abstract and begins to be identified increasingly with society. In short, the whole movement of the state has been from a mere mechanism separate from society, to part of the organism of society, so that the two are inextricably intermeshed. The question which remains, however, is the extent to which this organism has left itself within the flux of a larger force: the technological growth and Americanization of North America. This is not the place to measure the extent. But this is the place to note that the instrument for reversing this drift in Canada has always been the state. Canadians have not, from the early years of its conservative tradition, been greatly adverse to the use of the state; and herein may lie Canada's hopes for plotting a more independent course in North America. Let us now look at Canada's place in North America and beyond.

4 Canada in the World

We have noted the increased interdependence between the state and society and the potency of the state for federal integration and for defining Canadian society. More difficult, however, is to assess the extent to which the state and society in Canada are themselves caught within larger international forces that may prove more powerful than either the state's capacity for internal development or society's. The foremost international patterns are the international market place, the pressures of technological transformation, and foreign influence over domestic priorities.

To some extent Canada has developed and has met its inner economic needs by explicitly subordinating itself to some of the needs of the international market place by engaging in resource extraction for other developed countries of the world. Canada has not been able totally to rely on this, however, and the state has had to help foster other activities as well. To some extent this framework, together with state supplementation, persists. Canada's place in the international and North American continental framework of the 1970s can be introduced by observing its trade patterns, its relations with the United States, and other dimensions of its foreign policy, especially defence and diplomacy. The recent reforms to integrate the external activity at the Federal level will be outlined at the end of this chapter.

(1) *Trade, Commerce and Investment*

Canada's trade patterns are obviously a major part of its political

97

and economic future. Its exports are probably a more important component of its economic growth than is the case in any other major industrial nation. In the early 1970s over-all exports were equivalent to 20 per cent of the country's gross national product – a greater proportion of GNP than is the case in Japan. Yet Canada is the only major industrial nation in the world without direct participation in a market of a hundred million or more people. Canada's most important export market is the United States (approximately two-thirds of Canada's exports go to the US each year). The United States also consumes over three-quarters of all of Canada's manufactured exports each year. Yet Canada's over-all access to the American manufactured goods market has never been very impressive. It is likely to remain unimpressive given the protectionist tone of the Americans and given Canada's disinclination to move to freer trade with the United States. Compared to member countries of the OECD, Canada's percentage of workers employed in the manufacturing sector is low – 23.3 per cent. compared to 36.3 per cent in Britain and 38.2 per cent in Germany. Canada wishes to develop its manufactured and processed exports outside of America, yet it recognizes that, in the Pacific, it will have to compete with three aggressive export traders, the Japanese, the Americans, and the Australians; in Europe with the United States; and in Latin America with the United States again. It is true that Canadian aggressiveness in promoting such exports in these regions goes beyond preliminary promotion efforts. But it has not appeared to come to grips with ambitions for a labour-intensive industrial strategy, or with the readily apparent competitive factors of the international marketplace, especially in the Pacific. An aggressive, imaginative attempt is necessary to identify the skills and services that Pacific, Latin American, and European nations lack and which Canada could supply. Such an approach might also help to orient the priorities of Canada's research, development and education strategies. For example, Canada's work in marine research, transportation, harbour development and planning and engineering of its resources, could all be exported in the form of consulting and engineering services, prototype supplies, tool and die exports. Canada is also clearly qualified, as the 1970 Federal White Paper on foreign policy notes, to provide technical expertise in the fields of telecommunications, grain storage facilities, hydro-electric equipment, pulp and paper machinery, specialized aircraft, subway, road and rail equipment, nuclear reactors, airport construction, aerial surveys, and educational equipment. Identification of capabilities and potential, combined with the freeing of export opportunities for foreign subsidiaries in Canada is imperative if Canada is to increase its exports of fabricated materials, end products, and services.

To pursue all these options is in essence to pursue more vigorously the conventional Canadian trade strategy of relying on about two-thirds of Canadian exports going to the United States together with *ad hoc* attempts to develop exports outside the United States to decrease this dependence, at least incrementally. This strategy, if vigorously pursued, might afford some important increases in Canada's exports outside the United States. Yet some Canadians are generating at least three fundamentally different perspectives on the whole approach.

There are always those (notably British Columbia's premier W. A. C. Bennett in 1971) who call for an end to the insistence that non-American markets should be pursued as a 'counterveiling force' to US trade. This argument is that Canada should aim primarily for a 'free trade common market between Canada and the United States'. This view is evident in the Canadian Chamber of Commerce, in government circles in a number of provinces, and in a massive 1975 report of the Economic Council of Canada.

On the other hand, a small but growing number of Canadians are beginning to glimpse the congruence between Canada's problem of dependence on resource exports and its difficulties in generating exports of end-products with the problems of a number of many developing (if less wealthy) countries. Canada and a number of developing countries are facing the problem of having to export more resources to pay for the same amount of end-products imported from industrialized countries (80 per cent of the foreign-exchange earnings of developing countries come from exports of primary commodities). Canada, according to this logic, might be wise to consider initiating more discussions with developing countries to begin a concerted re-examination of their common problems. Perhaps the energy crisis will spur this.

Another school of thought argues that any of these strategies (including the conventional one) cannot be pursued effectively by any Canadian Government as long as all the disincentives against making such strategies work continue to be sown into Canada's industrial structure by the foreign ownership of its economy. To some extent this view was supported in a private paper produced for the cabinet on foreign investment. It was not accepted by the cabinet but was subsequently published by the *Canadian Forum* in December 1971. It is the premise of this school that foreign ownership of key sectors of Canada's economy must be lessened before any strategy emphasizing either less dependence on trade with the United States or (its opposite) free trade could be workable. To try to alter present patterns without lifting the 'dead hand' of foreign ownership on Canada's export performance (according to this argument) is to pursue a Quixotic policy. This view is not confined to this report, or to a wing of the New Democratic Party but appears to a lesser degree as well in the October 1971 analysis of the Science Council of Canada.

It is difficult to predict how important these three radically different strategies will be in the 1970s, but there should be no mistaking that they arise in part out of a growing widespread concern about the efficacy of the conventional strategy. One result is certain, however, Federal government leadership will be vital no matter what strategy is chosen.

The considerable disparity in size and structure between the American and Canadian economies, and the diversity of the economic relations between them, have forced the two countries to perceive their mutual economic problems in fundamentally different ways. The United States is Canada's most important trading partner; American reliance on Canada for its trade, while sizable, is less pronounced. Economic issues of great importance to Canada are most often handled in a multilateral context by the American government. The impact of an American policy decision on Canada may not be considered any more seriously than its impact on a number of other countries likely to be affected. Frequently, American relations with a third country determine policies which affect Canadian interests. For example, in an attempt to amend what was considered a disadvantageous trade position with Japan, the United States reinforced the administration of its anti-dumping laws, with some pernicious consequences for Canada. Another example is the US Tariff Commission's 1970 report, recommending retention of tariff exemptions for re-entry of American-made parts assembled abroad. This clearly benefited Canadian manufacturers. Yet the exemptions were jeopardized by AFL-CIO pressure directed not against Canada but against the number of factories set up in Mexico, Formosa and South Korea which have been using cheap labour to assemble parts re-entering without duty.

The obvious remedy for such situations has been for the Federal government to establish Canada's status as a special case in those areas of vital interest directly affected by American economic policy. In wartime and the early postwar years, for example, Canadian importers were assisted in the purchase of scarce but vital commodities by the Hyde Park principle of sharing adopted by the two countries in 1941. Since then the Canadian government has treated this concept of 'sharing' gingerly, because it smacked of 'integration' and would have given the United States an undesirable bargaining advantage in the conduct of economic relations. Yet, in certain areas, Canada has sought various forms of 'special status'; for example, with respect to privileged access for certain Canadian exports such as crude oil, for exemption from the US Interest Equalization Tax, in Defence Production Sharing Agreements, in modified free trade in automobiles, and so on. Frequently Canada's special interests have usually been recognized as such by the United States because they coincided with the important interests of its own, yet frequently they have been overlooked in Washington. Two examples of such oversights are the original blanket imposition of the Interest Equalization Tax in 1963, and the Immigration Act of 1968 (now being amended) which so reduced the quota of Canadian immigrants into the United States as to make company personnel transfer between the two countries extremely difficult.

More difficult is to identify the extent of 'special treatment' and the lack of it in all the economic dimensions of American-Canadian relations. The subject matter of Canadian-American economic relations is vast and varied, covering such problems as the alignment of wheat prices, the administration of customs duties, the continued export of Canadian softwood lumber which is threatened by western lumber interests in the United States, the effort to secure an exemption for Canadian-produced books from the manufacturing clause of the United States Copyright Law which inhibits their importation, and the annual problem of commodity trade between two countries with different growing seasons.

Three particular issues, however, have ranked highest on the agenda of Canadian-American negotiations in the 1960s and 1970s because of their impact on Canadian society and the challenge they present to state leadership. They are: natural resources, trade and capital movements, and the ownership of Canadian industry.

The issue of 'resource sharing' is not new to American-Canadian relations. Five provinces – New Brunswick, Quebec, Ontario, Manitoba and British Columbia – have hydro-electric power hook-ups with American states. Most attention, however, has been directed to the subject of Canadian exports of crude oil to the United States which were breaking all records in early 1970, and were then cut back by presidential decision. To many Canadians, the decision appeared to be a deliberate effort to force Canada to agree to a free market in energy resources. Now it is Canada that wants to limit these exports, not the United States.

Canada is unique among nations in being both an importer and an exporter of oil. It is an exporter by virtue of a favourable quota, originally granted by the Eisenhower Administration on the grounds that Canada could be considered a militarily secure source of supply. Since 1973, however, Quebec and the Maritimes have received their supplies from sources more costly and judged to be more insecure (Venezuela and, to a much lesser extent, the Middle East). Therefore when an East-West oil pipeline (which the Canadian oil industry now considers economic) is built, it will remove the temptation for Canada to enter the American market to compete for limited oil supplies in the event of an international crisis cutting off present overseas sources.

Including oil and gas, two-thirds or more of Canada's overall imports come from the United States [as noted the same proportion of Canadian exports are usually purchased in the United States]. Canadians who are concerned about this reliance on the American market naturally take satisfaction in seeing new trade markets open up in other parts of the world. At present no nation other than the United States takes as much as 10 per cent of Canada's sales abroad, and maintaining and extending access to all foreign markets has therefore been a recurring hope of Federal government policy utterances on trade. To do this, Canada has tried to discourage the development of protectionist blocs in the United States and elsewhere, and has applauded American efforts championing free trade. This explains Canadian enthusiasm for the formation of GATT (General Agreement on Trade and Tariffs) and Canada's careful efforts to ensure American membership. It also explains its lukewarm attitude to the European Common Market's external tariff structure. In the 1970s it is obvious once more that it is in establishing decreasingly protective international standards of commercial behaviour that Canada hopes to restrain protectionist sentiment in the United States and in the EEC. Protectionist sentiment is always feared, not only for its effects on Canadian exports but for the antagonism it could arouse among other trading partners. An economy as heavily dependent on trade as Canada's could be mortally wounded by a mounting wave of trade protectionism. Typically, within months of the August 1971 announcement of the 10 per cent American surtax on imports, the Canadian trade minister announced that the Canadian government would open a new offensive for more liberalized trade in the Western world.

To open up more markets outside the United States and to open up opportunities for more manufactured or processed exports everywhere now appears imperative to the Federal government because of the relationship between bilateral trade and the movement of American capital into Canada and within Canada. The standard pattern of the postwar years has been that of a Canadian current account deficit with the United States compensated by a capital account surplus. An important anomaly explaining this capital account surplus is that Canadians, who are among the highest savers in the world, have considered themselves in the past to be unable to fulfil their own capital requirements. Counting foreign reserves accumulation as a capital export, Canada was a net exporter of capital in 1970 for example. (Speeches by provincial premiers indicate that most of them believe that the need for selected amounts of foreign capital will continue in the 1970s as well.) This domestic capital deficiency has been variously attributed to the lack of a merchant banking facility able to provide risk capital at medium terms; to the inherent caution of Canadian investors; to the use of Canadian savings for American takeovers instead of for new enterprise; to the high Canadian investment outside Canada; and to the un-doubted magnitude of Canada's capital needs. To argue that Canada has been short of capital may therefore be incorrect; it may be more accurate to say that it is in the *organization* of mas-sive investments for large resource and industrial developments that New York and Chicago have outdone Toronto and Montreal. The Federal government may now move to alter some of this with its foreign investment review legislation.

Also central to trade and capital movements between the two countries is the emerging problem of the slow growth of the manufacturing sector in Canada, particularly after noting the strength of the Canadian manufacturing sector in the early 1960s. The chairman of the Science Council of Canada has argued that Canada in the 1970's is in real danger of becoming a post-industrial state that does not have the industrial base to sustain its economy.[1] Since American policy-makers in the 1970s are also concerned about the deterioration in their trade balance with Canada, this fear is well-founded. After decades of Ameri-can trade surpluses with Canada, it appears that Canada emerged in 1970 with a surplus (although, according to prelimin-ary indications, this surplus declined almost to nothing in 1971). The Auto Pact, the defence production sharing agreements, and growing Canadian oil exports were the major contributors to the 1970 surplus. Canada's foreign exchange reserves have climbed to record levels in the 1970s as well. In December 1968 the govern-ments in Washington and Ottawa agreed that Canada no longer needed to keep a ceiling on her reserves, but that the Canadian government should nonetheless exert its efforts to hold down Canadian borrowing in the United States. By 1972, however, this emphasis had lessened in Washington. American efforts to increase its economic leverage in Canada centred on a strategy to increase Canada's imports of manufactured goods from the United States *and* to allow foreign investments to develop Canada's resources for export. New to US-Canadian relations is the hardening American attitude towards capital outflows, the Auto Pact, and other trade questions. As a result Canada's current account deficit widened greatly from 1972 to 1974 and 1975. All this must lead to a tough and coordinated effort of will at White House and Federal cabinet levels in this decade. This is in significant contrast to much of Canadian-American relations since the Second World War. In a paper written towards the end of the 1960s, based upon a number of interviews with senior career officials of the Canadian Departments of Finance, External Affairs, and Industry, Trade and Commerce, in October 1969, a University of British Columbia political scientist was able to suggest various inhibitions on both the United States and Canada against pressing either's power too far in their relations with each other.[2] He explained this primarily by reference to the 'diplomatic ethic and culture', between the two countries, not simply the 'mutuality of interests' which exists between them. This ethic and culture helped to explain how agreements were reached 'without wide publicity' and with a 'mutual feeling of ease and frankness'. He argued also that the 'willingness of the agencies of one government to act in the interests of another [government]', the relative absence of 'spillover of conflict from one issue area to another', helped to keep the diplomatic culture acting in a way which leads to (what each country saw as) 'responsible behaviour'. This he concluded, could to a certain extent make diplomatic relations 'immune to the vagaries and personalities of the top level'. It appears now that this characterization no longer reflects US-Canadian relations on major questions of trade. This is yet another burden for the Canadian Federal state. Not only must it continue to negotiate agreements, but now it must do so amidst considerable publicity because of the centralized nature and general notoriety of the negotiations.

Another area of international economic policy where acts of state initiative and control will be more evident than in the past is Canada's whole approach to lessening, or at least monitoring, foreign ownership of its economy. In addition to the well documented extent of foreign (mostly American) ownership of the Canadian economy, there are other dimensions of this problem which will increasingly involve government action from Ottawa and from provincial capitals.

Foreign acquisitions of Canadian business, for example, increased alarmingly in the later 1950s and early 1960s. Horizontal mergers – those involving competitors selling the same products in the same market – accounted for about one-quarter of foreign takeovers and about half of domestic mergers. Vertical mergers – acquisition of suppliers or customers – accounted for 18 per cent of the domestic and 31 per cent of the international mergers during this period. Approximately 80 per cent of both domestic and international mergers occurred in the manufacturing and trade sectors of the economy. The causes of foreign acquisitions can be traced to rather prosaic micro-economic realities. A study for the Economic Council of Canada examined data on mergers in Canada between 1945 and 1961 and found that the number of foreign takeovers of Canadian companies tended to rise as a function of increasing merger activity in the United States, declining levels of corporate liquidity in Canada, and increases in business failures in Canada.

What also continues to aggravate many Canadian observers is that the extension of American control is largely financed within Canada once the American interest has marshalled the initial capital and assumed the initial risk. Recent statistics of the US Chamber of Commerce show that retained earnings, depreciation and depletion allowances provided approximately 66 per cent of the capital funds raised by a selected group of Canadian subsidiaries – principally for new investment and for the takeover of other Canadian companies from 1963–5. Further, in 1968, 20.3 per cent of these funds were raised on Canadian money markets and only 4.9 per cent on American. Between 1963 and 1968 the subsidiaries surveyed (which represent a fairly good sample of all American affiliates in Canada) raised $1,244 million in the United States and $2,007 million in non-American – mainly Canadian – money markets.[3] It is clear, then, that foreign-owned industries are absorbing substantial quantities of indigenous Canadian capital. This absorption has prompted complaints that 'Canada is being bought out with its own money'.

Others regard this way of articulating the problem as deceptive, since about two-thirds of capital funds are cash flows generated from retained earnings, depreciation and depletion allowances. And if these assets are considered to be foreign-owned, then these sources must be viewed similarly. Also it is clear that foreign investment can be of substantial benefit in the long run in ways unacknowledged by its critics. Summarizing the usual argument on this latter point, one Canadian economist points to the fact that over half of all the direct profit from foreign investment remains in Canada in the form of: corporation income tax payments to the government; withholding taxes on external dividend payments; and dividends received by Canadians who directly or indirectly hold equity in foreign-controlled corporations in Canada. Additional benefits accrue to Canada through the indirect effects of foreign investment: in raising the earnings of domestic productive factors, including labour; and in increasing productivity and/or reducing prices.[4]

These benefits are important. Nevertheless, this emphasis should not be allowed to obscure the fact that dividend payments are but one of a number of reasons which force multi-national corporations to maintain foreign subsidiaries. For example, to the extent that a more or less assured market exists for the component or finished exports of a parent at prices that can be manipulated by the parent, this surely involves a 'cost' to the host country. American investors, in particular, prefer wholly owned subsidiaries (unlike the Japanese, who are prepared to take a minority equity position), for this facilitates a strategy of taking the main profits through the parent. And the decisions on how to price products sold among subsidiaries can be made dependent on the tariffs and taxes prevailing in each country.

Many Canadian economists dispute the relevance of much of this. For example, it may be true that with respect to some allegations of poor subsidiary export and research performance, suspicions of a number of foreign subsidiaries are largely speculation. Yet it is difficult to argue that the present pattern of multinational corporate activity in Canada, at the manufacturing level, does not, on occasion, open the way for a shifting of profit from Canada to the parent through high management fees, overcharging subsidiaries for goods bought from the parent or its other subsidiaries, and through heavy charges for services supplied by the parent. It is also difficult to argue against the proposition that one of the sources of Canada's underemployment can, in some instances, be traced to an uncreative manufacturing sector and the purely extractive nature of some resource industries; and this can be a result of some types of foreign investment. The encouragement in Canada of miniature replicas of foreign (largely American) product lines can fulfil market needs profitably enough, and the subsidiary can therefore be discouraged from pursuing its own research and development in order to produce a different product, specifically Canadian, and suitable for export.

The deepest dent made in Canadian public opinion about

American influence in Canada may have been made by President Nixon on 15 August 1971, when he slapped a 10 per cent surtax on a number of American imports, at least 25 per cent of which affected Canada. Before this, the nationalist writers were probably more successful in reaching public opinion on the political, rather than economic, aspects of their case. In a Gallup poll published as early as January 1971, 59 per cent of Canadians said that a growing concern over Canadian nationalism was a good thing for the country. Only 8 per cent said it was not. This mood can be traced in part to the fact that the experiences of Canadian and American societies have diverged rather radically in the last ten years. Such developments as the American urban crisis, and the Vietnam War, have given Canadians the occasion to gain some sense of national attributes and national objectives which distinguish them from Americans. Many will say that these distinguishing features are not defined. Yet at least the search is a fact, and demands for sovereignty and freedom of action have unquestionably emerged. What is notable is that the state must meet these demands with little help or encouragement from the forces in society that are foreign-owned. Yet the state has had to act because of its own inner needs and because of outside realities.

Canada's economic linkages with the United States can endanger the potency of the Canadian state in at least six important ways: the potential threat of generalized retaliation against undesired Canadian behaviour; the threat of specific retaliation for actions of economic policy detrimental to American interests; the inability to affect business policies because of the transfer of decision-making to the United States; the extra-territorial application of American laws and regulations in Canada; the 'penetrative influences' of American multi-national corporations as carriers of American cultural values and political influences promoting American objectives; and involvement by implication (for example, defence production sharing agreements).

It may be true that it will prove very difficult for the Canadian Federal government to change much of this overnight. To many observers 'interdependence' seems inevitable. In its less palatable version, the argument of interdependence is a forthright statement of the inevitability of *dependence*. Judd Polk, an American banker, in a paper prepared for a Columbia University Conference on Canadian-American relations in 1970, argued that the most significant continental linkages are simply not susceptible to national treatment on Canada's part. The Canadian tax structure cannot diverge too radically from the American; wage pressures in the more advanced industrial economy are bound to be communicated north of the border, and so on. Even by itself, the catalogue of linkages appears to make an overwhelming case for continued interdependence: the paper estimates that 54 per cent of Canada's GNP is the product of American investment and imports; financial and money markets are one; financial institutions are intermeshed; foreign ownership and most of its effects are facts of life; and to consider breaking the links is to think the unthinkable.

This is an argument more noteworthy for its psychological than its intellectual power. But it suggests very strongly that the economic relationship does yield definite parameters which have governed Canadian freedom of action; that there is an immovable *structure* concealed beneath the mass of day-to-day dealings between Canada and the United States. The great imponderable confronting observers of the Canadian state is that these parameters have never been tested much before this decade, and thus the power of the Canadian state to alter that structure has not been fully tested. Until the late 1960s, it was evident that most of the assumptions of the key policy-makers and advisers in the public service and outside promoted the idea that the Canadian economy could only be harmed if disincentives against foreign investment were allowed to slow down the growth of the Canadian economy, especially in the resource centres. A mildly 'nationalist' budget prepared by the finance minister, Walter Gordon, in 1964, had to be prepared in part by himself and a small group of outside advisers because of the lack of enthusiasm for it in his department. That the Federal and provincial governments have not acted too vigorously on this question of foreign ownership, no doubt reflects the fact that the dangers of inaction have not revealed themselves until recently. The state has only just begun to feel public pressure for some action and to question whether the very potency of the state itself may be in danger if nothing is done. Already it is reorganizing itself at the Federal level to integrate its external activities so as to organize better its approach to this and other areas of external policy.

(2) *Other Dimensions of Canadian Foreign Policy: The Decline of Voluntarism Beyond North America*

It would be easy to forget, in the above emphasis on Canada's international economic problems, that Canadian foreign policy, especially since the Second World War, has exhibited an 'internationalist' thrust. At times, it has appeared to be almost altruistic, e.g. when Canada agreed to serve on the peacekeeping mission in Vietnam in 1973. In most cases, however, the internationalist emphasis has not been difficult to square with Canadian national interests. Canada's interest in world trade liberalization is complemented by a Canadian emphasis on internationalism. Canada's impotence to affect through its own power any world military configuration has also made it useful to support NATO and NORAD where at least formal consultation with allies is provided. Canada's search for both material and symbolic counterweights to the United States has led to a Canadian cultivation of European contacts, vigorous efforts to hold the Commonwealth together and relentless efforts to help prop up and sustain the United Nations. Canada's inability to affect the arms race on its own has left it with little option but to exhibit enthusiasm and patience for any potential East-West disarmament or mutual security agreement. Canadian fears that small crises can escalate to major power confrontations have led to a Canadian willingness to contribute to UN-sponsored peacekeeping ventures and to steadfast, if monotonous, Canadian requests to the belligerents 'to come to the conference table to settle differences peaceably'. Clearly, then, 'internationalism' in most cases has been generated by Canadian 'national interests'.

Until recently, another characteristic besides 'internationalism' has been present in Canadian external policy. Canada's postwar contributions to NATO and to peacekeeping can be understood in part as expressions of a trait unique to Anglo-American experience – the 'voluntarist' outlook of the key makers of Canadian foreign policy. This is exhibited in Canada's emphasis, when talking about distant international constellations, on the importance of acts of faith and goodwill and good atmosphere, all of which emphasizes empirical restraints. Geographical, and to some extent historical separation from the European continent helped at one time to contribute to this 'voluntarist' outlook on world affairs in Canada and within the Department of External Affairs. The tradition of national rivalries, suspicion and hostility in Europe has appeared to the United States, Canada and Britain to have made crude national pre-eminence the goal of most of European diplomatic activity. Yet Canadians and Americans, and to some extent, the British, watching this scene from afar, have been impatient with, and somewhat uncomprehending of, continental Europe's Hobbesian strategems, selfishness and conflicts. In the past, voluntarist Canadian and American diplomats have appeared as if they were more attracted by opportunities to forge new principles into international relations, to try to elevate the whole nature of these relations above the unsavoury business of balance-of-power politics.

'It was European policy, European statesmanship, European ambition that drenched this world in blood', complained the Canadian delegate to the First Assembly of the League of Nations. Prime Minister Arthur Meighen congratulated his delegate for stating so frankly 'the price the world has paid for European diplomacy of the last hundred years'. This attitude so shaped the view of Europe held by the key members of the Department of External Affairs that it was both continued and transformed when Canada played an active, even an initiating, role not only in altering the nature of the Commonwealth but also in the creation of the North Atlantic Treaty Organization from late 1947 to March 1949. Superficially this latter immersion in European balance-of-power politics might appear as the end of the voluntarist syndrome in Canadian foreign policy. Yet the Canadian attitude to the alliance was even more voluntarist than that of the United States. During the preliminary negotiation of the treaty, the Canadian participants appeared to be the only nation anxious to concentrate on the ethical necessity of a better world order, instead of relying solely on the existing unhappy conditions of power balance in Europe. In accord with this, the department invented and worked steadfastly for the inclusion of Article 2 into the treaty organization's Charter. This Article, commonly called the 'Canadian Article', expressed the intentions of the signatory nations to develop relations not only in the military but in the economic and cultural fields as well. (Canada's heavy participation in peace-keeping ventures, its unstinting effort in disarmament negotiations since the early 1950s have flowed, in part, from this voluntarist outlook as well.)

By 1960, however, the world did not seem to be accommodating itself to anyone's projects of voluntarism, let alone Canada's. Progress through peacekeeping, the UN, NATO, and disarma-negotiations, was imperceptible, if not non-existent. This resulted in considerable introspection about Canada's world role.

Voluntarism was not jettisoned by Canada in the 1960s but the impulse was redirected in most instances into a more limited context. It was redirected by Canadian diplomats and the political leadership into an emphasis on Canada's duty to help to hold 'international' organizations together (the UN, NATO, the Commonwealth), as well as an emphasis on Canadian contributions to international police actions, and on calls to belligerents to come to the conference table. It may not be far-fetched to describe this as Canada's 'federalist' approach to world politics, because the 'organization-maintenance' and brokerage tactics the Pearson Government found essential within Canada from 1963 to 1968 could be comprehensibly transposed to the international system. This tendency to put organizational viability before purposes of organizations, to present ambiguous schemes for peacekeeping, and to put insistent emphasis on the curative powers of negotiating tables began, however, to be attacked by spokesmen in all major political parties by 1967. By the time the decision was to be made on NATO in April 1969 by the new Trudeau Government it was clear that the Atlantic Alliance had proved to be an expensive and profitless arena for the proponents of voluntarist action. The organization-maintenance arguments for heavy Canadian contributions to NATO were also wearing thin because Canada's influence in the alliance was either chimerical or, if real, could be destroyed if Canada boasted of it in public. All this experience in the military arena combined nicely with the new emphasis of the Trudeau Government, (in the Privy Council Office primarily) which dismissed the helpful fixer role of the 1950s and 1960s as an inadequate basis for policy on its own terms, useful only if it could be clearly linked to national interests. As a result, the Trudeau Government found Canada's NATO commitments too expensive in terms of the country's other national interests in foreign policy, and Canada's contribution to its European Contingent in NATO was halved.

It now appears that the emphasis on voluntarist action has contracted somewhat. Canada's nationalist position in Law of the Sea conferences resembles the old Europeans in its emphasis on protection of national sovereignty and integrity. A more nationalist emphasis is evident in the Trudeau government's idea of the continental defence of North America. In fact, there is something false in describing Canada's North American military activity as an exercise in continental defence. It is to phrase it in a way more attuned to the perceptions of Canadians in the 1950s than the 1970s. A majority of Canadians may now be as worried about defence of their territorial sovereignty against Americans as about military defence against Russians or Chinese. In all three major Federal political parties, the rise of anti-continentalist movements, and the concern for pollution controls, arctic sovereignty and fishing rights, combine to put a whole new perspective on the old meaning of the 'defence of North America'. In fact the 1971 White Paper on defence ranks 'the defence of North America in cooperation with US forces' as a second priority. The first priority is 'the surveillance of our own territory and coastlines, that is, the protection of our sovereignty'. As the defence White Paper makes clear, Canadian military activity will concentrate increasingly on tasks *within* Canada designed to protect and affirm Canadian sovereignty. Canada, in the words of one shrewd defence analyst, is moving from an alliance-oriented defence policy to an independent defence policy, which provides a framework in which 'we would offer to our allies what we had instead of providing ourselves with what they wanted'.[5]

Events of the late 1960s and early 1970s may also point to a similar perceptible shift in the character and motive of Canadian external policy in policy areas other than defence. This shift may have been both obscured and exaggerated by some critics who have portrayed it as a movement away from an 'internationalist' emphasis to isolationism. In fact the Trudeau Government, if anything, broadened the geographical context of Canadian attention. It attempted to move beyond the old 'Atlantic triangle', 'Commonwealth', and 'UN' cornerstones of Canadian external policy through its emphasis on more contacts with China and the Soviet Union, on francophone Africa and Latin America in its aid programs, and on increasing trade in the Pacific.

It is not 'internationalism' as such that has diminished as a feature of the new Canadian external policy; it is its old 'voluntarist' component. The old Canadian voluntarist emphasis on acts of faith and 'moral exhortion' has diminished. We have seen that Canada's defence priorities have shifted to an emphasis on 'independence' and 'sovereignty protection'. The residual value of its NATO commitment seems primarily symbolic (that is, Canada continues to support Western Europe in a clear case of Soviet attack) and selfish (membership allows Canada to keep itself informed). Although the government agreed to a peace keeping role in Vietnam in 1973 Lester Pearson's voluntarist readiness to contribute to peace keeping is clearly played down in both the Defence and Foreign Policy White Papers of the Trudeau government and also in its threat to withdraw from Vietnam if the shooting re-commenced in a major way. Canada's disillusionment with the results of 'good intentions' in its peace keeping in Cyprus, the Middle East and south-east Asia (through the International Control Commission) has contributed to profound uneasiness in Canada with these ventures.

Canada's membership in the Commonwealth remains intact. But it is the voluntarist emphasis on moral action in this organization, so evident in both Lester Pearson's and John Diefenbaker's actions over Rhodesia and South Africa respectively, that has disappeared. Perhaps the clearest example of this new attitude is Prime Minister Trudeau's view of the Commonwealth which he explained in a press conference before leaving for the Singapore Commonwealth Conference on 5 January 1971. It is obvious that, compared with the past image of 'active mediator' cultivated by Canadian Prime Ministers Pearson and Diefenbaker, the shift in emphasis is dramatic. While at the conference, the prime minister argued further against 'the helpful fixer' role for Canada and the Commonwealth, and suggested that in the future the Commonwealth ought to concentrate less on 'immediate problems' and spend 'two or three days in a general discussion of the world political situation and the world economic situation'. (Somewhat ironically, however, Mr Trudeau ended up, apparently against his will, accepting a place on a committee to study the volatile issue of arms exports to South Africa.)

Another example, not of a declining internationalism but of a marked decrease in simple altruistic voluntarism, is the mode of expenditure in Canada's aid programme. It is clear that the programme now opens windows on areas of the world hitherto rather hidden from Canadian foreign policy. Canadian aid is no longer concentrated in Colombo Plan countries. In 1970–1 bilateral disbursements saw $172.4 million go to Asian countries, $30 million to Francophone Africa, $19 million to the World Food Programme. Disbursements of development assistance almost doubled from 1968–9 to 1970–1 to $354 million. This is an increase in internationalism. Yet the Canadian government's slowness in untying its aid hardly indicates a dramatic revival for simple altruism.

Given the nature of Canada's international economic problems, this decline of voluntarism was perhaps inevitable. And the unwillingness of increasing numbers of Canadians to perceive symbolic and voluntarist actions in foreign policy outside North America as sufficient counterweights to American influence in Canada may also have contributed to the decline in the appeal of voluntarist action outside North America.

The Making of Canadian External and Defence Policies

The growing complexity of international relations and of its world role have not left Canada's foreign-policy machinery untouched. Today not only the Department of External Affairs but also various divisions of other departments are involved in external policy. For example, the Department of Finance directs Canada's posture in the international monetary world, and is also responsible for preparing tariff changes. The Department of Industry, Trade and Commerce is engaged in the commercial side of external policy, such as export promotion, identification of foreign markets and the subsidization of various export industries. In addition the Department of National Defence not only has tasks for deterrence, defence, peacekeeping and reconnaissance but it also has liaisons with External Affairs on a number of foreign policy issues and with Industry, Trade and Commerce on issues of military procurement.

In short, the supremacy of the Department of External Affairs in Ottawa on questions of foreign policy is no longer unrivalled. Still, it remains a useful focus for anyone who wishes to understand how foreign policy is made. This department has grown from its inception in 1909, when it consisted of its undersecretary Joseph Pope and six clerks, to a department today which has over two thousand personnel (about half of these are posted abroad). By 1970 it had eighty-nine embassies and twenty-eight high commissions and other missions abroad. Even today the department retains something of its early personality. With a tiny staff for the first thirty years of its existence, it developed a reputation as an elite corps of generalists whose prevailing organizational philosophy seemed to be that everyone should be ready to do almost everything. Few specialists were hired, and recruitment standards to the department emphasized adaptability, common-sense and general intelligence. As late as 1964 the Royal Commission on Government Organization criticized the department for its lack of specialists, its few imports from other departments, its eclectic and swift rotation of foreign service officers and the lack of response of the generalist head office to officers in the field.

Yet this generalist style had great advantages. If the Treasury is the breeding ground for future top civil servants in Whitehall, so it could be said that in Ottawa the Department of External Affairs was the breeding ground for future deputy ministers, privy council secretaries, even prime ministers. The intelligence, commonsense and adaptability of the more able External Affairs personnel helped to suit them for executive tasks in other departments. The access of many members of the department to the prime minister helped (the prime minister remained secretary of state for external affairs until 1946). Louis St Laurent and Lester Pearson as secretaries of state for external affairs not only had considerable influence on the prime minister but became heads of government themselves. This no doubt has helped the department's leaders to gain pre-eminence in Ottawa since the Second World War to the end of the 1960s. Canada's importance in world affairs immediately after 1945 also helped.

Today the status of the department is more ambiguous. Increased emphasis on the non-diplomatic activity of the department explains this. Economic analysis and work with other departments on questions of trade, investment and technological development have forced the department either to yield some influence to other departments on a number of foreign policy issues or to lose influence altogether. For example, officials from Finance, Industry, Trade and Commerce did the major work in preparing Canada's representations to Washington after the 10 per cent surcharge on a host of imports was applied by President Nixon in August 1971. Prime Minister Pierre Trudeau ordered Privy Council Office personnel to reassess External Affairs' 1969 recommendation not to cut back Canada's NATO contribution. He has used one of his aides, Ivan Head, to do scouting expeditions on Canadian policy in Africa and elsewhere.

The department has been reorganized to allow the top command to concentrate on broad policy and to participate more effectively in schemes to integrate Federal government programmes which have external implications. Reorganization of Ottawa headquarters was the key step here. In the words of the department's memorandum on its organization to the House Standing Committee on External Affairs and Defence, 5 May 1971:

> The main body of the department is composed of a number of bureaux whose formation has been the principal focus of the new headquarters organization. The bureaux have either (I) area, (II) functional or (III) administrative responsibilities and each is managed by a director-general.[6]

The four area bureaux then established were: African and Middle Eastern Affairs; Asian and Pacific Affairs; European Affairs; and Western Hemisphere Affairs. Management of operations in these regions 'including country programme planning, resource planning and control and policy guidance to missions' is the authority of the director-general for each bureau. The functional bureaux then established were: Economic and Scientific Affairs; United Nations Affairs; Public Affairs; and Coordination, which includes 'Federal-Provincial Affairs; in their international context'. Since domestic departments of government are also in large measure organized on a functional basis, the Department of External Affairs believes their functional bureaux reflect those 'areas of direct concern to other government departments'. The primary responsibility for ensuring cooperation and coordination with other departments falls to the Interdepartmental Committee on External Relations (ICER). The undersecretary of external affairs chairs this committee, which includes the deputy heads of departments and agencies with major operations abroad, the Department of Industry, Trade and Commerce,

Manpower and Immigration and the Canadian International Development Agency plus the secretary to the cabinet and the secretary of the Treasury Board. This committee attempts to make all departmental programmes in any given country consistent with one another and with the Government's over-all objectives. ICER's overall performance since 1971 is unclear. Since it is chaired by the External Affairs undersecretary, other departments have been known to resent ICER's attempts to coordinate them. Also to integrate support services for foreign operations of all Canadian government departments and agencies, its Personnel Management Committee is to try to coordinate policies on recruitment, career development, classification, pay and allowances, etc. as well as develop criteria for the selection of heads of missions. Progress however has been slow even at this level because of a lack of inter-departmental consensus on what to integrate.

The department has attempted to free the top command, the undersecretary, associate undersecretary, and the assistant undersecretaries for concentration on policy formulation and direction by delegating general operational control of the bureaux to the bureaux directors. The top command engages in a wide range of sensitive and vital policy activity. To quote the departmental memorandum again :

The assistant undersecretaries now have greater freedom to participate in discussions on specific problems with foreign governments, to undertake special assignments in the areas of the world of particular current concern to them, to consult closely with other departments whose interests are reflected in our foreign activities and to attend conferences at home and abroad.

Canada's Department of National Defence has a firm reputation for subordination to civilian control. The most striking instance is the recent abolition of the army, navy and air force and the unification of Canada's armed forces. The budget of the department has shrunk steadily as a percentage of the Federal budget. It is 10 per cent for 1975–6. Of the Canadian Defence Department's budget not much goes to capital expenditure (for the fiscal year 1975–6 little more than 13 per cent).

The department engages in a host of varied activities. The government considers that Canada contributes to a stable deterrent system but not to all the components of the system.

Canada, to quote an aide to the minister of defence before the House Committee on External Affairs and Defence, 29 February 1972, is clearly 'not in the business of providing retaliatory capability; that is the United States. On the other hand we have in the past made pretty substantial contributions in the way of providing warning, warning against air attack and attacks coming from the sea. We also have played a role in terms of North American defence . . . the anti-bomber defences which now exist.'

Canada provides warning against the threat of bombers (whether nuclear-equipped or not) through its operation of the DEW line system. Canada's defence contribution against nuclear missiles is effected primarily through its maritime role, where in both the Atlantic and the Pacific it helps to 'provide warning against the possibility of a hostile submarine buildup'. A minor contribution is that the American-operated BMEWS system for warning against missiles is communicated in part through Canada.

Canada's much publicized decrease in its NATO forces abroad did not really decrease the cost of NATO to Canada. The ministerial aide quoted above also suggested that

if one looks at the amount of money involved in the estimates of our contribution to NATO, which includes much more than forces in Europe – it includes a share of the forces in the Atlantic and a share also of forces in Canada which are committed to Europe – one finds that the amount committed to NATO *per se* has not declined.

As already noted, the Canadian armed forces have also taken part in international peacekeeping. Early in 1973 there were three hundred Canadian troops serving in the Indochina peacekeeping venture, and a similar number of troops were stationed in Cyprus as UN peacekeepers.

The Defence Department has a fairly long history of assisting civil authorities in national development. It constructed and maintained the Northwest Territories and Yukon Radio System from the mid-1920s up to the mid-1960s. It was engaged in much aerial photography, mapping and charting of Canada until the mid-1950s. It is engaged in short-term programmes to hire additional employees to meet short-term unemployment needs such as the 1971–2 Work Intensive Programme. Many examples of spin-off from its research work can be cited, notably the industrial applications of gas laser development by the Defence Research Establishment. Although its involvement is not as close as the involvement and power of the US Federal Corps of Engineers in American development, its field engineer squadron has constructed bridges and airfields in the north.

This department, too, has undergone considerable organizational reform at headquarters, most of it in 1971–2. At the top of the organizational scheme is the minister who, as before works closely with his deputy and the chief of defence staff. The reforms occurred under this level. Under the chief of defence staff is the vice-chief of the defence staff (rank of lieutenant-general). Reporting to the vice-chief is the deputy chief of defence staff (Operations) who is responsible for operational planning, programmes and training and for intelligence and security. The deputy chief of defence staff (Support) is responsible for personnel administration of both military and civilian staffs, for logistics and medical, dental and chaplain services.

These deputy chiefs work closely with the assistant deputy ministers who come immediately below the deputy minister in the organization chart. Each civilian ADM has an associate ADM of major-general rank. There is now an ADM (Policy) responsible for strategic studies, policy and capabilities planning and programme analysis. The ADM (Finance) no longer has these policy responsibilities, though he retains the financial responsibilities and responsibilities for management advisory services. The ADM (Personnel) develops the personnel policies of the department for both the civilian and military staffs. The ADM (Material) is in charge of the research establishments, engineering services and the centralized procurement and supply service. There is also an ADM (Evaluation).

The Defence Council is the department's senior policy committee where the minister is briefed. It is predominantly civilian; its chairman is the minister, other members being his parliamentary secretary, the chief of defence staff, the chairman of the Defence Research Board, the vice-chief of the defence staff, the ADM (Policy), and the ADM (Evaluation). However, one new reform which complicates an assessment of civilian power at the deputy's level is that the new reforms no longer leave him with a purely military and a purely civilian staff : there is now a mixed staff.

All of this reorganization has come as a result of the department's efforts to improve coordination of its programmes and operations in the wake of the recommendations of the Royal Commission on Government Reorganization in 1964 and other management consultant recommendations since then. It also reflects the much publicized, indeed remarkably thorough, integration and unification of the navy, army and air force. Before integration and unification, each force tended to plan, programme and budget in an unrelated way. There was no overall system of defence programming. Now there is an integrated programme, complete with a five-year plan.

5 The Federal Public Service: Mediator, Adviser, Policy-Maker, Administrator

(1) *Its Scope and Resources*

The functions of the public service in Canada cannot be understood in isolation from its social and political context. Both society and the state in Canada are deeply engaged in structures and beliefs which attempt to promote such values as economic growth and technological progress. The public service as part of the state ought not to be singled out for special blame or praise for promoting these wider values. The public service does not create all of the state; instead its growth and character is at least partially a result of the state's magnetic field. The public service is the bureaucratic expression of the state.[1] Yet each part of the state has its own unique contribution to make to the promotion of the structures and beliefs of the state and society. The Federal public service's most vital contributions include its strategic power to give policy advice and its work at what is commonly thought to be the job of the politician, that is to mediate between the various levels of the state and between the state and society. The public service thereby helps to ease, unconsciously perhaps, the insinuation of the state into society. Because of its tactical and substantive knowledge of what society is ready for, its close contact with, and in some cases monopoly of, expert knowledge, and because of the political executive's requests to the public service for policy advice and for communication with those inside and outside the Federal public service, the bureaucracy helps to mediate between state and society.

(2) *The Structure of The Federal Bureaucracy*

The public service and those government employees outside public service classifications for all three levels of government in Canada account for over 12 per cent of the country's work force.[2] By 30 May 1970 the total number of Federal government employees reached 379,000, and provincial (not local) government employment almost equalled this number.[3] The extent to which government is an employer in Canadian society may not be obvious in Ottawa because of the division of government employment into Federal, provincial and local levels and because of its geographical dispersal. (Considerably less than half of Federal employees work in Ottawa.) Also, a large number of employees are engaged in activity which is not visibly 'governmental', such as the work of the Crown Corporations (approximately one-third of all Federal employees are engaged in such corporations).

Levels of government employment are an uncertain measure of the significance of the public service in the over-all life of society. More important is the nature and extent of public service activity itself. In Canada at the Federal level the administrative machine is made up of widely disparate units pursuing many different activities. By 1970 the Federal government was made up of twenty-seven departments, twenty-five boards and commissions, and forty-six Crown Corporations.

Let us look first at departments. Table 3 (overleaf) gives a list of departments of the Federal government on 1 May 1973.

All departments except for the Privy Council Office have this much in common: they have been created by statute. This is in contrast to Britain. Yet in Ottawa the cabinet now has liberal discretionary power to alter the duties of departments, thanks to the Transfer of Duties Act of 1918.[4] A department's functions are, of course, defined in large measure by those Acts of Parliament which the minister is expected to administer. The rationale for any group of agencies to be placed into one department or ministry of state varies, from the need to group common functions (such as External Affairs), or common clienteles (Agriculture), or similar processes (Supply and Services), or similar missions (such as the Ministry of State for Science and Technology created in 1971). Other departments are Irish stews, congeries of

Table 3
Departments of the Federal Government

Department of Agriculture (established 1867)
Department of Communications (established 1969)
Department of Consumer and Corporate Affairs (established 1957)
Department of Energy, Mines and Resources (created 1966)
Department of the Environment (created 1970)
Department of External Affairs (established 1909)
Department of Finance (created 1869)
Department of Fisheries and Forestry (established 1969)
Department of Indian Affairs and Northern Development
(established 1966)
Department of Industry, Trade and Commerce (established 1969)
Department of Insurance (established 1875)
Department of Justice (established 1868)
Department of Labour (established 1900)
Department of Manpower and Immigration (constituted 1966)
Department of National Defence (reorganized 1968)
Department of National Health and Welfare (established 1944)
Department of National Revenue (known as such since 1927)
Post Office Department (constituted 1867)
Privy Council Office (considered as a department of government
under the prime minister for administrative purposes,
constituted 1867)
Department of Public Works (constituted 1867)
Department of Regional Economic Expansion (established 1969)
Department of the Secretary of State
Department of the Solicitor General (under a minister since 1945)
Department of Supply and Services (established 1969)
Department of Transport (now included within the Ministry of
Transport)
Treasury Board (Statutory Committee of the Privy Council since
1869, separate department of government since 1966)
Department of Veterans Affairs (established 1944)

---

widely diverse activities (such as the Department of the Secretary of State). Departments also vary widely in size, and in policy influence from the small but powerful Department of Finance to the enormous yet less powerful Post Office. Some are so enormous and multi-faceted, such as Transport, that they have recently had to be fundamentally reorganized to allow the minister and his top public servants time and opportunity to concentrate on at least a minimum of comprehensive policy assessment. A few new departments comprise a large number of staff and executive personnel who have had little experience in the public service (such as in Consumer and Corporate Affairs). Some departments have been at the centre of the Ottawa scene for decades, such as Finance, Justice and External Affairs, and they have enjoyed a good deal more prestige than either their size or their budgets would suggest. Even more striking is the diversity in the geographical dispersal of departments. Some departments, such as Agriculture, Environment, Veterans Affairs, Transport, Manpower, Immigration and Defence, have over three-quarters of their personnel posted outside Ottawa. Some, such as Finance and Justice, have almost all of their personnel in Ottawa. Some departments are deeply involved in fundamental long-range policy-planning, such as the Department of Finance's research branches (in concert with the Bank of Canada's research branch) and some, such as the Department of External Affairs until the late 1960s, have indulged in little long-term policy-planning. These wide differences in departmental characteristics are no doubt typical of most bureaucracies in any country. A striking feature of Canadian departmental history is the prescience of the fathers of confederation. In 105 years the numbers of departments has only grown from fourteen to twenty-seven. Another feature of Federal departments, however, is the tendency to organize departments around what foreign observers would quickly recognize as uniquely Canadian assets: for example the Department of Indian Affairs and Northern Development, the Department of Fisheries and Forestry, and the Department of Energy, Mines and Resources.

That part of the administrative machine most answerable to Parliament is both *de jure* and *de facto* the government department. Within each department are 'branches' or 'divisions' or 'services' which in turn are usually made up of sub-units ranging in name from corporations, to councils, to agencies. At the top of the departmental pyramid is the minister who is responsible to Parliament (and also to the prime minister and the cabinet) for the work of his department. He is chosen by the prime minister, is a member of the prime minister's political party, and is a Member of Parliament or, very infrequently, a senator. Aside from the 'parliamentary secretary' (another MP who assists the minister in ways defined by the individual minister), the minister is the only official 'political' actor in the department. All 'public servants' in a department are constitutionally subordinate to the minister. In public, departmental solidarity and loyalty to the minister is expected. (Unlike the case in Britain, ministers in Canada do not have 'private secretaries' seconded from the public service to help them with personal political and public relations duties. Instead it is the 'executive assistant' who helps the minister most in these functions. These 'EA's' are usually chosen from outside the public service. A large number of these appointments are filled by young men who are party members and look to a career in politics rather than in the public service).

Although not appointed under the provisions of the Civil Service Act, the chief public servant in the department, responsible to the minister for running it, is the deputy minister (or in the case of some departments the 'undersecretary'). In the past, the 'DM' was usually a product of many years experience in the public service: more often than not his experience was in the department in which he was the deputy. Now it is no longer unusual for a prime minister who wishes to shake up a department, or who wishes to give it a new sense of mission, to choose someone from outside to be its deputy. A number of deputy ministers were changed after Mr Trudeau took over from Mr Pearson as prime minister in 1968. Some were appointed from other departments and some from outside the public service. (For example, a western Canadian businessman was named deputy minister of Energy, Mines and Resources by Mr Trudeau, and a close personal aide of the prime minister was named a departmental deputy minister in early 1973.) The power of the deputy minister is only what the minister chooses to give him except for some managerial authority delegated to him by the Treasury Board and the Public Service Commission. Underneath the DM there are usually assistant deputy ministers (ADM's) or assistant undersecretaries. Departments vary in the number of positions at the ADM level (usually around four). Reporting to ADM's are directors of divisions, or similarly senior line managers. These officers, plus those in ranks immediately below, comprise most of the 'executive' class of the public service. (There were 618 members of this class in 1971).[5]

The most durable image about the bureaucratic part of the government of Canada is that it is a gigantic administrative pie sliced into hermetically sealed, rigorously hierarchical, departments. This way of looking at the Canadian government is useful as an organizing device for budgetary reporting, for coping with parliamentary accountability, and for certain types of administrative convenience; it is only partially useful as an image of how the government's work integrates or fails to integrate. Although this chapter will concentrate on the role of public servants in *departments* in the formation of public policy it would be remiss not to note that the non-departmental branches of the governmental apparatus, the boards, corporations and commissions, account for a large part of the bureaucratic machinery. In fact the administrative part of the government of Canada is a collage of departments, boards, commissions, Crown corporations, supradepartmental control and initiating agencies and Federal-provincial committees and interdepartmental committees. More of this collage is represented not by a list of departments but in the list of the bodies and agencies responsible to the 'Ministry'.

The 'Ministry' of the government of Canada is composed of ministers whose answerability goes beyond the mere obligation to answer for departments in Parliament. Most ministers not only represent departments but are answerable in part for the activities of various boards, corporations and commissions. The list on page 130–4 (as of 1 May 1970) gives the names of the various Ministries of the government of Canada and the departments, boards, commissions and corporations which report through the minister to the House of Commons. It must be noted that although ministers are completely responsible for all work done in departments there are other agencies in his Ministry for which he acts only as a 'spokesman' to Parliament. He is not responsible for their activities.

The Federal government contained seventy-one boards and corporations in 1970, a smaller number than in some provincial governments. For example, by the early 1960s Alberta had 123 such bodies and Ontario had 97.[6]

Canada's Federal Crown corporations are important allocators within the Canadian state. They account for considerable resources and expenditures. For example, in the fiscal year 1969–70, Crown corporations obtained from the Federal government a net amount of $2,162 million, comprised of $1,075 million in loans; $656 million in subsidies and other payments to cover operating and capital expenditures; and $449 million for other purposes such as payments of subsidies to private businesses.[7] A substantial portion of Federal government resources – equal to about one-fifth of the total Federal budget – went to Crown corporations in that year. There were twenty-seven Crown corporations classified as business enterprises, seventeen of these supporting the infrastructure of the economy in transport, communications and finance. Those not classified as enterprises were on the whole engaged in economic or social support services: these include 'thirteen engaged in economic development and support functions of various kinds, six in health and welfare, four in culture and recreation . . . and three in other functions.'[8] Canadian Federal Crown corporations are not involved in judicial functions or day-to-day political considerations and they 'perform at least one of the functions of managing capital assets, lending, making transfer payments and research'.[9]

The growth in the number of these corporations and commissions is noteworthy, but perhaps not exceptional. All countries try to exempt some functions of government from the restraints and patterns of their public service commissions, such as rules on job classification, promotion, staffing and pay. Exemptions are also sought from Treasury departments with their standardized budgetary and financial procedures. All countries also try to take a number of explicit public functions out of 'politics', so that the minister will not have to be answerable in more detail for the operations of certain public activities than he ordinarily would wish. Canada is no exception. If anything, Canada is becoming unusually prone to those temptations at the Federal and the provincial levels. Still some parliamentary communication is expected from most of these quasi-independent bodies. It has been suggested that the proliferation of such bodies in this century in Canada is in all probability a concession to American influences. Yet apart from a few bodies, such as the Public Service Commission, Canadian agencies bear little resemblance to the 'independent' executive agencies in Washington in that a minister is expected to supply responses from such bodies to Parliament, even if he does not meddle much in their activity. Even the most 'independent' of Canadian agencies is at least expected to provide a minister with information if he asks for it.

Federal boards have considerable independence and power of regulation. The powers of Canadian boards include powers to study, to make policy, to grant licences and to publicize. Some Federal agencies give considerable power to interest groups by giving them representation on the boards; one example is the representation of producers on Federal boards for the marketing of agricultural products. It is also clear that a number of Federal boards wield considerable allocative, structural and regulatory power with little or no cabinet or ministerial influence until the minister decides to change the statutes under which such agencies operate, or unless public or interest-group pressure grows intense enough to force a minister to attempt to persuade such agencies to shift their policy. For example, the powerful Canadian Radio and Television Commission is to be free of political influence, and its mandate includes the power to prescribe classes for broadcast licences, to allocate broadcasting time, to determine time that may be devoted to advertising, and to prescribe the nature of political advertising by political parties. The policy powers of the Canadian Transport Commission are vast. They involve major allocative and regulatory activities. For example under the National Transportation Act (see Bill 231 in 1967) the grant of power to the Commission under Section 3 of the Act is no more detailed than the direction to investigate for the 'public interest'. The guidelines for granting pipeline licences are little more explicit than 'to serve the public convenience and necessity'. Also 'the Commission shall make investigations, including the holding of public hearing, as in its opinion is necessary or desirable in the public interest', or further 'it may disallow acquisitions if in the opinion of the Commission such acquisition will unduly restrict competition or otherwise be prejudicial to the public interest'. In considering an application for a pipeline certificate the Commission 'shall take into account such matters as appear to be relevant'. However the Commission is expected to be aware of over-all ministry policy in areas concerned.

Most boards, commissions and crown corporations, because of their members' fixed tenure of office and statutory power, are officially expected to operate free of political influence. In practice this expectation is occasionally qualified. First, there is the tendency of the cabinet to appoint to these positions many members who have been party supporters. Second, there is the necessity for many boards or commissions, such as the Canadian Transport Commission, to integrate some of their policy emphases within over-all Ministry and government policy. Third, it is politically advisable for good public relations that corporations such as Air Canada or the Canadian Broadcasting Corporation, or regulators such as the St Lawrence Seaway Authority, agree to explain to parliamentary committees their policies on various matters. Yet these opportunities for parliamentary probing should not lead one to conclude that such agencies are little different from those agencies clearly integrated into departments. Since there are countless issues with which these independent agencies deal and for which the cabinet and the minister would prefer not to be fully 'answerable' in Parliament, ministers are happy, in most instances, to grant them *de facto* power of decision, they simply report their decision to Parliament or let their officers explain the rationale of their decisions in parliamentary committees. (As yet the Government of Canada has not allowed Parliament to question appointees to boards or commissions before the appointee's actual assumption of office.) Table 4, a list of the Ministries as of 1 May 1970, gives some idea of the diversity of the boards and commissions in Ottawa.[10]

Table 4
Ministries of the Federal Government

Minister of Agriculture
    Department of Agriculture
    Agricultural Products Board
    Agricultural Stabilization Board
    Canadian Grain Commission
    Canadian Dairy Commission

Table 4
Ministries of the Federal Government–continued

    Canadian Livestock Feed Board
    Farm Credit Corporation
Minister of Communications
    Department of Communications
    Canadian Overseas Telecommunications Corporation
Minister of Consumer and Corporate Affairs and Registrar
General of Canada
    Department of Consumer and Corporate Affairs
    Prices and Income Commission
    Canadian Consumer Council
    Restrictive Trade Practices Commissions
Minister of Energy, Mines and Resources
    Department of Energy, Mines and Resources
    Board of Examiners for Dominion Land Surveyors
    Canadian Permanent Committee on Geographical Names
    Atomic Energy Control Board
    Atomic Energy of Canada Limited
    Eldorado Aviation Limited
    Eldorado Nuclear Limited
    National Energy Board
Secretary of State for External Affairs
    Department of External Affairs
    Canadian International Development Agency
    International Joint Commission
    International Boundary Commission
    Roosevelt-Campobello International Park Commission
Minister of Finance
    Department of Finance
    Inspector General of Banks
    Anti-Dumping Tribunal
    Bank of Canada
    Industrial Development Bank
    Canada Deposit Insurance Corporation
    Department of Insurance
    Tariff Board
Minister of Fisheries and Forestry
    Department of Fisheries and Forestry

Table 4
Ministries of the Federal Government–continued

    Fisheries Research Board of Canada
    Canadian Salt Fish Corporation
    Eastern Rockies Forest Conservation Board
    Fisheries Prices Support Board
    Fresh Water Fish Marketing Corporation
    International Fisheries Commission
Minister of Indian Affairs and Northern Development
    Department of Indian Affairs and Northern Developmen⁺
    Commissioner of Northwest Territories
    Commissioner of Yukon Territory
    Historic Sites and Monument Board
    Nation Battlefields Commission
    Northern Canada Power Commission
Minister of Industry, Trade and Commerce
    Department of Industry, Trade and Commerce
    Dominion Bureau of Statistics
    Corporation and Labour Union's Returns Act Administration
    Export Development Corporation
    National Design Council
    Standards Council of Canada
Minister of Justice and Attorney of Canada
    Department of Justice
Minister of Labour
    Department of Labour
    Canada Labour Relations Board
    Merchant Seaman Compensation Board
    Unemployment Insurance Commission
Minister of Manpower and Immigration
    Department of Manpower and Immigration
    Canadian Manpower and Immigration Council
    Immigration Appeal Board
    Canadian Wheat Board
    Public Service Staff Relations Board
Minister of National Defence
    Department of National Defence
    Canada Emergency Measures Organizations
    Defence Construction (1951) Ltd

Table 4
Ministries of the Federal Government—continued

    Defence Research Board
Minister of National Health and Welfare
    Department of National Health and Welfare
    Canadian Council on Nutrition
    Dominion Council of Health
    Medical Research Council
    National Advisory Council on Fitness and Amateur Sport
    National Council of Welfare
Minister of National Revenue
    Department of National Revenue
    Tax Appeal Board
Minister of Public Works
    Department of Public Works
    Dominion Fire Commissioner
Minister of Regional Economic Expansion
    Department of Regional Economic Expansion
    Atlantic Development Council
    Cape Breton Development Corporation
Secretary of State of Canada
    Department of the Secretary of State
    Canada Council
    Canadian Broadcasting Corporation
    Canadian Film Development Corporation
    Canadian Radio Television Commission
    Company of Young Canadians
    National Arts Center Corporation
    National Film Board
    National Library
    Board of Trustees of the Museums of Canada
    Public Archives
    Public Service Commission
Solicitor General of Canada
    Department of the Solicitor General
    Canadian Penitentiary Service
    National Parole Board
    Royal Canadian Mounted Police
Minister of Supply and Service and Receiver General of Canada
    Department of Supply and Services

Table 4
Ministries of the Federal Governmen–continued

    Ploymar Corporation Ltd.
    Canadian Arsenals Ltd.
    Canadian Commercial Corporation
    Crown Assets Disposal Corporation
    Royal Canadian Mint
Minister of Transport
    Department of Transport
    Air Canada
    Canadian Meteorological Service
    Canadian National Railways
    Canadian Transport Commission
    National Harbour's Board
    Northern Transportation Company Ltd.
    St Lawrence Seaway Authority
Minister of Veteran's Affairs
    Department of Veteran's Affairs
    Army Benevolent Fund Board
    Canadian Pension Commission
    Commonwealth War Graves Commission
    War Veteran's Allowance Board

Another bureaucratic activity omitted in a list such as this is the network of formal and informal contacts with provincial governments. Generally these are carried on by departments. As we saw in chapter 2, the work of provincial governments affects the work of countless departments of the Federal government and vice versa. A good example of this is the description of a key branch in one department, the Department of Regional Economic Expansion:[11]

PLANS FORMULATION BRANCH
The primary responsibility of this branch is to assist the department in the development, jointly with the provinces, and in collaboration with other Federal departments, of development strategies, plans and programmes.

The branch is organized both regionally and functionally. Small regional groups – for the Atlantic region, the central region (Quebec and Ontario) and the western region – are responsible for working directly with the provinces on strategy and plan formulation.

The four sectoral planning groups – Natural Resources, Human Resources, Private Capital, and Social Capital – provide specialized expertise for the development of plans with the provinces and are responsible for programme development in their respective areas of concentration.

The role of the Social Capital Planning Section is the development of plans for social capital facilities needed to stimulate and assist economic growth; that of Private Capital Planning is the identification of viable and competitive industries for the slow growth regions and the assessment of plans for their attraction; that of Human Resources Planning is to develop programmes for needed human resource development and social adjustment; and that of Natural Resource Planning is to identify the patterns for efficient development and exploitation of regional natural resources.

During 1969–70, the main effort of the branch was devoted to the preparation of plans with the provinces for implementation in the special areas in 1970–1. Federal–provincial task groups reviewed provincial needs for economic expansion and social adjustment and recommended the establishment of special areas in order to facilitate growth. ...

In the Atlantic region, plans for highway development were drawn up with the provinces and financed through the agreements on special areas and highways signed in the following fiscal year.

A number of Federal-provincial planning studies were initiated to develop urban plans for Saint John and Moncton, New Brunswick, and work was continued on urban planning studies in Halifax. Plans were completed for a mineral development study in New Brunswick and plans were developed and negotiations carried out for the second phase of the Atlantic Mapping, Surveying and Titling Program. ...

(3) *Canada as a Modified Administrative State?*

Jean Blondel, in his *Introduction to Comparative Government* has characterized the 'administrative state' as one 'in which a very large percentage of decision-making is in the hands of the administrators and the authority of the administrators is recognized over a wide area of policy' and 'legitimacy patterns lead to the administrators or technicians and the people at large recognize this authority'.[12] Administrative patterns of authority over policy-making are indeed evident in a number of key policy areas.

In such areas of policy, managers and top administrators find themselves in the best position to wield decisive leverage on policy and hence become what could be called 'legitimate actors' in the Canadian policy-making system at the Federal level. For example, not only do the top public servants in departments occasionally hold 'departmental meetings' without the ministers, but ministers often allow deputy ministers, ADMs, and division heads and other public service executives to conduct vital policy negotiations with interest groups, with provinces, or with foreign states. Research by Robert Presthus indicates that public servants are well aware of their influence. Certain steps of coordination and rules of consultation can build up in the bureaucracy and these can become legitimized to such an extent that ministers have difficulty altering them. For example, one Canadian minister has spoken of difficulties he had with his department. After becoming a minister he

... soon realized that all the expertise needed to sustain me was available right within my department, and I'm sure that it is available to ministers of all departments. However, it seemed to me that everything was arranged to keep the expertise beyond my grasp. I found it very difficult to communicate, to seek out advice, when I needed it. I felt that the ritual of the paper work – the chain of command – made it virtually impossible to get the kind of information I needed when I needed it and I felt very helpless.[18]

Bryce Mackasey, then minister of labour (in the same speech to the Federal Institute of Management in Ottawa, 22 May 1969) went on:

... the best people in our public service seem always to be the busiest. The minister seeking to broaden the sources of counsel is always made aware of how busy everyone is with something else. On what? On 'running the railway' they say ... In the public service, where the policies are supposed to be developed leading to legislation, the ministers can't avail themselves of the very people they need because these people happen to be engaged in measurable *things* ... into getting the existing jobs done.

These busy men in the public service are in key positions not simply 'to run the railway' but to monitor, prepare and recommend policy suggestions. This is evident in descriptions of most positions in the executive class not only at, but below, the

Figure 2

Department of Energy, Mines and Resources (October 1968)

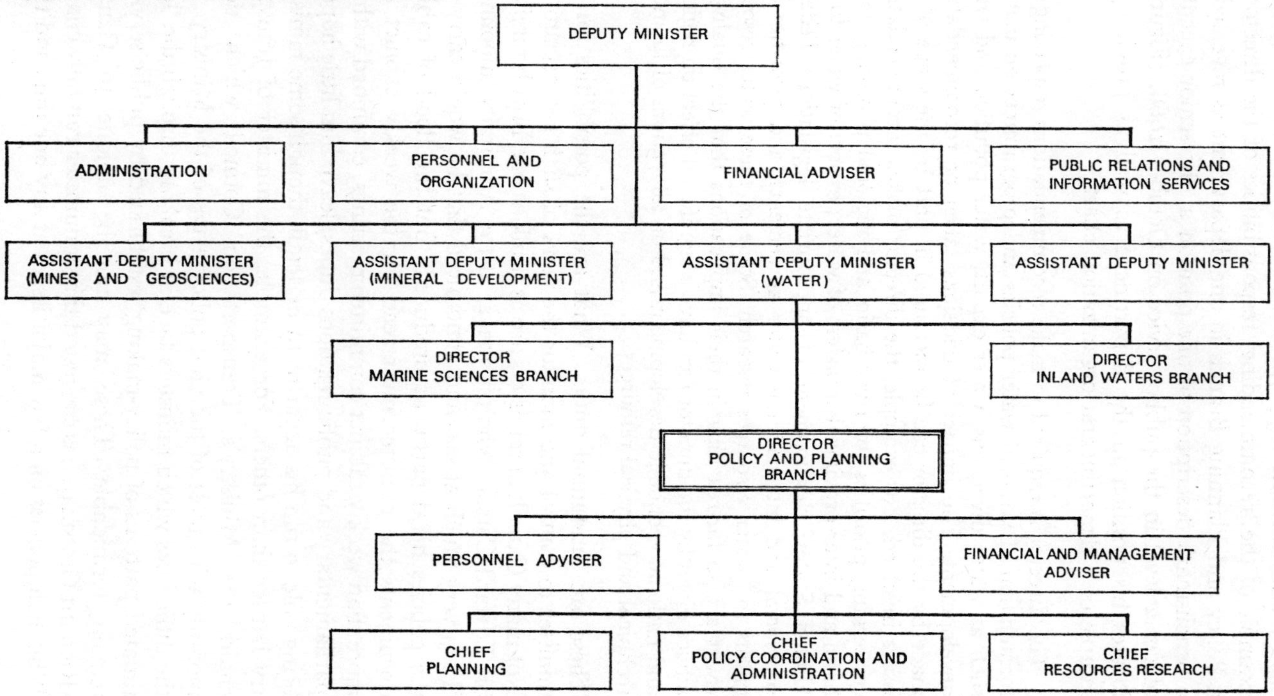

deputy and assistant deputy minister level. The following is an example of the 'recommending' responsibilities of the director of a Policy and Planning Branch in one department as revealed in a bench-mark description of one position at the senior executive officer 2 level in the public service on October 1968. (Figure 2 locates his position in the department as well as providing a sample of a departmental organization chart.)

The director is required to make recommendations respecting the formulation of national water policies and programmes on matters such as water diversions, water export, water pollution and water development. The impact of decisions taken or recommendations made by the director can be measured in part by the scope of the issues involved. For example, the director makes recommendations concerning priorities for river basin and regional planning; inter-basin and inter-provincial transfers of water; export of water to the United States; development of appropriate legislation; Federal-provincial and international water agreements, and priorities and grants for water resources research. Some of these water resource issues are so far-reaching in their implications that the quality of advice given by the director can have a significant effect on regional and national economic development and on allocations of financial, technical and physical resources . . .

These are substantial duties. What are the possibilities for the minister to control and monitor the work of such key executives? Not many Canadian ministers are as frank as one British minister, Sir Edward Carson, who on arrival at the Admiralty announced 'I am very much at sea' and announced that he would carry out the policies his department produced! But the flood of cabinet documents the minister must read for the weekly cabinet and more than weekly cabinet committee meetings, combined with his parliamentary and public relations duties, leave him little hope of being able to run his department in detail, though some ministers try harder than others. For example, the minister of transport chairs the Ministry's Transportation Council which deals monthly with most of the vital policy issues of the Ministry. Yet the difficulties which ministers face in breaking through the 'legitimated patterns of policy-making' established by public servants remain formidable. These may not be unique to Canada (Richard Crossman has suggested that a minister can only change Whitehall policies on a few major issues at any one time and then he will need powerful allies in the cabinet).[14] But a number of characteristics of the Canadian administrative machine are unique and suggest that the public service's patterns of legitimacy may be strong in Ottawa. Two characteristics, the absence of 'political party' representatives in a number of Federal-provincial and international policy negotiations, and the proliferation of inter-departmental committees, have been noted above. The webs of secrecy necessarily created by much of this activity can insulate public servants from those outside the bureaucracy. Other characteristics of the administrative state at the Federal level deserve a more extended exposition here because they reflect the peculiar characteristics of Ottawa's authority patterns, even though many of these tendencies may be evident in part in government bureaucracies outside of Canada.

Considerable patterns of authority are established by public servants in their day-to-day managerial, consultative and research duties. As Robert Presthus' recent research on Ottawa shows, public servants are as deeply involved in formal and informal contact with interest groups as are ministers. Departmental Annual Reports also reveal that almost every department is engaged in 'long-run' policy research (no member of the governing political party is a part of this activity, however, except perhaps the minister). The fact that public servants often have more specialized and comprehensive information than do outsiders on public policy makes them not only indispensable *sources* of information but, within countless areas of public policy, often authoritative on what is currently considered 'possible' or 'advisable'. Equally important, the management tasks of the executive class in the public service are so varied and far-reaching that their momentum and direction produce policy constellations that can be only vaguely comprehended by reading the statutory authority for these tasks. In short, authority patterns for policy-making, and constellations of autonomous activity and purpose, are naturally evolved by public servants. Harvey Lithwick, an academic charged with fashioning a new urban policy report for the minister in 1970, has written of how different was the momentum of housing policy-makers in the public service from the minister's aspirations for policy. All this renders the classical notion of the public servant as an implementor of ministerial 'rules' almost meaningless in many policy constellations. Much high level and middle level public service activity is far more akin to the business of 'working toward certain general purposes' than it is to simple rule implementation. As government's participation in the economy and society grows, a gap also grows between this positive activity of public servants and the formal nineteenth-century notion of rule and application. Jean Blondel has summarized the dynamic for most developed political societies thus:

> State intervention implies a philosophy of 'autonomous' action and indeed missionary zeal on the part of administrators. This philosophy can be found in all state activities concerned with the transformation of a service, social or economic, in order to achieve, first better results of the service itself, and later an improvement in the quality of the society as a result of the development of this service.[15]

One simply has to read the dialogues of MPs with public servants in committees of the House, especially during the Standing Committees' examination of estimates (after the minister has asked his public servants to 'amplify in more detail' the implication of government programmes), to see countless examples of this autonomous action. For example, the proceeding in one committee on 24 April 1969 heard the deputy minister of finance outline how his department 'worked out' a scheme for 'equilization of provincial revenues' and how his department acts as 'a sort of internal opposition' in financial questions in inter-departmental committees. In another discussion of estimates in 1970 committee members were able to question a deputy minister sufficiently to penetrate to the department's essential criteria for the awarding of regional economic expansion grants. These criteria emerged as far less comprehensive than the minister's stated guidelines. In the same year, officials explaining the lack of action on certain projects connected with the St Lawrence Seaway revealed that *their* preferences explained inaction far more than those of the minister. Countless more examples of the policy attitudes of officials who are charged with managing major activities are almost endlessly revealed (if little noted by the press) in committee testimony on the estimates. It would not be difficult to find evidence for Blondel's proposition about the ubiquity of 'autonomous action and missionary zeal' (implied in the goal of 'effective management') in the activities of officials who are theoretically only 'implementing' government programmes in Ottawa.

Of course, the policy inclinations and enthusiasms of the public service can be altered by ministers. In the absence of attempts to change their outputs, however, value allocations by public servants will more often than not remain decisive. This activity attracts little public notice because of a double cover of anonymity. First, there is the fiction that the minister sanctions all this activity, although in large departments he is probably unaware of much of its inner workings. Second, the perpetuation of the fiction that such activity is logically nothing more than an extension of statutory guidelines, and not a reflection of autonomous managerial activity, also keeps its importance hidden from parliamentary scrutiny and public curiosity.

Another feature of Ottawa's administrative activity which permits considerable bureaucratic influence is the ubiquitous phenomenon of delegated legislation and the lack of strong appeal provisions. It is true, of course, that almost all delegated legislation designates the 'governor-in-council' (in effect, the cabinet) or a minister, as the agency allowed to make regulations. In practice, however, most of this work is done by public servants and regulations reflect their decisions. A House of Commons Special Committee revealed that 420 of 601 Acts of Parliament provided for delegated legislation. Rarely is an appeal procedure against such regulations or their effect provided in a statute. An aggrieved party must, in most instances, work through the courts on the legal ground that such regulations are contrary to the intent of the statute. On the whole, these appeals have not been very successful, owing to the careful wording of statutes giving broad ambits of discretion. A particularly vivid example is the appearance in a number of Federal statutes of subjective terms which allow the 'governor-in-council' to make regulations, *as it deems necessary*, to carry out the purposes of the Act. This confers such wide scope as to allow almost no basis for appeal. Even more important is the fact that much administrative 'regulation' is not considered regulation in a legal sense and hence is not only unappealable but unpublished. Most departmental directives, handbooks and guidelines for such decisions as the awarding of loans, granting of contracts and criteria for inspection are not legally regulations, even though they no doubt codify the essential basis on which statutes are carried out.

Since Canada does not entrench the liberties of citizens in a written constitution, and since there is no 'Council on Administrative Tribunals' in Canada and no Ombudsman, there is inadequate legislative prescription of administrative procedure. Also, as mentioned above, there are many regulatory boards and commissions with power to decide cases from which no provision for appeals to a court is provided. (Canada has a baroque collection of antiquated laws on Crown privilege, expropriation and liabilities.) Although there has been some improvement in the relatively weak arrangements which exist for free legal aid to needy citizens, there is no formal procedure either within the Parliament of Canada or in provincial legislatures for settling the grievances of individuals against administrative bodies. In addition, the division of powers between the Federal and provincial governments has meant that some provisions protecting the citizen's rights against administrative actions vary widely from province to province.

It was widely hoped that the 1970 Federal Court Act would improve appeal procedures at the Federal level. Clause 28 of the 1970 Federal Court Act grants the 'Court of Appeal ... jurisdiction to hear and determine applications to review and set aside a decision or order ... [of a] Federal board, commission or tribunal ... [on certain grounds]'. Superficially, this section is an important change in that there are a number of statutes establishing Federal administrative agencies that do not provide for appeal. (For example, The Agriculture Products Board Act, 1952; the Anti-Dumping Act, 1968–9; the Atomic Control Act, 1952; the Fisheries Research Board Act, 1952; the Industrial Relations and Disputes Investigation Act, 1952; and the Parole Act, 1958.) Yet the wording of this clause does not provide right of appeal through the Appeal Court. The Appeal Court can only 'set aside' the decision of an administrative agency, which essentially means that the court can send the case back to the tribunal 'for determination in accordance with such direction as the [Court of Appeal] considers to be appropriate' [see S 52(d) of the Federal Court Act]. The tribunal may then render a different decision or it may not. Nor can the Appeal Court 'set aside' decisions of an administrative (as distinguished from judicial or quasi-judicial) nature unless the authority fails to give reasons for its decision and unless it fails to observe 'natural justice'. As one observer put it, this essentially means that the Federal Court of Appeal

> ... cannot interfere with an administrative agency's right and responsibility to develop policy where that agency has been given a statutory discretion to do so. For example, the refusal of an administrative board to make a loan or grant to an individual or agency may not be reviewed by the Court provided that agency acted within the limits of discretion given to it by statute.[16]

The Federal Court Act of 1970, therefore, did not on the whole improve the citizen's recourse against Federal administrative agencies. The Act does not require boards, beyond the rules of natural justice, to conduct hearings according to any minimum standards of procedure or to what an American might call 'due process'. In fact the new Act, in some respects, makes it more difficult for Canadian courts to maintain their effective right to review administrative functions of boards and commissions because it increases confusion as to the distinction between administrative and non-administrative functions (see section 28(1) of the Act).

Another large consideration in assessing the power of the public service is to note those controls that keep the public service from riding off in all directions according to their sectional policy preferences. The first set of controls, evident in all bureaucracies, are controls that come from the enunciation from the cabinet, refined by its staff agencies, of its over-all set of priorities for government policy. In Britain this is generally done through the influence of the Treasury in Whitehall together with the cabinet secretariat and the prime minister's staff. Agencies of central control in Ottawa are discussed in part in the discussion of the cabinet in chapter 7 below. Let us examine in this chapter the potency of some of the centralizing forces and controls aside from the cabinet.

An intriguing allegation which constantly recurs about the apex of the executive public service class in Ottawa is that there exists within it a club, ranging from three to fifteen top public servants (depending on who is doing the alleging), which dominates, coordinates and filters the work of the over-all policy process in departments, and sometimes even dominates the cabinet. Scholars have suggested that such a 'club' may exist, and disgruntled ministers have resigned in outspoken criticism of it. One minister in the Pearson government in the mid 1960s, Maurice Lamontagne, has written of how 'the establishment emerged and gradually became the centre of power within the Federal administration. . . .' If united the 'establishment got its way; if divided the cabinet failed to act'.[17] Another minister who resigned from the Trudeau cabinet in 1971, Paul Hellyer, explained his frustration as a minister this way :

You might say that I'm at war with the system – the way it operates, the way it has operated in the last governments. . . It's too rigid, a handful of people – a small coterie of a dozen or fifteen top men in the public service make too many decisions. . . . Their views are rubber stamped down the line by the cabinet; there's no way the cabinet can buck the prime minister and the in-group. Then the party in turn endorses the cabinet position.[18]

Complaints by another cabinet minister, Eric Kierans, who resigned later, contained almost similar sentiments.

The existence of such an inner group of powerful non-politicians is always difficult to prove. It might be argued in fact that, given the disparate nature of so much of Canadian policy-making in the Federal public service, it is perhaps inevitable that informal attempts are made somewhere – even by 'a coterie' of public servants – to keep an eye on over-all agency and departmental policy proclivities, and to attempt to discipline and clarify these tendencies through cabinet committees, central budgetary planning and other measures. This suggests first, that in Ottawa there will probably always be central control mechanisms, however general, at the top (through the Prime Minister's Office and the cabinet's administrative arm, the Privy Council Office), and through the Treasury Board's allocations and its financial reporting guidelines. There are also other warning systems set up through techniques such as cost-benefit analysis and programme reviews. In fact, two central control agencies, the Privy Council Office staff and the Treasury Board staff, have been unusually active since 1968. They are made up in part of rotating staff from other departments, so that the feeling for intrinsic departmental folkways, procedures and biases will not be absent at this level; yet the explicit responsibilities of the PCO and Treasury Board require that these two bodies endeavour to pursue some measure of control over, coordination with, and trading among, departments. The role of the PCO and PMO will be outlined, and then we shall examine the Canadian government's mode of central budgetary controls.

Since 1968 there has been an intense effort at the prime ministerial and cabinet level in Ottawa to integrate the activities of the Federal government, including federal-provincial relations.

As recently as 1940, according to Arnold Heeney who was the cabinet secretary at the time, the cabinet was run very informally : 'There was no agenda, no secretariat, no officials present at meetings to record what went on, no minutes of decisions taken, and no system to communicate the decisions to the departments responsible to implement them'.[19]

Much has happened since to improve communication, and policy control at the cabinet and top executive levels. A summary of Bruce Doern's excellent updating of this follows.[20] The respective roles of the Prime Minister's Office, the Privy Council Office, the Department of Finance and the Treasury Board remain complex but are now more clearly distinct. They are derived from the logic of their functional input into the policy. It can be said in summary that the PMO's role is to be the strategic source of political advice, while the PCO's role is the key source of over-all governmental advice. The overview of government activity by the PCO is bolstered by the Department of Finance and the Treasury Board, but on a more functional basis. The latter two organizations are too complex to be examined fully here, although it should be noted that the Treasury Board is a cabinet committee which functions in two distinct, if interrelated, areas of government: the Cabinet Committee on the Expenditure Budget, and the Cabinet Committee on Management. The Department of Finance, on the other hand, tends to view matters in terms of their impact on: (a) the government's ability to extract resources; and (b) the fiscal and economic consequences of government activity on the external society and economy. The Treasury Board seems more concerned with on-going resource allocations and with the internal financial administrative impact of established and proposed government activity.

The practice of debating most policy decisions during the Diefenbaker era at full cabinet level forced the cabinet secretariat within the PCO to concentrate most of its attention on the cabinet. The result was that secretariat members often found themselves entangled in half a dozen diverse policy areas. The Pearson government began an embryonic system of cabinet committees supported by a structured secretariat which allowed the PCO to specialize more and to do more than just serve the cabinet secretariat. Some structural differentiation evolved immediately.[20] The appointment of assistant secretaries to handle economic policy and resource issues, Federal-provincial relations, and security and intelligence, is the clearest indication of this. While they indicate a diffusion of roles, these changes did not presume that the members of the secretariat would be activists in policy development, even though the PCO included some policy units that were activist in form, such as the Science Secretariat and the Special Planning Secretariat. These two secretariats, special concerns of Mr Pearson, no doubt reflected the policy machinery needed for formulating policies on social development, particularly for the 'war on poverty'. Throughout this time, positions were being multiplied in both the PMO and the PCO. In the former, for example, a 'principle secretary' and 'programme secretaries' joined the correspondence secretaries and press secretaries of old. Mr Pearson's 'principle secretary' Tom Kent, and his personal initiatives, were apparent in such policy fields as the Canada Pension Plan, Federal-provincial relations, and economic development policies. By late 1971, there were 238 personnel in the PCO.

Many members of the public service were concerned that the strengthened PCO and PMO would lengthen the process of policy-making. To this Prime Minister Trudeau has replied that, on the contrary, such agencies would only expedite policy proceedings. Yet the former transport minister, Paul Hellyer, and the former communications minister, Eric Kierans, both contended that, while policy matters may have been somewhat expedited by these reforms, most decisions were heavily influenced, if not controlled, by a small group of advisers in both the PMO and the PCO. Gordon Robertson, the chief of the Privy Council Office, has attempted to lessen these concerns by explaining that the Privy Council Office's major activity is to advise on government matters and to communicate cabinet decisions to the relevant officials. As such the Office did not have the power either to administer specific programmes or of ultimate decision. It is clear however that its monitoring, coordinating and communicating activities have been exercised with vigour. Structurally the PCO embodies three main divisions; 'operations', 'plans' and 'Federal-provincial' affairs. In turn each of these divisions has numerous political tentacles. For example, the 'operations division' has five secretariats, each under an assistant secretary to the cabinet and each responsible for the work of one of the 'standing committees' of the cabinet. In pursuing its monitoring, coordinating and communicating activities the PCO collects data and presents 'policy papers'. This is to facilitate normative planning, or what is referred to in the PCO as 'converse incrementalism'. It was felt that the 'incremental' policy approach had allowed policy-makers, before the Trudeau period of office, to create new policy only by deviating slightly from the original tenets of any policy position, assigning at times additional resources which affected the output only on a marginal basis.

The policy role of the equally enlarged PMO appears more informal. Policy matters often arise in the PMO within a political fire-fighting context; yet the PMO claims it is also involved in various long-range policy discussions that occur in the PCO, the cabinet and its committees. (The heads of the PMO and the PCO confer with the prime minister most mornings for half an hour. There is also a weekly planning session between representatives of both the PMO and the PCO.) The other functions of the PMO involve communicating with the MPs for the prime minister, the processing of large quantities of mail, preparing of public statements, releasing press notices, briefing the prime minister before House question periods, assisting on appointments to top government jobs and scheduling the prime minister's time on a daily basis.

Another key reform was the revision of the cabinet committee system in 1968, which reduced the number of committees. In 1972 there were four coordinating committees: planning and priorities, Federal-provincial relations, treasury board, and legislation and house planning; and five functional committees: external policy and defence, economic policy programmes, science policy and technology, social policy, and cultural affairs and information. At the same time provisions were made for an increase in and greater regularity of committee meetings in the hope that there would be a more systematic and orderly consideration of problems for submission to the cabinet. Since the cabinet committee system had been initially set up to lessen the work of the whole cabinet, the cabinet committees have now taken over an increasing amount of responsibility for making what is in practice the final decision on policy. The old practice of moving policy questions from the full cabinet to cabinet committees has been reversed. Now cabinet committees have the power not simply to recommend courses of action to the cabinet but to take specific decisions. There is a provision however, whereby a minister who is not a member of a particular committee can have a committee decision discussed in full cabinet before it becomes effective. If no such reservations arise, items on the full cabinet agenda annex are to be taken as approved by the cabinet and are to become part of government policy. The chief of the PCO, Gordon Robertson, suggested in 1971 that in comparison with the situation before these changes, the 'cabinet is dealing with a larger volume of business but taking only half as many cabinet meetings to do it'. The number of cabinet committee meetings has more than doubled since 1968. These cabinet reforms have not necessarily diminished the influence of public servants. The heavy emphasis on cabinet committees may allow departmental public servants to be heard more often than before. Deputy ministers, assistant deputies and heads of divisions now attend many cabinet committee meetings. Some ministers complain in private that the public servants often do more talking than the ministers or members of the PCO. This is in marked contrast to the previous system in which most major issues were aired at full cabinet with very little participation from public servants.

The cabinet committee on 'planning and priorities' which is chaired by the prime minister and includes eleven other ministers is the key cabinet committee. Its work now includes more than the financial aspects of policy. According to Mr Robertson, this key committee gives attention to the broad objectives of the government and to policies which have long-term implications.[21] Robertson refuses to describe this committee as an 'inner cabinet', however, arguing that like any other committee it must have its decisions and recommendations go to the cabinet for confirmation or for debate and final decision. Yet there are in fact significant differences between this committee and the others. Its major function is to formulate a policy perspective for all the other committees. It has extensive powers of review over other committee decisions. Ministers cannot attend the priorities and planning committee unless they are a member or are invited to attend. Significantly the task of setting the agenda for cabinet meetings, if largely a prime ministerial prerogative, also receives input from this committee.

Another major attempt to enforce central guidelines has been through the budget preparation reforms since 1967. One useful way to assess the mode of operation of this endeavour in Canada, as well as the 'programme budgeting' orientation and the 'systems control' mechanisms in financial management, is to look at the criticisms and recommendations of the Glassco Royal Commission which reported in the mid-1960s on these matters, and to compare its recommendations to reforms in place ten years later. The Glassco Commission's main criticism of government planning and budgeting was that both had been designed around an approach which compared only the two previous years' budget figures to the new budget year. This also meant that a department's efficiency was measured simply by comparing the percentage increase in expenditure between the two years; no scientific methods such as work measurement, cost analysis or statistical sampling were employed. To remedy the Burkean, incrementalist, assumptions of this procedure, the Glassco Commission recommended among other things that:

More objective standards for analysis and comparison be developed and employed by senior departmental management and Treasury Board in a process of over-all programme review and that all departments and agencies be required to prepare and submit to the executive long-term plans of expenditure requirements by programmes.... Based thereon, an over-all forecast of government expenditures and prospective resources for a period of five years ahead should be prepared annually.

To meet this request the government of Canada adopted what is called a 'Comprehensive Programme Budgetary System' in which over-all government operations were divided into major functions:

General Government Services
Foreign Affairs
Inter-governmental Fiscal Transfer Payments

Economic Measures
Social Measures
Education Culture and Recreation
Public Debt[22]

(By 1972 the functions of government were outlined somewhat differently. See for example the Summary of Budgetary Estimates for 1975–6.) In turn, each of the functions in table 5 is divided into sub-functions and further broken down into departmental programmes. The division into departmental programmes was to permit the work of the government to be assigned to different agencies. The departmental programmes were divided into activities which were to be designed to assist resource allocation decisions, to provide headings under which the department will negotiate for funds, and to provide the focus for planning by the department in deciding how to achieve programme objectives.

Table 5
Summary of Budgetary Estimates for 1975-6 and Forecast
Expenditures for 1974-5* by Function (in millions of dollars)
Source: Estimates for Government of Canada 1975–6 (Ottawa, 1975), p. 1–32.

	Estimates 1975–6	Forecast expenditures 1974–5	Change Increase	Decrease
General government services	1,436.6	1,214.0	222.6	—
Foreign affairs	700.9	512.2	188.7	—
Defence	2,802.1	2,511.7	290.4	—
Transportation and communications	2,080.2	1,933.4	146.8	—
Economic development and support	4,656.7	4,341.9	314.8	—
Health and welfare	7,853.9	7,023.0	830.9	—
Education assistance	672.5	643.2	29.3	—
Culture and recreation	690.4	580.2	110.2	—
Fiscal transfer payments	2,624.6	2,631.4	—	6.8
Public debt	3,575.0	3,175.0	400.0	—
Internal overhead expenses	1,149.3	886.5	262.8	—
	†28,241.9	†25,453.0	2,788.9	—

* *Total 1974-5 expenditures forecast as at 31 December 1974.*
† *Details do not necessarily correspond to totals due to rounding.*

Each programme is then shaped internally for presentation to Parliament in an 'estimates' format which in essence is a structure of 'votes'. Each programme consists of one vote. The vote is then subdivided into three sub-votes: Operation and Maintenance; Capital; and Grants and Contributions. However, the government has deviated from the rule of 'one vote per programme' whenever the 'Capital' or the 'Grant and Contributions' sub-votes exceed the sum of $5 million. In such a case, the particular sub-vote becomes a separate vote and the programme funds are controlled by more than one vote.

In practice, all of this budgeting by departments is done by the preparation of two documents – the programme forecast and the estimates.

The programme forecast is a long-range plan for the department and extends over a period of five years. This document consists of a statement of objectives for particular programmes together with a descriptive analysis of how the department plans to meet the stated objectives. A number of schedules are submitted identifying the financial and manpower resources required to carry out the plan. To accomplish its stated programme, it is sometimes expected that the department will do 'sensitivity analyses' of its plans. Each department is also expected to determine the effect that different expenditures will have on the level of service provided by the programme.

Once approved by the department's head, this 'programme forecast' document is then sent to the Treasury Board, where it was originally expected that an in-depth analysis of *all* departmental plans would be made by the board. Here the contributions made by the various departmental activities towards the fulfilment of various *overall* governmental functions and purposes were to be analyzed. (This analysis has been occurring but not without considerable devolution to departments for help. In many cases departments have not been cooperating satisfactorily.) Decisions are then made, based in part on Treasury Board information, by the cabinet committee on priorities and planning as to the level of service to be carried on for each function. It is unclear how independent are the studies done for this committee compared to Treasury Board studies. It is doubtful that this cabinet committee is able on its own to produce detailed and comprehensive sets of assessments of all major Treasury Board recommendations on programme levels, although some different assessments undoubtedly do occur, especially on the weight to be given to political considerations and broad priorities. The Treasury Board then takes the documents back and determines the budgetary targets for each department based on the guidelines set by the cabinet committee.

In practice however, there is still room for manoeuvre after this step. When departmental targets have been announced by the Treasury Board, departments start the task of detailing expenditures for the next fiscal year in view of these targets. In effect the following sequence of events occurs after the programme review: if their objectives and targets are changed, departments are asked to update the first year of their five-year plans in the light of these changed targets. Some critics have suggested that although this whole five-year 'programme forecast' exercise continues, not all departments take it very seriously. The key exercise, they allege, is seldom the programme forecast. As before in those departments not submitting controversial long-range programmes, the key struggle is the preparation and acceptance of the estimates each year. The 'estimates' are the documents detailing the next year's phase of the long-range plan. Once next year's estimates are completed, they are sent from the department to the Treasury Board where they are screened in order to assess their fidelity to the five-year plan. (However, the Treasury Board has asked departments to submit 'X' budgets each year outlining their 'real priority requirements' for the impending fiscal year in order to help the Treasury Board pare costs if necessary. Most departments have not produced what the Treasury Board feels are realistic X budgets. The most any department has done is simply to prepare an X budget which reflects what it might do if it participated in any reasonable continuing cost reduction programme.)

From this brief description we can see that budget planning *in theory* definitely takes the emphasis away from the traditional year-to-year estimates preparation, format and cycle, and is now focused more in a long-range planning context, which, again in theory, may enable the cabinet to make better value judgements and control over-all priorities. The insertion of the 'programme forecast' as the main planning tool ostensibly takes the emphasis away from short-term planning and puts more weight on long-term planning. Yet this will be true only to the extent that long-term plans cannot be fabricated by departments in such a way that they are not simply elaborate smoke screens for next year's *ad hoc* and incremental preferences and demands. There are doubts about the extent to which the exercise of long-range programming really does prevent this kind of mystification. It remains obvious that after the long-range five-year 'programme forecast' document is completed, the haggling by departments with the Treasury Board over their estimates document each year remains as important as ever in the department's success in attaining funds. Yet, thanks to the long-range format, it can be insisted with some confidence that the cabinet and the Treasury Board may be better able to determine the long-term costs of some new programmes and of those on-going programmes it wishes to maintain for at least five years. Yet even here full confidence is not easy to maintain for a number of major Federal activities. Spending levels on conditional grants with the provinces have a way of growing beyond the Federal government's control, and these amount to over 25 per cent of the Federal budget each year. It is not clear how many of these programmes have been affected by this long-range planning process. For example, Federal finance ministers continually complain about what they describe as 'uncontrollable expenditures', i.e. those which arise from these conditional grants. It is also difficult to see how a number of deeply ingrained Federal activities are greatly affected by this long-range planning (e.g. Old Age Pensions, or the charges on the public debt).

Another problem of control is the lack of precision in the 'estimates' document itself. The estimates are the documents which give departments the legal authority to spend funds. Following the Glassco reforms, this document is to appear as follows:

(1) Departmental estimates are to be prepared on the basis of programmes of activity and not by standard objects of expenditure.
(2) Where appropriate, revenues are to be offset against related expenditure, and the votes shown in the estimates are to be expressed on a net basis.

153

Without going into all of the merits of the new form of the estimates, it does not relate expenditures to each specific sub-activity, only to broad 'activities'. The disciplining and clarifying effect of the new estimates format should not, therefore, be exaggerated. Departmental activities and programme costs are not in fact outlined in detail in this document.

This leads inevitably to the question of a department's actual capacity to alter its spending within the set estimates passed by Parliament and approved by the Treasury Board. The power of departments reassert itself when one recognizes that other 'control' mechanisms over finances have in fact been relaxed since Glassco. Side by side with increasing the Treasury Board's power the Commission, following the somewhat contradictory injunction of 'letting the managers manage', recommended that departments be given more autonomy in managing their more detailed financial affairs. This opens more opportunities for departments to make smaller allocations with less central control. Specifically, Glassco recommended that:

(1) Departments and agencies be given the necessary financial authority and be held accountable for the effective management of the financial resources placed at their disposal;

(2) responsibility be placed on departments for certifying to the comptroller of the Treasury that expenditures will be lawful charges and that funds are available;

(3) the responsibility of the comptroller of the Treasury be limited to ensuring that the departmental officers providing this certificate are properly authorized;

(4) the appointment of the senior financial officer in each department and agency be subject to the concurrence of the Treasury Board.

In response to these recommendations, under new regulations by the Treasury Board, departments are now given more power to transfer funds between activities and between sub-votes where the sub-vote is under a certain amount ($250,000). Also, with the amendment of the Financial Administration Act in 1967, the authority of the comptroller of the Treasury has been reduced. Departments are now responsible for certification of availability of funds and for commitment control. The comptroller of the Treasury now issues cheques at the request of departments as long as there are funds available under the vote and as long as the issuing of the cheque is properly authorized by the department. Each department now has its own senior departmental financial adviser who is responsible for financial matters.

Another frequent form of control over the public service is the expenditure audit. This audit is the responsibility of the office of the auditor-general and his staff of over 280. The auditor-general is an employee of Parliament and not of the public service or of the executive. He is responsible for reporting on the audit of the accounts of the government of Canada (including departments, boards, commissions, Crown corporations and other Federal public bodies). His office also audits and reports (on a cost recovery basis) the accounts of international and other organizations. His report always attracts a fair amount of publicity each year and the indiscretions revealed range from the tantalizing to the grotesque. These revelations, however, are confined to an outline of failures to expend funds effectively or failures to spend as authorized. The auditor-general is not expected to report on expenditures in a larger policy context.

Other developments in the Canadian public service also indicate that departments and other non-departmental parts of Ministries have far from capitulated to central control agencies. Since 1967 the Public Service Commission of Canada has lost its function as the official 'employer' of the public service to the Treasury Board. Though the Commission retains its statutory control function as the sole staffing agency committed to the preservation of the merit system, it has delegated most of this staffing function to the departments and agencies. (It has retained the role of 'auditor of performance' in these areas of delegated authority.) On the whole the Commission has moved to a position more akin to that of adviser and trainer rather than regulator, through its emphasis on its Bureau for Staff Training and Development and its analyses of needs for training, for advanced courses, and for employee facilities.

Without clear and detailed guidelines, it is difficult for an agency such as the Public Service Commission which has responsibilities for investigating activities of various departments and agencies to wield much power if it lacks clear support from the key members of the public service. Another example of this is the delicate position of Canada's Official Languages Commissioner, who is charged with monitoring the progress (and enforcement) of bilingualism in the public service. In a country which is over one-quarter French-speaking this is a vexed problem. (In 1970 only 15 to 20 per cent of executive, technical and administrative positions were filled with French-speaking Canadians). In an interview granted a few months after his office was established to implement the Official Languages Act, the commissioner argued that most of his work would be effective only if it was looked upon as something like 'a free confidential consulting service' to deputy ministers and heads of Crown corporations. As he put it 'we will be just like chartered accountants but specializing in linguistics. I'd like the office to be like a mirror of Canadian society, not a kind of Mafia promoting a French plot'.[23]

A similar development which affords power to the bureaucracy over non-financial as well as financial matters is the considerable opportunity which exists for public servants to do little to implement the principles or sentiments of a statute or order-in-council because of the tendency for Governments in Ottawa to have statutes or orders-in-council written in a general manner and in many cases lacking coercive content. This is a tendency not unique to Canada. Political executives (or key public servants) are often uncertain or unclear about the standards they wish to see applied or the specific outputs they would like to see emerge from various high-sounding statutes. Statutes which are little more than expressions of good intentions encourage the public servants who prepare them to write broad delegations of power and vague guidelines into the terms of the legislation. They allow officials to divine later how determined their political masters are about the bill's sentiment or how far the sentiment can be carried into practical action.[24] This penchant for writing generalities into statutes is particularly obvious in some of the more hastily devised bills of the government of Canada in the late 1960s, as for instance in the Act setting up the Company of Young Canadians in 1965, or the legislation of the Consumer and Corporate Affairs department since 1965, the legislation to screen foreign investment, and the Textile and Clothing Board Act.[25] Another example is the (as yet unclear) meaning of many standards in the Federal Competition Act. Important here is the way in which the department will interpret the 'credulous men' test in its attempt to discourage misleading advertising. The legislation to screen foreign investments in 1973 was also so devoid of specific standards that the standing committee on finance had to make it more explicit in its 12 July 1973 report.

Specialist and Technicians and their Influence on Canadian Public Policy

The influence of specialist or technical public servants, and the extent to which they can be controlled by the political executive, is another important problem. The amount of executive control over specialists in Ottawa no doubt varies by department. It is notable that Canada's federal bureaucracy has thirty times more employees in the scientific and professional than in the executive category (18,099 to 618 as of 31 December 1971). Unlike an underdeveloped country, some career options may exist for technicians outside the Federal government and this may increase their sense of over-all career safety and encourage them to push for their values in the bureaucratic system. Within the Federal government in 1965–6 the turnover in this category was 12 per cent; in 1966–7, 13.2 per cent; in 1967–8, 10.5 per cent; in 1968–9, 10.1 per cent; and in 1969–70, 13.5 per cent.

The growth of the state in Canada cannot be attributed primarily to the technical and specialized resources lodged in the state. These resources may account for some of the state's growth but many restrictions bureaucratic, political and ideological hedge and circumscribe the specialist and the technician. These two groups are expected to be concerned with their speciality and it should not be surprising if they are expansionist about their sphere of public activity. Jean Blondel has suggested that technicians and specialists become 'sectionalists' insofar as they become involved in proposed technical advances rather than with persons or organizational structures. Technical specialization is, of course, a major characteristic of the tasks of various agencies within Canada's Federal departments: for example, research and experimentation within the Department of Agriculture; the Northern Science Research Group in the Department of Indian Affairs and Northern Development; various forms of research by the

157

Canadian Transport Commission; the generation and application of laws concerning corporate disclosure, combines, mergers, bankruptcies, copyrights, and trade marks within the Department of Consumer Affairs; the main function of the Forestry Research Service; some of the fundamental research activities conducted in Canada's Energy, Mines and Resources Department; analyses within the Department of Industry, Trade and Commerce to assist manufacturing and processing industries to adapt to changes in technology; and the specialized medical research of many of the branches of the Department of National Health and Welfare, such as the Medical Services Branch and the Food and Drug Branch. A number of marine service operations, including aids in navigation, nautical and pilot services, and a number of air services such as the meteorological branches of the Department of Transport, are obviously specialist in emphasis. The work done by the Defence Research Board and the National Research Council, and the policy research done for Crown corporations, may be further examples of sectionalist pressures from technical and scientific personnel.

The amount of 'sectional' pressure that specialists or technicians may wield in a bureaucratic system will no doubt depend in part upon the hierarchical levels at which technicians are placed in their department's agency and in the over-all department itself. As suggested earlier, there are a number of government departments which include more 'groups', 'branches', 'divisions' or 'agencies' which are dominated by technical, specialized and professional research and argument than other departments. It seems clear that in the Department of Health professional expertise will account for much of the managerial and policy attitudes within certain agencies and advisory boards. This specialist influence no doubt occurs also in a number of other departments, such as within the Department of Justice, the Department of Communications, the Department of Agriculture, the Department of National Revenue, the Department of the Solicitor-General, the Department of Supplies and Services, and the Department of Veteran's Affairs; and on purchasing decisions in most departments, especially National Defence and Transport. Because of the nature of the work done within these agencies, sectional demands for technical efficiency and for high-level technical achievement might be expected to characterize large parts of these departments. Yet to assess the over-all amount of sectional pressure and influence of technicians in Ottawa's departments is difficult. Where 'non-technical' managers are, relatively speaking, in control within a department, they may act as filters and isolate the technicians. The conditions for this no doubt exist, to some degree, in Ottawa simply because of the career patterns of the executive class of the public service of Canada. This top class of the public service spends a high percentage of their career years in the public service (and not outside in a specialized professional or technical occupation) before their appointment to their executive position. This may suggest that executives have had little time to build up technical and scientific biases in careers outside the public service. For example, in a survey taken of executives in the Federal public service in July 1967 (there were then 625 executives, known as senior officers 1, 2, 3, deputy ministers and deputy heads), the total career years spent in various 'experience areas' was 28.2 years for this class, of which 65.9 per cent were spent in the public service (3.9 per cent was spent in manufacturing, 2.4 per cent in university (non-student), 2.8 per cent in provincial government, 14.8 per cent in business and self-employment, and 9.9 per cent in the military).[26] Significant here is the fact that only one-third of the total career years of executives was spent outside of the federal public service. In 1971 the Public Service Commission's Annual Report reveals that, of appointments to the executive category that year, 18 per cent came from outside the public service. This suggests that professional and technical standards of value, generated outside government, such as in universities and in business, may not be as pervasive at the executive level in Ottawa as in the United States, for example, where there is a high percentage of total career years spent outside government by those in the executive class. This 'in-house experience' of the Canadian executive may serve as a partial filter against technical and specialized interests outside the public service. For example, the influence of technicians has apparently been minimized in the United Kingdom because of the lower status given to technicians in the managerial hierarchy of the United Kingdom. In Canada, the Public Service Commission and the Treasury Board also attempt to keep purely technical and specialized activity at a somewhat lower place in the hierarchy compared to executives. But as mentioned above, the nature of the work of various departments in Ottawa makes some departments somewhat specialized by nature and therefore the status of technicians in these departments will be higher than in other departments. In the classification scheme of the public service, it is clear that the technical skills and duties are kept out of descriptions of most executive jobs. The technicians will also clearly make little impact on the executive class in departments where there are low levels of technical expertise needed to do the work of the department. This is probably the case for some of the key activities in the Department of External Affairs, the Department of Indian Affairs, and a number of the agencies underneath the secretary of state of Canada.

The most potent control on technicians and specialists is probably the socialization process of Canada and of Ottawa: i.e. the values which lead them into accepting the processes of the political system. Certainly it must be assumed that the Canadian educational system is not systematically geared to producing widespread dissent about the values and processes of the Canadian political system. This, combined with the lack of experience outside government of public servants at the executive level, suggests that there is probably considerable socialization of technicians and technician-managers to accept the hierarchical controls implied by ministerial responsibility. It could be argued, therefore, that the technicians and specialists have been conditioned into agreeing with the proposition that the minister should be responsible for the most important decisions, even if these decisions have considerable adverse impact on the technical achievement of the speciality with which certain public servants are concerned. One of the great utilities of the principle of ministerial responsibility is that it provides a rationale for technicians to abandon their sectionalism. Although it is difficult to surmise the extent to which these elements of socialization are present in Canada, it would be foolhardy to insist that they are absent.

The division of Canada's public sector into Crown corporations and administrative agencies, the division of the administrative agencies into Federal, provincial and local offices, and the duplication at the provincial level of technical expertise generated at the Federal level, may also contribute to a breaking down of the technicians' sense of unity. Recent research on Canadian Federal-provincial relations at the middle-range bureaucratic level (e.g.

wild-life management, resource management, etc.) indicates that technicians and specialists within provincial governments are developing sufficient research and expertise to enable them to follow policies which are not necessarily those of a similar agency at the Federal level.

Another emerging force contributing to agency loyalty from technicians is the growing diversification of university educational and technical institutions in Canada. This has led to more diversity in specialized education, and the old pattern of the technical-managerial public servant graduating from the same two or three major Canadian universities no longer occurs. There are, of course, a number of associations of specialists, such as the Canadian Medical Association, which cut across the boundaries of agency loyalty; yet it is difficult to identify many such associations which are sufficiently cohesive to combat effectively all the divisions arising from the structures to which technicians belong.

This fragmentation of a good portion of the Canadian technical and specialist bureaucratic class in Canada, and the considerable control over these groups in many departments, may go far to explain why these classes seldom overtly challenge executive and political control. Yet there is a burgeoning set of forces in modern Canada which may admit more credence and influence to one type of technical rationality than ever before. This is the influence of 'the ideology of functional and technical efficiency' which has been growing in Ottawa since the Government Reorganization Act (1966) and the Financial Administrative Act of 1967. In addition there have been a number of solid indications from the government since then that a heavy emphasis is to be placed on systematic and technical excellence in the analysis of public policy, through the reorganization of the cabinet around functional committees, the massive infusion of systems analysts and cost-benefit analysts for programme evaluation, etc. This development, however is not logically at one with the sectional values and enthusiasms of specialists and technicians in various departments. Instead this 'ideology' is primarily preoccupied with efficiency and optimization and is not logically allied with sectional and technical enthusiasts in departments. Yet insofar as it puts a premium on 'hard data', and on quantifiable policy outputs and outcomes, it may give more influence to those technicians in departments who can argue their case in the language of the new ideology. This may allow their analyses to receive greater respect at Treasury Board and executive levels. Yet the necessary compromises inherent in Federal-provincial relations, and the difficulties in the technical measurement of a number of key policy areas, suggest that much policy-making will remain resistant to this ideology. For example, the success of intimate relations of Federal public servants with their provincial counter-parts will be determined as much by compromise and negotiation as by anything else.

(5) *The Public Servant – Executive Alliance*

An even more fundamental source of public service leverage over policy-making in Ottawa is the protection officials enjoy from penetration from Parliament. At the turn of the nineteenth century much of the colonial bureaucracy was appointed by the governor and by the Colonial Office in London. This made appointed officials dependent on their superiors in London. Since members of Assemblies were elected from the colony itself, they in contrast were more dependent on local attitudes than was the bureaucracy. The gap that eventually widened between politician and bureaucrat was one of the burning issues in the American Revolution. In the words of one scholar, the revolution in the United States 'created a permanent suspicion of executive power which has stood ever since in the way of developing responsible government'. In Canada, the bureaucrats were more successful in withstanding the challenges of the politician. 'Loyalist' sentiment in the colony may be a partial explanation. The brevity of most Assembly sessions may be another. Also, it appears that British North America had a more muted and pragmatic spoils system than did the United States. R. Macgregor Dawson explains:

> The government could and did fill offices with its supporters [but] 'rotation in office' was adopted in the United States as a principle and a right, but it never attained such dignity in Canada. Rotation never became an end in itself or a political virtue about which to boast. When removals from the Canadian service occurred, they were made somewhat furtively, and the onus of proof always rested on the government to justify its action.[27]

When responsible government was achieved in 1848 in the provinces of Canada and Nova Scotia and soon thereafter in the other provinces, the Assemblies wrested control of the Ministry and patronage from the governor. This achievement ushered in a brief period when bureaucratic unity and strength was broken by powerful Assembly committees and by a widespread, though still furtive, spoils system. Yet immediately after confederation in 1867, the unity and insulation of the bureaucracy from Parliament was restored. The control of the elected House by John A. Macdonald's Liberal-Conservative 'Party' or 'coalition' led to a central-initiating political executive which could dominate the majority of the legislature as well as the bureaucracy. This mode of domination over the bureaucracy should not be confused, however, with the American notion of Congressional control (through committees) of the bureaucracy. What developed in Canada was what L. S. Amery has described as the 'Tory notion' of strong and stable government; a unified, central, energizing form of responsible government which does not permit legislative procedures to render the executive impotent or fragmented. This notion took hold in practice. It is quite different from the notion of a fragmented Congress controlling a fragmented public service and executive. What developed in Canada, even during an extension of the furtive spoils period for the first two decades after confederation, was a mode of executive-bureaucratic control of the 'government'. If it can be said that the cabinet could manipulate the bureaucracy with little difficulty (through the spoils system), it might also be acknowledged that the executive was allied with the bureaucracy in its adversary role against the most vocal adversary parts of Parliament, 'the Opposition' (the minority) and the obstreperous private members with their endless numbers of private bills.

Some minor civil service reforms to lessen the more obvious abuses of the spoils system were instituted in 1882. Some competitive examinations for entry to the public service were established. As a result of pressures (from the parliamentary Opposition and from a Royal Commission), the Laurier government passed a Civil Service Act in 1908 which established an independent civil service commission, with life tenure, to institute genuinely competitive examinations for 'inside' positions in Ottawa. As a result of reforms in 1918, patronage was to be removed from Federal positions outside Ottawa as well. Yet as late as 1944 most 'outside' Post Office appointments had remained, on the whole, political party appointments. On balance, however, since 1918 Ottawa has had a 'neutral' public service in the sense that it is free from most of the furtive spoils which had previously characterized it. (Patronage today has shifted more to appointments to quasi-independent boards, commissions and corporations and to contract work done by private legal firms, consultants, etc.) These reforms from 1882 to 1918 have left the public service free from arbitrary dismissal by dissatisfied ministers. Even though it no longer needs to be an alliance based on party preference, these reforms have cleared the way for the public service's alliance with the political executive of the day. These public service reforms of 1882, 1908 and 1918 do not alter the public servant's 'alliance' with the political executive in the operation of the government against the opposing minority in Parliament. In this sense, then, the public service is not neutral. Neither 'responsible government' of 1848, nor a neutral public service operating on the merit principle, changes the public servant's relationship to those parts of the elected assembly which are opposed to the political executive. This is keenly felt by Opposition MPs who are usually frustrated if they attempt to extract much more than public information from the public service in private.

The bureaucracy therefore has always played – with a brief interruption in the mid-nineteenth century in most provinces and somewhat longer in New Brunswick – a central, protected and allied role in relation to the political executive. Its role has not been one of *de facto* subservience to the legislature. Instead it has been subservient to one part of the legislature, the cabinet, which in turn controls the parliamentary majority. Jack Pickersgill, one of Canada's most experienced public servants and politicians, put it this way in his 1972 Clifford Clark Memorial Lecture: 'While bureaucrats should not be partisan, they do not have the right to be neutral between government and opposition. Public servants owe loyal service to the government in office whether they like its politics or not.' As J. E. Hodgetts puts it, the public servant, 'for all practical purposes . . . is not a servant of Parliament but a servant of the executive'. His appointment and 'classification of office' are matters for 'executive determination'.[28]

Given their historical protection from the obstreperous parts of

Parliament, given the many opportunities for public servant influence on both major and minor policy, and given the informal legitimacy patterns that encourage deference to administrative modes of consulting, negotiating and collaborating on policy, it is not difficult to find in Canada many of the attributes of an 'administrative state', or to find disgruntled ministers hinting about the power of public servants even to 'scuttle' ministers.[29] In Ottawa's case, however, the image of an administrative state should not convey an impression of a tightly woven blanket of complacent officials smothering all ministerial initiatives. Nor should the opposite image be perpetuated of a united, ruthlessly aggressive public service devoted to its own programmes of reform which it bulldozes through cabinet and Parliament by skilfully moulding ministers and systematically mystifying the public and Parliament. That the public service cannot be totally unified in spite of Treasury Board, Privy Council Office, Department of Finance or cabinet schemes aimed at unity and coordination has been indicated earlier. Problems of coordination are particularly acute when provincial officials can stall or frustrate Federal schemes of coordination. What is more pertinent than the possibility that the Ottawa public service might be a united conspiracy is to assess the conditions in which ministers are most likely to reverse or change the inclinations of their officials.

(6) *The Impact of Political Leadership from Ministers, Cabinets and Prime Ministers*

The amount of leverage a minister actually exercises with his officials varies, among other things, according to the personalities involved, the prestige of the minister, the length of stay of the minister in his portfolio, and most important, the prime minister's, or the cabinet's (or its staff agency, the privy council's) willingness to back up the minister on his policy initiatives to overcome the objections and delay tactics from officials in his department. Although public servants in most situations will probably look to their minister's leadership, and do not look to ways to frustrate it, there are enough examples to indicate that ministers frequently need help from outside their departments if they are to prevail against the established view of their own mandarins. Paul Hellyer as defence minister received full backing, almost a *carte blanche* from the prime minister, to integrate the armed forces in the mid-1960s. This, in Hellyer's mind was essential if the naval, air and land forces were to be helped to integration with a minimum of delay. The reorganization of the Department of Transport into a complex new 'Ministry' form in the late 1960s and early 1970s has required not only full backing from the prime minister but a vigorous determined minister, frequent help from the Privy Council Office, and the appointment of a one-time highly placed privy council official into the Ministry as deputy minister. The insertion of a number of officials from Trade and Commerce into the Department of External Affairs since the 1970 White Paper (which called for a greater trade and technological emphasis in Canadian foreign policy) can also be taken as an example of the kind of help the minister may need, apart from his own efforts, to implement the new priorities in his department.

Of course the Canadian public service is filled with constellations both of inertia and of policy enthusiasts. Yet it should be remembered that both constellations are sustained in some measure by political leadership or by the lack of it. In fact, either constellation may depend upon at least occasional acts of ministerial initiative or cabinet conciliation if they are to continue to persist at all. Robert Bryce, perhaps the most influential public servant in Ottawa since the Second World War, has referred to the cabinet's key role for reconciling or deciding on policies 'when ministers disagree'. This may be just another way of saying that the cabinet is vital for breaking log jams when 'the key public servants and their ministers' disagree. Second, and more important, is the optical illusion which mistakes highly aggressive activity by public servants as totally self-induced. In fact such officials may simply be following the express will of the political executive. Public servants who are enthusiastically following their ministers' decrees may therefore produce new programmes or energize old constellations of inertia and become so active as to become noticed even by the press: for example, two officials in the secretary of state's office who were delegated by the minister to push some of the department's difficult programmes in 1972.[30] Some officials also may be thrust into prominence by the prime minister or the minister in order to give their tasks new prestige within the bureaucracy. Encouraging the new deputy minister of energy, mines and resources to make public speeches on the need for conservation safeguards in northern development may have been a deliberate attempt to enhance these values within his department and within other departments.

Nor should it always be assumed that constellations of inertia in the Canadian public service are always the handiwork of public servants. Canadian political history is filled with examples of prime ministers or ministers taking rhetorical postures, or producing high-sounding legislation, devoid of specific content, the primary aim of which appears to be more to deflect critics who find a government unconcerned with an issue than realistically to cope with a problem. In this situation, it is missing the mark to accuse the public service of failure to elaborate programmes which transform postures into detailed commitment. Surely the tiny budget, obscure guidelines, and elaborate rhetoric behind the setting up of the Company of Young Canadians is an example of this initial lack of real commitment. It would not be fair, for example, to blame officials in the Department of Labour for failing to produce policies for protecting workers to be affected by technological change if the cabinet had not made it clear before 1971 that it would be uneasy with such a policy. Equally it is unfair to criticize the failure of the Department of External Affairs' Internal Task Force on Europe in 1969–70 to recommend a decrease in Canada's military role in NATO when its minister at the time clearly did not favour such a recommendation.

In short, both inertia and aggressiveness in the public service are related in many instances to the preferences of the political executive. On occasion, nothing can be more dangerous than for a public servant to be prematurely right (as officials, who advocated a Canadian Development Corporation in 1964 and saw it derisively shelved and not dusted off for reintroduction until 1971, will attest.) Equally, nothing is more difficult than for a key official to stay on in a department once the old preferences of a department have been reversed by a unified and determined minister or prime minister or cabinet. It is difficult to imagine the incumbent deputy minister staying on in the Transport, the External Affairs, the Energy Mines and Resources, and the Indian Affairs Departments after the Trudeau government had given notice it was going to overhaul these departments and point them in new directions. As expected, these officials were 'laterally shifted'.

In the absence of firm political leadership, however, the public service retains considerable power and leverage over policy. A minister who idly suggests a policy idea will probably be met by public servants carefully outlining all the problems. Ministers seeking to impose unpopular policies on the bureaucracy will often be met not only with political resistance but a stunning array of bureaucratic log jams and inter-departmental stalling. Left without clear political leadership from a minister, backed up by the prime minister and key members of the cabinet, the public service should not be blamed if it produces policies that are safe and uncontroversial.

Sources of outside expertise and pressure, however, emerge in reports of royal commissions, task forces, even parliamentary committees. These in many instances have pointed to new policy directions supplemented by careful research and often by public hearings. However, the public service is usually asked to assess these recommendations, giving it considerable influence at the legislation preparation stage. Still, if the recommendations are often ignored at this stage, at least the public expectation of some new government initiatives forces some results from most royal commission and task force reports.

What gives the key personnel in the public service their unusual leverage in policy development and control in the Canadian political process in the last fifty years can be traced not simply to their abilities and knowledge and the other conditions mentioned above. The infrequency with which the political executive generates policy values which explicitly challenge those produced by the powerful arbiters in the public service is also important. A survey conducted by Professor Robert Presthus in the mid-1960s found that not many top level public servants in Ottawa ranked 'party policy' as an important influence in what they did compared to other influences. This attitude, of course, may only reflect the fact that the governing Liberal Party has not frequently generated policy values too different from those of the public service, and has not therefore felt it has had to impose its values on the bureaucracy. If this is a governing party's assumption, controls over the public service will be pursued less from the cabinet level than through internal devices shaped by the bureaucracy itself. If, however, a political party assumed power with substantially different policy values from those of the bureaucracy, the Canadian system might go through successive waves of extra-bureaucratic controls, urged not only by the parliamentary caucus, but meticulously enforced from the cabinet or privy council or PMO levels. We have seen that the Trudeau Government, mostly in the interest of consistency and integration and optimization, has pursued some such controls from the cabinet and PCO levels. What may be missing, however, is the sense of a fairly specific policy mandate to which the Trudeau Government was sufficiently committed in an election campaign so that the cabinet and the parliamentary caucus would insure that their commitment could not be altered by the public service.

In a larger sense, even a specific mandate would simply alter some of the internal relationships of the bureaucracy to their political masters. Given the ideology of all the political parties, and the internal needs of the bureaucracy, a mandate would not halt the growth of the state. In summary, it can be said that Canada, especially at the Federal level, exhibits many characteristics of an administrative state. Yet the nature of the state activity can never be thoroughly comprehended by identifying these administrative characteristics.

It is almost impossible to conceive of a diminution of participation by public servants in policy-making without a diminution of the state itself. To be able to respond coherently and effectively to ministerial and public demands for policy, contacts of the public service with the environment have become crucial for interpreting problems, proposing solutions and deflecting uncongenial demands. These contacts also become indispensable to any political executive or minister searching for interpretations of the nature of the problem to be solved. Yet it must be remembered that the public servant is usually reporting on a condition in the environment in which the state is already involved. In fact the state may have set the framework giving rise to the condition or problem in society in the first place. Yet the employees of the state are asked to diagnose as well as to prescribe. The state thereby becomes increasingly abstract. It reports on and prescribes for society while in fact it is responsible for much of the nature of that society. It is not difficult to see how all political parties and ideologies in Canada have the primary function of making further demands on the state. A call for separation between society and state does not emerge from these forces. Whenever difficulties arise, most of society waits for the decision of the state. Whenever disturbances occur, Canadians bemoan the incompetence of the state. The state is driven to increased superordination in relation to everything around it. The public service, of necessity, plays a crucial role in mediating and extending this superordination, a task made somewhat easier in Canada by the principle of a neutral public service.

6 Parliament as Catalyst

The Canadian Parliament is legally sovereign in Federal jurisdiction. Nothing becomes Federal law unless Parliament passes it. Although Federal public servants have immense influence in making policy and in writing legislation, although Federal-provincial relations affect these activities, and although the political executive's power of leadership is also important, Parliament can say no to all of these agencies of decision. It can refuse to pass their legislation. Any part of Parliament, the governor-general, the Senate or the House of Commons can do these things.

Yet as all observers of Canada's Parliament know, the governor-general has almost never exercised his prerogative to do these things in this century and the Senate alters legislation mainly on details. The House of Commons alters some details of bills, occasionally derails or stalls a bill, and often embarrasses the political executive. But in times of majority Government, most of the Government's legislative programme is whipped through the House. In times of minority Government, the same occurs until a minor party's cooperation with the Government ceases.

Parliament's legal sovereignty can mislead the observer who wishes to understand the normal position of Parliament in the political and policy process. This chapter will trace first the overall position of Parliament in the Federal state. Then it will examine the potent functions which remain to the House of Commons in the policy-making process and in political life. Even if the House of Commons' legal sovereignty does not mean it is all-powerful in the day-to-day business of the Federal State, its actual activities remain far from negligible and these deserve an extended exposition. Let us first introduce the other parts of 'Parliament', the governor-general and the Senate, before moving to this discussion of the House of Commons.

(1) *The Crown and the Governor-General*

The relevance of the Crown to the government of Canada appears to be everything or nothing. The monarchical language of the BNA Act makes it appear as though the governor-general runs the country. In fact, most of these powers have atrophied and his relevance is now almost completely nominal in the field of policy-making. As confirmed in the 1926 Balfour resolution and effectively established somewhat before, the parliamentary functions of the monarch are performed in Canada by the governor-general. He operates without any reference back to the monarch in Britain or to the British government. The official parliamentary functions of the governor-general now include the summoning of the House of Commons, the appointment of senators, assenting to legislation, and recommending financial measures to the House. As we saw earlier, these functions were vested in the governor-general primarily to retain centralized executive control of the government (especially to prevent private Members of Parliament taking the initiative on money bills) and are now all, in effect, carried on by the prime minister and the cabinet. Except for some squabbles between the governor-general and the prime minister over appointments of senators in the last century, no governor-general, since the 1880s, has refused to follow the prime minister's advice on these matters. The real potency of the governor-general is to dissolve Parliament and to name a Government. This power can in fact – in extreme situations – be decisive. These functions are usually left to the prime minister if he clearly commands a majority. Yet there have been occasions when it was ambiguous which party could command a majority in the House of Commons and in such cases the governor-general may re-enter the picture. The governor-general's exercise of this prerogative became contentious when he exercised it in the teeth of the advice of the incumbent prime minister in 1926 (he refused to grant a dissolution of Parliament to the prime minister soon after an election because he thought the leader of another party might have been able to form a Government and command a majority).

But 1926 was the last time such a confrontation occurred, because since then the governor-general has followed the evident will of the House of Commons. It is possible, however, that his performance in the minority Parliament elected in 1972 may become contentious.

The governor-general can play an integrative role in Canada through his travels, speeches and receptions, which can help to affirm advances in Canadian society and promote national feeling. His ceremonial and social activities no doubt also free the prime minister to concentrate more on matters of governmental and political importance. Since 1952 governors-general have been Canadians.

(2) *The Senate*

The Senate is the senior house in Canada's bicameral system. It is made up of 102 seats. The Senate's original representation under section 22 of the British North America Act was to be split in thirds between the maritimes, Quebec and Ontario. By 1915 the four western provinces had been established as a fourth division with twenty-four senators. The entry of Newfoundland into Confederation in 1949 brought six more senators to make the total of 102. Senators are no longer appointed for life but those appointed since 1965 are now to retire at the age of seventy-five. In effect all senators are appointed by the prime minister.

A diligent reading of the British North America Act would suggest that the Senate and the House of Commons are roughly equal in power. Yet the Senate, as a non-elected – an appointed – House, has seldom risked its own abolition by exercising its legislative powers in a way which might seriously displease the cabinet and the majority of the House of Commons. Its control over policy and appropriations can in no way be compared to the American Senate. In its caution, it resembles the British House of Lords, yet there are some important differences. Unlike the House of Lords, the Canadian Senate has had no inherited peers. The Canadian Senate is weaker than the Lords in the sense that it enjoys no legal provision for delaying government bills with a suspensive veto. It simply must reject a bill, amend it or pass it. Yet in another sense it is stronger because the House of Lords can be over-ridden (when pressed, the Senate usually backs down – e.g. in the cases of the 1969 pesticides and the 1974 wiretap bills).

Although the Senate does much useful work in tidying up legislation, it seldom defeats a bill or amends it on matters of substance.

If Canadian senators enjoy some social prestige, it cannot be said that the Senate has ever enjoyed much self-confidence in the Canadian political system. Too frequently, appointments to the Senate have been used by the prime minister as plums to reward party stalwarts or as safety valves for prime ministers who wish to 'promote' certain cabinet ministers 'out of the cabinet'. (In one celebrated instance during the early 1920s, a cabinet minister embroiled in a scandal over customs administration was hastily 'promoted' to the Senate by the prime minister.) Nevertheless, as mentioned, the Senate does do considerable work 'cleaning up' sloppily drafted bills. This is an activity which its large proportion of lawyers do quite well. The Senate cannot, however, introduce or increase, and seldom will it amend, a money bill. The Senate has conducted a number of well researched and well publicized studies and inquiries and has thereby helped to spotlight the importance of the subject-matter under study. (For example in the last ten years the Senate has produced careful studies and investigations of employment, land use, science policy, poverty, ageing, the mass media, and Indian problems.) Observers note that this chamber operates with less party partisanship than does the House of Commons. Its lower political temperature no doubt helps it to do the tasks of legislative draftmanship and investigation quite well. However the heavy representation of corporation lawyers and businessmen in the Senate affects it in a partisan way by keeping these business interests informed of what the government may be thinking and by providing access for these interests to ministers. The senators have, in fact, reacted rather partisanly on issues close to their pocket books, such as tax reform. (The Senate in the summer of 1971 recommended a host of retreats away from the reform suggestions of the cabinet in its White Paper on taxation.) Yet it has also reported on situations in the private sector that criticize its operation, such as in its report on science, the mass media, and poverty.

(3) *The House of Commons*

The key part of Parliament then is the House of Commons. Its power comes from its position as the directly elected House of Parliament and from its principle of representation. Like most parliamentary lower Houses, the Canadian House of Commons' principle of representation is to reflect the distribution of population. The Senate, in contrast, is designed more to provide regional equality. The elaboration of this principle of representation in the House of Commons is not without some Federal or 'regional' backstops. Representation is apportioned by provinces and altered after each decennial census under a complicated set of guidelines. The 'Federal' or 'regional' backstops include a minimum number of seats for each province (otherwise Prince Edward Island's 110,000 people would not have four members) and a 15 per cent limit on the reduction of a province's representation after each census. The 'population' principle of the House's representation emerges in the basic calculation for representation. Each province's share is calculated by dividing the total population of the provinces by 261 and the quota thus obtained is divided into the population of each province. Constituency boundaries are decided under the direction of the Speaker of the House based on the work of a representation commissioner working through ten *ad hoc* non-political boundary commissions in each province working under guidelines which allow a – not inconsiderable – variation in the size of constituency populations within each province.[1] Representation in the House as a result of the 1961 census and used for the 1972 election is given in table 6 below.

Table 6
Representation in the House of Commons by Province

	(a)	(b)
Prince Edward Island	4	4
Nova Scotia	11	11
New Brunswick	10	10
Newfoundland	7	7
Quebec	74	75
Ontario	88	95
Manitoba	13	14
Saskatchewan	13	14
Alberta	19	20
British Columbia	23	27
Yukon Territory	1	1
Northwest Territory	1	1
Total	264	279

(a) as of 1974 election

(b) proposed Federal Government redistribution introduced 21 November 1974 for the next Federal General Election

All members of the House are now elected from single-member constituencies. However, given the rather wide variation in the size of constituency populations, it is rare to find a party's over-all representation in the House proportionate to its popular vote. Only twice since 1930 has the majority party in the House secured a majority in the popular vote. In 1968, for example, the Liberal Party polled 45 per cent of the vote and secured 59 per cent of the House seats. Another peculiar result of the electoral system has been its tendency, with the exception of the 1958 election, to produce far fewer seats for the Progressive Conservative Party in Quebec in Federal elections than its popular vote warranted. For example, this party attracted approximately 19 per cent of the popular vote in the province of Quebec in the 1972 Federal general election, yet secured only two of the province's seventy-four seats. Other informal characteristics of the House should also be noted. The turnover of members from one Parliament to another is large, usually around 40 per cent, and the occupational (and class) distribution of members is woefully malapportioned. There have been very few members from the non-professional wage-earning part of society and there has been a dramatic over-representation of lawyers. In fact in the past approximately one-half of the members of the House have been lawyers. Perhaps the 1975 increase in the parliamentary indemnity to $24,000 a year plus further tax-exempt allowances of $10,000 and the 1974 Act granting partial public funding of election campaigns will make it easier for the less wealthy to run for Parliament.

Other prescriptions affecting the nature of the Canadian House of Commons should not be forgotten. Unlike Italy, for example, where public servants are sometimes also parliamentarians, no one can sit in the House who holds an office of profit or emolument under the Crown. The life of a Parliament can run for five years, but usually a Parliament lasts for four because a prime minister will not want to narrow his options on when he can call a general election at a time propitious for his government. Parliament must hold one session a year, although there are no requirements as to their length. (For example, the third session of the twenty-eighth Parliament began in late 1970 and did not conclude until early 1972, whereas another session in 1940 lasted only a few hours.) Most sessions last somewhat less than a year, with breaks in the late summer and at Easter and Christmas time. There is no constituency residence qualification for members of the House.

(4) *The Relevance of the House of Commons And Its Relationship to the State*

The position of the House of Commons in the growth and nature of the state in Canada cannot be understood without recognizing its historical genesis. 'Responsible government' was achieved in the provinces of Canada, Nova Scotia and New Brunswick in 1848, Prince Edward Island in 1851 and Newfoundland (effectively) in 1855. Most historical commentaries in Canada describe this event – the achievement of responsible government – as the final destination on a long constitutional journey. It is seen as a long overdue wresting of control of government power and patronage from the influence of the Crown's viceroy, the governor, in each province. Yet for our purposes it is better to see this event as a landmark on a continuing journey. The practical result has been executive (not parliamentary) control of the government between elections. Because of party discipline and the paucity of parliamentary reforms to alter executive dominance, this dominance was not altered by the events of 1848 to 1855 in the provinces. 'Responsible government', which was demanded in the name of freedom, produced in fact a greater efficiency and a greater systematization of the apparatus of the state. The idea of liberty and of responsible government became defined in the power of the state, not defined by society's resources against the state. Since 1867 the idea of responsible government under majority, and most of the time under minority, Government became increasingly integrated into state power. Responsible government ceased to mean meticulous and systematic control of the executive by the Assembly. It became almost (but fortunately not entirely) what the executive – if it had a firm majority – could safely allow the Assembly to do between elections. With this 'revolution' of 1848, the state grew stronger by pledging to secure the very value it largely absorbed: 'responsible government'.

Parliament retains legal sovereignty today in that nothing becomes law unless Parliament passes it and no executive can last in office without the support of the majority of the House. Yet beyond its importance for legitimatizing a Government's right to office, the notion of 'responsible government' should not be extended too far as a way of understanding day-to-day executive-parliamentary relations under majority, and some minority, Governments. When the possibility of dismissal of an executive or 'Government' in the House was not remote, the principle of responsible government could be a meaningful deterrent to bad or unpopular government. After the events of 1848, the Assembly of the province of Canada was a model of Walter Bagehot's elaborate notion of responsible government, i.e. the lower House was an 'elective', 'choosing' and 'deliberating body'. From 1854 to 1864, there was enough fluidity among groups and factions, and party discipline was sufficiently weak, to make it difficult for any political executive to control a majority in the Assembly for very long. During this time at least nine ministries were forced to resign or to change their leadership because of adverse or threatened adverse votes in the Assembly. No ministry survived intact (without a major re-alignment) for what may now be called a Government's normal life (which is the period from a general election until the leader of a Government asks for a dissolution at a time of his choice near the end of the legislature's allotted span). During this decade, the executive's responsibility to the Assembly was based fundamentally, and without ambiguity, on the political willingness, not simply the legal potential, of the Assembly to choose a ministry without having to submit to a general election before the end of the Assembly's allotted life (usually four years). This 'elective' power was, in Bagehot's theory, the lower House's most important function. On this hung all hopes for meaningful day-to-day control; on this rested the power of the Assembly to ensure that it fulfilled its 'teaching', 'expressing' and 'legislating' functions vigorously and without intimidation from the executive. This brief period when Assemblies were able to exercise their pre-eminence over the executive in Canada is a pristine example of the logic and implication of true responsible government. Yet it has also given rise to the confused complacency with which the whole idea of responsible government is viewed today. This confusion and complacency comes from overlooking the fact that responsible government operates today within the context of disciplined parties in Parliament. Ever since the ascendancy of mass disciplined political parties in Canada was confirmed in 1878, the 1848 notion of responsible government has, except for its legal accuracy, grown increasingly unhelpful as a rubric under which other characteristics of cabinet-parliamentary relations are to be understood.

It is well known that during the first decade after confederation, party discipline in the Federal House was still somewhat weak around the edges. Direct parliamentary influence from all parts of the House on the government and on legislation was perceptible. Yet when the simultaneous and secret ballot was introduced into the Federal election of 1878, almost all candidates for the House submitted themselves to the continuous discipline of a political party. (In fact Prime Minister Alexander MacKenzie created a constitutional novelty by resigning after the election without meeting the House of Commons because it was clear that the party of Sir John A. Macdonald would command a majority in the impending Parliament).[2] Commentators who insist that Parliament – the House of Commons in particular – has declined, usually refer to the growth of executive functions since the turn of the century. In fact the most fundamental decline in the House occurred in 1878 when party discipline began to erode the power of the House between elections.

To ask, however, if the House of Commons' roles in government and politics have declined *since 1878*, is to ask a more complicated question. The Canadian House has declined in one fundamental sense since that year in that the number of private bills which can be debated and the length of time during which they can be discussed have been rigorously prescribed. Now the House spends less than 3 per cent of its time on such bills.[3] (My calculations of the session in 1969–70 show 2.5 per cent of the time of the House was spent on private member's public and private bills[4] and 4 per cent on private members' notices of motions, motions, and resolutions.)[5] The House may have declined in another sense, in that the length of members' speeches and of certain set-piece debates (including supply) have been shortened or eliminated by reforms to the standing orders. These and other reforms will be discussed later. It is difficult to argue, however, that these changes in parliamentary procedure have drastically altered the House's effect on the executive since 1878. Since 1878 when the secret ballot cut down on intimidations and simultaneous elections made 'loose fish' candidates (who would support any ministry) almost extinct, two mass, office-seeking, national parties monopolized Canadian politics until 1921. One-party Governments, and to a large degree one-party Oppositions, became a regular feature in Parliament until 1914. The effective threat that the House of Commons might choose another Government *between* elections, without reference to a general election, has seldom been credible. All but one change in the Government of Canada has occurred, not because of a parliamentary reversal, but because of a vote against the government in a general election. The twenty-ninth Parliament, elected 30 October 1972, may in fact break this pattern. The official opposition may be able to attract the support of a minor party to take over without an election before this Parliament's time expires. Except for what may happen in the twenty-ninth Parliament, this reticence to allow the House to choose a Government between elections can be praised as a triumph for direct democracy insofar as it signifies a direct influence of the people on the choice of a Government. Yet for the purposes of understanding the House of Commons' role in Canadian politics, one must be clear about the implications. We now have a situation in which the assessments of A. H. Birch, speaking of Westminster, may be appropriate for Canada. What has developed, in his words, 'is not so much a form of parliamentary control of the executive as a form of voters' control, exercised in parliamentary elections. And since elections take place infrequently, it is not clear that the word "control" is appropriate.' The idea of 'responsible government' in itself does not provide for an effective sanction against government mismanagement or dishonesty in Canada. Much more must be added to the remote deterrent of a parliamentary defeat if majority Governments are to be made responsible. In fact, crises that once could crumble Governments and dissolve legislatures (such as the combined sectional onslaughts that toppled the Hincks and Morin Government in the Assembly of the province of Canada in 1854 or the Macdonald Government in the House in 1873), have served primarily as an occasion for Government MP's to rally even more loyally around their leader. Far from testing their party's actual conviction in Government action in times of crisis, prime ministers are prone to be very critical of any rebel behaviour, absenteeism, or lukewarm support in their party during such crises. Also, as is well known, in times of crisis prime ministers can, if they wish, grip even more firmly to the reins of power until public attention is diverted to new policies and pre-occupations. Such deflections can allow a Government to return to a position of electoral popularity before allowing the electorate to express its view on the party in power through a general election. In this sense, part of the idea of government 'responsibility' is now completely reversed in Canada. What A. H. Birch suggests for Britain is true of Canada : a Government is now said to be 'taking responsibility' when it takes a collective decision to use the whip to ensure parliamentary support for itself. It is perceived to be 'evading' responsibility if it permits a free vote.[7]

(5) Influence in the Interstices

Even with the operational realities imposed by executive-dominated parliamentary majorities the House of Commons has found much to do since 1878, and it fulfils functions that give it influence at least within the interstices of this matrix of executive dominance of Parliament.

First, the traditions and ideals of Parliament help to entrench various 'rights of the opposition'. Before confederation provincial Assembly procedures, as a legacy of the struggle for responsible government, were something of a procedure of opposition. The House carried the spirit of these procedures almost intact into its Standing Orders and in the Speaker's rulings for almost fifty years after confederation. Although parliamentary sessions in the nineteenth century were short by contemporary standards, each day's business was studded with lengthy speeches and inundated by floods of private bills. Little occurred to reverse these charac-teristics until 1913.[8] Since then there have been episodic but infrequent attempts to cope with the Government's need to have all of its ever-increasing legislation debated and hopefully passed, yet all the while meeting the time-honoured 'procedure of opposi-tion' of the House of Commons.

There can be little doubt that if they have not systematically decreased the opposition's dominance of debate, the effect of various reforms since 1913 in the Canadian House has been against the opposition's supposed right to talk almost as long as it wants in all debates. Several new rules were introduced in 1913, but the most drastic renovation was the introduction of a closure rule. This permitted the Government to end debate in the house after twenty-four hours notice and the motion itself, which remains in the Standing Orders today, is not debatable. Up until the twenty-ninth Parliament, however, it had been used on only eight bills in all, and only three times on all stages of a bill. Far more effective in terms of its systematic effect on House activity was another new rule which cut down on the number of debatable motions. In effect this rule guaranteed the Government that Supply, as well as Ways and Means, would get to the Committee of the Whole on Thursdays and Fridays during most of the session. Other motions left off the list of 'debatable motions' cut down in effect on the number of stages for debate as a bill passed through the House.

Little further change occurred until 1927, when the rights of most members to speak almost endlessly on a motion were formally reduced. The new rule stated that no member other than the prime minister, the leader of the opposition, a minister moving a motion, or the first member to reply to a motion, was to be allowed to speak for more than forty minutes. (The forty-minute rule did not apply in committee, however.) A rule for 11 o'clock adjournments was also passed, thwarting another familiar opportunity for attempts by the opposition or a private member to wear out the Government by speaking long into the evening.

Few further changes occurred until 1955. Several thoughtful reports and recommendations for reform emerged from revision committees in the House from 1944 to 1951 but the Government did not see fit to act on many of these. However, the House passed some amendments to the rules in 1955 in order to abbreviate certain set-piece debates. The length of speeches in the Committee of the Whole was cut and a maximum number of days was established for such debates as : the debate on the Address in reply to the Speech from the Throne; the budget debate, and the motion to go into Committee of Supply. Further amendments in 1960 cut speeches on these occasions to thirty minutes and the length of the first two debates to eight and six days respectively.

Finally, the interminable House debate on the resolution for a new Canadian flag in 1964 brought matters to a head. The Canadian House is still feeling its way through the changes provoked by the events of 1964. In 1964 a near-unanimous feeling swept through the chamber that if all legislation and all House business were to receive an appropriate amount of time some method of time allocation was necessary. As rarely before in the history of Canadian parliamentary reform, an all-party Special House Committee on Procedure and Organization was able to agree on a number of reforms.[9] The Pearson government followed the committee's recommendations completely in some cases and tentatively in others, for example abolishing certain appeals to the Speaker's rulings and setting up more active standing committees.[10] The most contentious reform, introduced in May 1965 and adopted provisionally for three years, was the insertion of a guillotine rule into the Standing Orders. A new guillotine rule was incorporated into the Standing Orders in 1968 but was not used until late 1971 when it was applied to the Income Tax Reform Bill. (The rule, however, is widely believed to be faultily drafted. It appears that if the opposition parties could agree on time allocation the Government party may not be able to use the rule. However, the use of it in 1971 allowed the Speaker to avoid ruling on this possibility since it appears that the opposition parties could not reach agreement among themselves on allocation of time.)

Perhaps the most important 1968 reform was the limitation of the business of supply in each session to not more than twenty-five days, plus three days for supplementary estimates brought in after the main estimates. These are now also called 'opposition days'. In the past, much of the consumption of House time came in the committee of supply because supply debates were wonderfully convenient pegs on which to hang almost any kind of speech on any subject (see table 8). And since one of the uses of a guillotine would be to shorten supply debates, the guillotine is not needed for these debates since supply days are now restricted by Standing Order. As a result of the 1965 and 1968 reforms, the examination of the Government's estimates of expenditure for each year – 'supply' – is now conducted primarily in the Standing Committees of the House of Commons instead of in the whole House. As table 7 shows, 110 meetings of Standing Committees were held to discuss estimates in the second session of the twenty-eighth Parliament. The Opposition can use its Whole House 'Supply days' or 'opposition days' to debate reports of Standing Committees on the estimates. Yet this is seldom the Opposition's main concern in these debates. The opposition parties decide on the topics to be debated during supply days and they chose, for example, to debate estimates on only one of the twenty-five days allotted to them in the first session of the twenty-eighth Parliament. The new procedure for the business of supply is not an unqualified gain for the opposition because it is a break from tradition in that it does not allow the opposition the time-honoured right to hold up supply in the Whole House.

Another specific time limit built into the Standing Orders in 1968 and begun by the 1965 reforms is the reform limiting the 'oral inquiries of the ministry' to forty minutes each day the House is in session. (However, this still adds up to a substantial amount of House time, 17 per cent of all oral debate in the 1969–70 session.) Another reform designed to save time in the House was the removal of opportunities for the opposition's dilatory behaviour on questions of procedure (for example, spontaneous questions of privilege arising out of proceedings outside the House are forbidden). Another restriction is the abolition of the four debates to go into the Committe of Supply in each session. Another is the reform which eliminates the right of appeal from the Speaker's decisions on points of order. Another abolished the resolution stage of money bills.

The new order that public bills 'unless otherwise ordered' are to go to Standing Committees for their committee stage is especially important. The prime minister expressed the hope in his speech on the reforms in 1968 that the major debate on Government bills would come at the report stage in the Whole House after the bill was examined in committee, instead of at second reading before a bill went to committee for close study. However, experience since 1969 has shown that on most bills the opposition prefers to spend more time in debate on second reading (20.3 per cent of the time of all oral proceedings in 1969–70) than on either the report stage or the third (and final) reading stage (both together comprised only 10 per cent of the time of all oral proceedings in 1969–70, see table 8). This proclivity may be a result of the tendency of the Government to agree to some minor, or even to more substantial, changes to some of its legislation in the committee stage. This proclivity to spend more time on debate before, not after, the committee stage may also be a consequence of the opposition's calculation that the mass media will expect a bill to receive its major wounds not at report stage but at the second reading and committee stages. After this second reading or committee stage, it is not unknown for the Government to withdraw a bill or to give in on a host of details (see, for example, the history of the Corporation Disclosure Act in 1970, part of the Act to amend the Criminal Code in 1970, the Broadcast Act in 1965, the Transport Act of 1966 and the Public Service Bills of 1969–70).[11] It is also clear that private motions sometimes become Government legislation after having been referred to a committee (such as the bill on Indian education in the twenty-eighth Parliament.)

By far the most important impact of the reforms of 1965 and 1968 has been on the role of committees of the House.[12] Until then, standing committees had never been very potent. Since 1968, however, all estimates and most bills go to standing committees. The wide-ranging activity of these committees makes them appear to be something of a combination of Westminister's Standing and Select Committees. Yet in another sense they are similar to France's six commissions in the Assemblée Nationale because Ottawa's standing committees exist permanently unless the Standing Orders are amended. A standing committee is able to conduct general inquiries into matters of public policy, although in fact the Government majority must agree to allow it to do so. The increase in standing committee activity is dramatic. In 1966, in the second session of the twenty-seventh Parliament, standing committees began to take the committee stage of a number of bills. They examined all parts of seven Government bills and the subject-matter of parts of six other bills. By 1969, forty-two Government bills were being dealt with by standing committees.[13] In committee, it is not unusual for Government bills to be considerably altered on details as a result of suggestions by members and by interest groups testifying before the committee. Some bills (such as some Criminal Code amendments in 1970–1) have been shelved after the committee ordeal precisely because the bill was far more contentious and faultily drafted than the government originally thought.

Standing committees have also been active in the unwieldly business of discussing the estimates. In Westminster, scrutiny of the estimates is done by the Estimates Committee through subcommittees. In Canada, as in France, most of the substantive standing committees examine the departmental estimates relevant to the committee. For example, the Standing Committee on Agriculture examines the Department of Agriculture's estimates, and so on. Discussion seldom settles into a systematic item-by-item scrutiny. Instead discussion, usually dominated by the opposition, is made up of exchanges of opinion and queries on broad policy and of close scrutiny on a pot-pourri of individual items. (For example, in four hours of scrutiny of the minister of transport on departmental estimates on 9 April 1970 ninety-three separate topics were raised.) Although the new format of the government estimates now expresses government expenditure in a programme budgeting format (to enable members, it is said, better to relate expenditures to purposes), members prefer to ignore this attempt to lift their thoughts to more rarified heights. Instead they concentrate on keeping the minister on firm ground with their emphasis on constituency problems, questions on equipment purchases, and so on. Members also use examination of the estimates to question public servants, not simply ministers. The range of public servants is much broader than that which appears before the commissions of the French Assemblée Nationale, for example. This has helped to lessen the anonymity of key public servants and the impenetrability of their duties. On occasion, members have provoked fascinating revelations of public servant (not only ministerial) attitudes on policy (see, for example, the proceedings in committee in 1970 on the Transport Department estimates and the Regional Expansion Department estimates).

Also in 1969 a Commons committee recommended the establishment of a parliamentary committee to scrutinize statutory instruments. By mid-1972, a joint Senate-Commons committee (eight senators and twelve MPs) was made ready for duty. It is not designed to act as an Ombudsman, taking up public or individual complaints; its role is to examine nearly all regulations made by public servants, boards and other government bodies to ensure that they follow statutory authority and do not infringe on individual rights. (The law now also requires all regulations to be published in the weekly *Canada Gazette*. Only regulations dealing with national security, international relations or Federal-provincial relations may be excluded from publication.) In essence this 'review' will comment on those regulations which seem to be inappropriate in terms of the above guidelines. Yet there is some evidence to suggest that the committee will be sensitive to submissions it receives from people or groups with grievances against government regulations, and although it won't officially carry their case for them – as an Ombudsman would – it may use these submissions to help them in its reviews.

Standing committees, such as that for External Affairs and National Defence, have also spent considerable time conducting inquiries into major issues of public policy (see table 7) and on some occasions, even under majority Governments, have produced reports openly critical of the Government (see, for example, the External Affairs Committee's critique of the Government's White Paper on foreign policy of 1970). This seems to happen to a greater degree in Ottawa than in Westminster. Some committees have recommended policy at variance with Government intentions. For example, one standing committee recommended the declaration of sovereignty over the Arctic archipelago, another recommended 51 per cent Canadian ownership of most of Canadian industry; both stand vividly in contrast to Government policy. Standing committees have also produced reports, which if they were not blunt criticisms of the Government, have made it awkward for the Government to ignore its opinion.

Table 7
Meetings of Standing Committees of the House of Commons,
*Twenty-Eighth Parliament, Second Session**

Total number of meetings	Meetings devoted to estimates	Meetings devoted to legislation	Meetings devoted to inquiries	Other meetings
596	110	169	315	2

* Calculated from the Canadian Government Publications Catalogue, 1970 (Information Canada, Ottawa, 1971). These are totals not of committee publications but of meetings.

This recent, increased activity of Canadian House of Commons standing committees is not in contrast to recent British experience but it is to contemporary French experience. In 1971, for example, the French Assemblée's six standing commissions held 279 meetings in all, whereas in Ottawa House committees held 596 meetings (see table 7) in the second session of the twenty-ninth

Parliament. Clearly the activity of select and standing committees in Westminster has increased in the last few decades. It has certainly reached the level of activity experienced by the Canadian committees since 1966.

However, burdened by all this work, Government and opposition members in Ottawa are not completely at ease with the advance of standing committees as these forums are time-consuming and often fail to attract publicity. Opposition members complain that Government members too often simply show up to vote without previous participation. Frequently, too many meetings are scheduled for the same day and it is difficult to muster a quorum. Some opposition members wonder if the role of the opposition in committee does not become too collegial, in that they may simply end up helping to improve a minister's bill, thus insufficient partisan advantage is gained from all this work. Complaints are also heard that the committee chairmen (who are, with one exception, The Standing Committee on Public Accounts, Government back-benchers) are sometimes unfair in their treatment of the opposition. There are the inevitable complaints that the Government gives the appearance of not taking the opposition very seriously. Government back-bench members complain that minsters do not appreciate too much probing of ministerial or departmental activity by government members in committees, nor do ministers always find it flattering to have to be helped in committee deliberations by Government members. Not surprisingly, Government members find much committee activity tedious and embarrassing. Some committees also have difficulty in getting their reports debated in the Whole House, if they go beyond the Government on policy.[14]

As already mentioned, committees sometimes have difficulty in mustering a quorum, though this is eased now by the fact that House Standing Orders permit one member to substitute for another in committee. One observer calculated that in the second session of the twenty-eighth Parliament the average substitution was 2.4 members per meeting. In the third session this increased to 3.4.[15] Part of the explanation for low committee attendance and high substitutions is that members are often out of Ottawa Mondays and Fridays, caucuses usually meet Wednesday mornings, and some committees hold travelling hearings. Not surprisingly, it has been found that in committee work, if workload is measured by attendance, some parties work harder than others and some members much harder than others. Dorothy Byrne's calculations show that 27.1 per cent of Liberal back-benchers did 52.8 per cent of the work, 25.0 per cent of Conservatives did 52.9 per cent of the work, 52.4 per cent of the New Democrats did 72.5 per cent of the work.[16] The Créditiste members had very weak attendance records. Of the many causes for this variation in workload-sharing, perhaps the low importance given to committee work by French-speaking members, compared to English-speaking, is one explanation.[17] Dorothy Byrne also suggests that a potential remedy for the administrative problem of scheduling meetings would be to schedule one week per month as 'committee week'.[18] The Government will sometimes temporarily deactivate most standing committees, as in the autumn of 1971 when it put its massive tax reform bill before a committee of the whole in the House of Commons to keep the bill moving under control. (No time allocation rule can be applied in standing committees.) Yet it seems clear that standing committees will continue to play an uncomfortable but increasingly active role in the Canadian policy process in refining legislation, in initiating major policy ideas, and in igniting controversies which lead to pressure on the government.

The fear, often advanced by British MPs, that any major increase in the role of specialized committees would produce 'consensus politics' and diminish 'political debate' in the Whole House is not confirmed by Canadian experience with its standing committees. There are some examples of committees producing consensual policy recommendations after its general studies into a policy area, such as with the Foreign Policy White Paper in 1971 or with the demand for a declaration of sovereignty in the north in 1970. There is little evidence, however, of 'consensus politics' in committee work on estimates and on the principles of most government bills. Examples of committee consensus on changes in details of government bills are not hard to find, but this does not necessarily imply a consensus on principles of the bill. Even more important, there is little evidence that the committees have diminished partisan political articulation during a bill's other stages. This should not be too surprising. In France, for example, even though commission reports by *rapporteurs* sometimes reflect criticisms of the opposition, much more remains for the opposition to say in the Assembly itself. Two results of the increased activity of standing committees in Canada, however, has been an improvement both in the calibre of debate and in the quality of the information produced in the debate on the report stage and in the third reading stage of government bills. These debates, however, are often dominated by those members who examined the bill in its committee stage. As Oscar Wilde once remarked on returning from the premiere of one of his plays, 'The play was a success but the audience a failure.' Many Canadian MPs feel similarly about debates in the Whole House after their committee has exhaustively examined a bill or a problem.

(6) *The Use of the Agenda of the Whole House of Commons*

The Canadian House of Commons indulges in various forms of catalytic and deliberative activity in addition to debating government bills. Before the parliamentary reforms of the mid–1960s, in the second session of the twenty-fourth Parliament in 1960 for example, about one-third of the time of the House was spent debating government bills; this was also the case for the second session of the twenty-eighth Parliament in 1970. The rest of the time in the Whole House was spent as indicated in table 8.

Even with the diversity of House set-piece events, the use made of debate by members of Parliament does not vary greatly according to the occasion. Partisan adversary use of the House dominates most occasions. Yet some nuances are worth noting. The debate on the 'Address in Reply to the Speech From the Throne' is a rather formless six-day debate made up of Government expressions of pride in its performance and in its promises for policy leadership in the future. The opposition concentrates on reinterpreting the Government's performance across many areas of public policy. The later days of the debate are dominated to a large extent by back-bench members discussing eclectic national grievances and various local matters. The 'Debate on the Budget' is restricted to six days. This is usually a major opportunity for the opposition to criticize the Government's economic leadership. Yet a natural balance reasserts itself. There are few parliamentary occasions that place the press and the mass media in such a position whereby they become almost 'information allies' of the

Table 8
*Debate on Legislation and Supply as a Percentage of all Oral Debate in the Whole House**

	Pre-Reform Session Third session, 24th Parliament (1960) Per cent of total time	Post-Reform Session Second Session, 28th Parliament (1969–70) Per cent of total time
Supply days (known as opposition or allotted days since 1968)	33.3	13.3
Government bills	33.1	33.6
Second reading	20.6	20.3
Committee of the Whole	11.2	3.3
Report stage	n.a.	8.0
Third reading	1.3	2.0
Private member's bills and resolutions	5.7	6.5
Other	27.9	43.6

* *Calculated after subtracting blank parts of pages and written documentation and replies from all proceedings in the House Debates for these two sessions.*

Government. The budget debate is one of the most important sources of 'hard news' in any given session. Therefore, the first few days of media discussion on the budget concentrates on exploring what the budget means to the average Canadian. Comments by opposition leaders are given brief prominence in the first few days but it would be foolish to expect that they would attract much attention as they are inevitably buried beneath the more important news of government announcements on tax and tariff changes. The use of the House of Commons during debates on government bills varies, but as noted, in general, the first reading is simply an announcement of the bill in the House and no debate is conducted. The debate on second reading is usually the lengthiest. After a bill goes to the standing committee (or to the Committee of the Whole) for its committee stage, it returns to the House. The Speaker marshalls the amendments proposed by the opposition and the debate is conducted on the amendments at the report stage. As we have seen, the debate at the report stage is usually brief. The debate on the third reading is usually the shortest of all. It is in debate on second reading that opposition members roam and comb at will over all the incomplete or wrong-headed principles of the government bill. At the report stage the opposition delivers an abbreviated but often more pointed and informed critique of the bill.

The topics for debate in the twenty-five supply days in the whole House are left to the opposition to decide. In fact these days are now called 'supply days' or 'opposition days' or 'allotted days'. The opposition usually employs these occasions to express concern with various government actions or inactions on a selected topical issue each day. The debate on the adjournment or 'the late show' at 10 p.m. which occurs three days a week allows for three different ten minute exchanges on various problems. An MP, usually a member of the opposition, makes an argument for up to seven minutes, and a minister (or, more often, a parliamentary secretary) replies for three minutes. The topics must be submitted to the Speaker in advance. These exchanges are not unlike a mini-supply dialogue or an extended question period exchange.

Another important House occasion is the 'oral inquiries of the ministry' which extends for forty minutes each day the House is in session. Here all but a small number of the inquiries are made by opposition members. This is an opportunity for the opposition to publicize certain issues, to attempt to embarrass the Government for its contradictions or obscurantism, and (through well-organized supplementary questions) to apply pressure on a minister to make an announcement or to act. The press gallery usually attends the oral question period, hoping no doubt to gain a sense of what issues may emerge as controversial and hoping to extract a piece of solid news from the prime minister or the ministers. Sir Ivor Jennings has called this period in Britain the 'parliamentary cocktail before the oratorical feast'. This epigram is even more apt for the Canadian oral question period because the questions do not have to be submitted in advance to the minister. They are popped without notice. Although the Speaker of the House since 1968 has become much more strict on supplementary questions, the trail of such questions often reads like a debate. Finally, the use of written questions (questions which are placed on the order paper for answer later in writing) is perhaps one of the House's most important functions, in that it forces the government to respond to certain questions in detail (there were over three thousand such queries in 1972–3). When a package of answers is tabled in the House every week or so, the responses to at least one or two of these queries prompt a story in the press, which often becomes a source for a series of further questions in the House in the oral question period.

When the use of the House agenda is examined it is clear, that except for the limitation on supply days and the limits on lengths of speeches, the opposition in the Canadian House is able to dominate debate and to bring up matters before they become overlooked by subsequent events. It is difficult to argue that the opposition has been seriously hampered in terms of scrutiny by the recent reforms of the House. In fact with standing committees meeting over a thousand hours in all in the session of 1969–70 for example, members of both sides of the aisle spent more time in sustained scrutiny of the executive than ever before. If the decline of Parliament is to be measured by the amount of time and effort members put into this activity, Parliament has not declined at all. Yet other reforms and changes of government attitudes would no doubt further the potency of the House. If more research help were afforded to members this might help. (In 1972, $400,000 was apportioned to the parliamentary parties for research assistance.) If cabinet ministers in question period were less secretive, this would help. If House committee meetings were better scheduled, especially those near the end of the session, this might increase attendance and improve debate at the report stage of bills. Finally, if legislation allowed for less delegation of authority to officials, boards, corporations and commissions, Parliamentarians might have less difficulty in getting ministers to answer for the major policy initiatives of these authorities.

(7) *Some Virtues of Adversary Politics in the House of Commons*

We have seen that even with political executive and public servant dominance of the operation of the state, at least there persists a systematic criticism of the Government of the day, thanks to the way opposition parties use the House of Commons, and to the provisions in the Standing Orders allowing this opposition debate and scrutiny. The House of Commons remains relevant to policy-making and to the political process in Canada precisely because of the inability of the state apparatus to absorb the opposition completely. A persistent complaint about this adversary process in Canadian politics is that Canadian political parties at the Federal level are not clear ideological enemies, that they do little more than conduct furious arguments about the minor issues which divide them. Lord Bryce in 1921 observed that party excitement in Canada, far from being a catalyst for thought, served 'as a substitute for thought', within parties.[19] Fifty years later an eminent Canadian political philosopher could write of the essentially 'consensus politics' pursued by the two major parties.[20] As a critique of the two major parties in Canada today, these aphorisms are still worthy of note. Even with the frequent failings of Canada's Federal parties to dramatically delineate their differences, the residual utility of the partisan adversary process in the House of Commons should not be overlooked. For the opposition parties to refuse to cooperate with the Government in policy-making, either because it is in clear ideological conflict with the Government or because it is merely a partisan adversary, is a more worthy enterprise than is usually acknowledged. (It is interesting to note that observers of the Austrian system of 'comingling of opposition and government' through coalition governments have written of the costs of this consensus for vigorous political debate in Austria.)[21] The House of Commons can act as a catalyst, driving the state to respond. For example, an advantage of systematic opposition by opposition parties in the Canadian House of Commons is that this activity can be an effective and open supplement, even a counter-weight, to the government's own carefully controlled – yet necessary – institutions of conflict resolution. The adversary activity of opposition parties helps to ensure that the executive cannot completely dominate the atmosphere in which decisions are made. The House of Commons will often be used by the opposition to compensate for the values or interests which are neglected, not only in the business-like structures of bureaucratic policy-making, but also left unchampioned by the operation of organized interest groups lobbying in Ottawa. In fact the circumvention of Parliament by many interest groups in their lobbying of ministers and of departmental officials can, curiously enough, have an unexpectedly good result. There is always a need in any society for a political agency which will articulate the quality and types of conflict that are not being resolved in the secret interest group-executive process. The marvellously diverse criticisms made daily by the opposition helps to do this. These efforts emerge as a key argument for the utility of adversary party opposition. Any Government's dislike of conflict or embarrassment will always lead it to threaten or entice cooperation from various parts of the political culture to 'talk things over in private'. Competitive non-coalescent opposition parties can seldom be intimidated or enticed under majority government.

Of course Canada's parties when in opposition are never completely open-minded. They are, to some degree, articulators of certain organized and well-financed interests. Yet it would be a wilful misreading of all House debate to suggest that the House is used primarily for promoting only these interests. An examination of Commons debates, not only on bills, but in question period, in supply debates, during the adjournment proceedings at the end of each day, and on other occasions, reveals the remarkably open tendency of the opposition to articulate the needs of unorganized groups. They do argue for values which are not articulated by associational and other organized group interests. This is an especially valuable activity in Canada because the needs of regions are often not articulated through provincial party positions and the grievances of unorganized interests are not always promoted by organized interests. Since opposition members find themselves in continual search for criticisms of the Government, they usually go far beyond the sounding of organized groups in pursuing their attack. In fact it can be suggested that opposition parties pursue at least four fundamental roles in their activity in Parliament in Canada.[22] Regardless of the nature of the party, all opposition parties use the House as a public forum, first to *check* on the government's integrity. They are in constant pursuit of evidence not only of government mis-spending of funds but of wider examples of dishonesty and arbitrary behaviour. Second, the opposition *prods* the government to act on behalf of certain interests, opinions and needs in society. Third, the opposition *probes* for information and although it seldom has success in eliciting hard information from the Government during the oral question period it can be remarkably effective (if it works at it) in eliciting such information in written questions and in committees.

Fourth, the opposition attempts to *re-interpret* the Government's performance in a way different from the Government's interpretation. This latter activity was pursued almost axiomatically by the more socialist-minded New Democrats in the last Parliament but it is pursued at length by the other parties in opposition as well. These functions of the opposition parties in the House when combined with surreptitious efforts by back-bench Government members to influence the cabinet, help one to understand more comprehensively the general role of the House of Commons in the political and policy process in Canada.

(8) *The Roles of the House of Commons in a Larger Perspective*

To understand the value of adversary politics in the House, a broader analytical approach than the 1848 'responsible government' notion of 'control of the executive' is imperative. This 1848 notion tells us where legal sovereignty lies but it does not capture the systemic value of the House. Two observers of the American legislative system, Malcom Jewell and Samuel Patterson, have argued for example that 'any legislative system will collapse and fail to act as an agent to preserve the political system' if it does not fulfil certain functions. These functions are the 'management of conflict' and the 'integration of polity'. They suggest that there are at least four ways in which a legislative system contributes to the management of conflict: the deliberative, the decisional, the adjudicative and the cathartic.[23] It is clear that these functions are filled differently in the American legislative system where party discipline is not strong, Congressional resources against the executive are potent and parties are less competitive or more coalescent than in Canada. As a structural-functional analysis of legislatures, Jewell and Patterson's is extremely culture-bound. But, curiously enough, even given their demands for a legislative system, if these functions were required of the Canadian House, the House emerges as more functional for the political system, even with its adversary debate (or perhaps because of it!) than many realize. Thanks in large measure to the opposition, the House partially fulfils all four of these functions, (even though it does it through a stylized adversary process) in addition to fulfilling its legal and constitutional functions to pass laws and to scrutinize the executive. First, although the decisive deliberations on policy usually occur outside the House of Commons in the bureaucracy and within the executive, a context can be set by the opposition for making various policies more urgent in its use of the question period, opposition days, etc. and in its attempts to speak to the *future* in debates on government bills. The House is, therefore, used by the opposition in Ottawa to publicize issues, to criticize the government or, as in the case of government MPs and ministers, to defend government policy. These debates add up to a 'deliberation' of sorts. Also, the House Committees, especially since 1965, have been producing reports based on hearings of witnesses and based on committee discussions of policy problems, bills and estimates. All this may help to define issues and to attract attention to their importance. In fact Government MPs have sometimes used these committee occasions to supplement their pressure on their leaders in caucus. To this extent the House retains, if not a key role, at least a not insignificant deliberative role by helping to set the agenda of public attention and by helping to focus and to publicize various interpretations of the Government's performance. Although the 'decisional' role of the House of Commons is legally unquestioned in that nothing becomes law unless the House passes it, informally, the role of the House is of some importance also. Government back-bench MPs are able to exert pressure in caucus, but also informally through members' discussions with ministers, or through skilful use of Whole House and committee proceedings to highlight issues. (Take, for example, the use of a committee by a Government back-bench MP in 1971 to publicize the possibilities of coastal oil pollution by oil tankers.) Even more important, the controversy provoked by the opposition in the House may also force the Government to make or to speed up a decision it ordinarily might prefer to postpone. (For example, the opposition forced the Federal cabinet to make a statement on Canada's role in Vietnam in the International Control Commission during the Pentagon Papers controversy in the United States). If the capacity to focus attention, to delay and to alter the context of some policy decisions are key sources of leverage in policy-making, the House – mainly through the opposition – enjoys some of this leverage on occasion and this can be significant. For example, the opposition was able to force changes not only in the Farm Marketing Products Act as a result of a filibuster in 1971, but also in the establishment of 'ministries of state' that year. Also during the first year of the minority Trudeau Government in 1973 the Government was forced by standing committees to make legislation more explicit and detailed, especially the legislation to screen foreign investment. Third, the House of Commons seldom 'adjudicates' a dispute but occasionally it will conduct inquiries through its committees, or it will help to publicize a scandal and hence can serve as a catalyst to force a governmental or judicial inquiry. Fourth, Canada's House sometimes plays a key 'cathartic' role in the Canadian political and policy process because the House sits over eight months each year. It is therefore the scene of timely umbrage and concern over political issues. To some extent, this activity is simply supplementary to the catharsis which occurs because of demonstrations, outside of Parliament or because of publicity in the mass media. However, timely questions in the House and hotly conducted House debates do on occasion permit immediate articulation of grievances, and this can be cathartic. 'Debates on the adjournment' and the special use of 'opposition days' in the House may not receive much publicity in the mass media, but it would be misleading to insist that House business can be structured so as always to be preoccupied with matters other than those of topical importance. In 1969–70, for example, the whole House spent 27 per cent of its time in the question period or in discussing government announcements on 'routine proceedings', 13 per cent in 'opposition days', and another 15 per cent of its time on occasions which were equally topical, such as the debate on the Throne Speech, the debate on the adjournment, the budget debate and private bills. None of these can be described as occasions which the Government can schedule so as to minimize topical controversy. (These comprised 33.6 per cent of House business in that session.) Yet even on other occasions opposition members can often wander into topical polemic without too much proscription from the Speaker. Government bills often invite topical controversy anyway. Therefore, the capacity of the House to play an expressive and cathartic role is also far from negligible.

In conclusion, even with the executive's ability under majority

Government to get its legislation through the House with most of its principles intact, the adversary use of the House fulfils many far from inconsequential functions. This makes Parliament far more relevant in the policy and political process (even under majority Governments or strong minority Governments) than many observers are willing to admit.

In fact if one adds the activity of individual MPs, both inside and outside the House (such as their quiet constituency liaison officer and ombudsman functions, well outlined in D. Hoffman's and N. Ward's study for the Royal Commission on Biculturalism and Bilingualism in 1970) to these overt activities of the House as an institution, the functions of MPs and of the House are far from negligible. The emphasis in the analysis in the previous chapters of this book centres on the coopting power of the state. Despite its frequently empty rhetoric, obvious partisanship, parts of the House remain as political agents which cannot be coopted by the executive. Still the thrust of parliamentary opposition, more often than not, is to urge more state responsibility and thus it too contributes to the state's continual generation of society. Although party discipline may to some extent alter grievances to suit party lines, the adversary nature of Parliament helps alternative values to be heard besides those implicit in the policy inclinations of the executive and bureaucratic establishment.

Parliament, therefore, plays the role of catalyst within the state. It helps to promote criticisms of the powerful agencies of policy decision within the state. This has had a dual, paradoxical effect on the state itself. Parliament, thanks to the opposition, can help to shake the smug complacency of some parts of the Federal state. It may even cause the key decision-makers some moments of self-doubt.

7 Political Parties, Political Leadership and the Executive

Given the incendiary quality of much of Parliament's work, and the social pluralism and political cleavages in Canada, it may still seem puzzling to a foreign observer how the Canadian state system has been able to grow and to integrate, and how the confederation has been maintained. After all, other federations with similar societal fragmentation and state penetration of society have not survived. This chapter will suggest that part of the answer to this lies in the peculiar nature of Canada's political parties and the operation of the political executive. These two agencies of Canadian political life have contributed to the maintenance of the federation and to the promotion of political stability not only through their willingness to try to compromise and to mediate, but through their willingness to allow the state to grow under their protection and guidance. Canadian political parties have done more than reflect social divisions; they have also contributed to the transformation of these forces at the level of the state. In Western democracies students of comparative government are often inclined to view manipulation of social forces as a phenomenon confined primarily to authoritarian states. Yet this view overlooks the power of the state and party systems in Western democracies to effect and even manipulate society, its demands and its perceptions. For example, provincial political parties help to transform and redefine many regional and local demands by appropriating much of the work of communication with the Federal level of government. As provincial political parties agree to continue their allegiance to confederation they thereby help to contribute to the integration of the state and society. But equally important in Canada is the fact that the Federal political parties also operate so as to promote societal dependence on Ottawa, not only through their mediation and compromise, but through their curiously direct connection with the mass, which enables them to communicate with the public without making themselves totally dependent on intermediaries. It is through this double dynamic that the Federal government has found a protective cover under which it has been able to grow and to increase its relationship with provincial governments and with society.

Let us look first at what are usually considered to be the most complete reflection of social and political forces in Canada at the Federal level, the Federal political parties. We will see that they are more than mere reflections of these forces.

(1) *The 'Mass Legitimacy' of Canada's Federal Political Parties*

In the first chapter we saw that the divisions over constitutional principles before responsible government in large measure gave rise – especially in the province of Canada – to the political parties. After confederation, the party system itself was potent enough to dominate the constitutional framework which had in large measure given rise to the party system in the first place. This was effected by the majority party operating with the inherited principle of a central initiating executive, thereby dominating the 'responsible Parliament'. The rise of party accomplished more than this. It effectively removed the Crown from politics. It made it possible for the political executive to largely dominate its parliamentary supporters and to secure the passage of most of its legislation. The rise of party altered the nature of elections. Under a fairly well disciplined two-party system until the 1921 election, the electorate had to alter somewhat its notions of political morality, as the ideal of the MP as a 'delegate' for his constituency yielded to a far more complicated set of standards. Loyalty to party became respectable and defensible. This is one of the key reasons why Canada's major parties became more than a reflection of social forces, they developed a measure of autonomy.

In essence Canada experienced a two-party system from 1878 to 1921. It may be that a two-party system usually originates from the growth of one party, which prompts those that oppose it to coalesce into a second party or coalition. It may be, too, that the first party is likely to be a conservative party, since it is often easier for the advocates of order to combine than the forces of reform, and if a revolution has not occurred it is usually the conservatives who have something to defend. The Macdonald coalition, at confederation, was in fact conservative; it wished to maintain the essentials of the confederation agreement, it did not want to disrupt the Church's power in Quebec, and it promoted various interests which would benefit from an ordered, and later a protected and expanding, transcontinental economic environment. The groups that coalesced into one formation to oppose Macdonald's party called themselves the 'Reform Party' and later the 'Liberal Party'. The most these groups seemed to have in common was their opposition to Macdonald's party and Government.

Soon, however, the two parties became something more than the mere sum of their parts. First, if each party was to compete coherently in Parliament and in elections they had to submit to internal party discipline. Second, issues and controversies which could not have been foreseen by the original coalitions at confederation soon transformed many of the interests and attitudes that sustained each party, and placed them both at a greater distance from these original interests. This two-party system survived in Canada until 1921. Macdonald's Liberal-Conservative Party – later known as the Conservative Party – decisively won the election of 1867. It won narrowly in 1872. It lost office in 1873 when Macdonald lost support because of the Canadian Pacific Railway scandal (Macdonald was accused of accepting money for party purposes from the railway owners). Alexander Mackenzie's Reform or Liberal coalition from 1873 to 1878 was diligent yet unimaginative. Also, it had to contend with an economic depression not of its own making. Macdonald's 'national policy' of protection, and his insistence on continuing 'the all-railway route to the west', swept his party back into office, where it remained until 1896. On Macdonald's death in 1891 four different Conservative prime ministers served until 1896 when Sir Wilfred Laurier, leader of the Liberal Party, reaped the benefit of a series of setbacks suffered by the Conservatives, especially in Quebec. Laurier led his party to election victories in 1896, 1901,

1904 and 1908. He was defeated by Robert Borden and his Conservative Party in 1911. Borden's party won that election thanks to a number of controversies, including the Naval Bill, allegations of corruption, reciprocity with the United States, and the rise of a third force in Quebec. A Conservative-Unionist coalition, which included some Liberals, governed from 1917 to 1921. In 1921, the Liberal Party began its long, only briefly interrupted, rule under Mackenzie King to 1948. Other developments made the 1921 election especially significant in Canadian history. When the Conservatives brought in conscription during the First World War, their support in Quebec was almost extinguished. The drafting of French-Canadians to 'fight English wars' proved to be electoral suicide in Quebec. This election also witnessed the appearance of a vigorous protest party, the Progressives, rooted primarily in the west. This party reflected prairie disenchantment with Ottawa's high tariffs, and with other policies which seemed to favour certain central Canadian interests. This party disappeared in 1935 but its message, if neglected, has never been totally forgotten in the west. Also during the 1920s a labour group began to organize, and by 1935 its successor, the Cooperative Commonwealth Federation, began to win seats in the Federal House.

The Liberals have governed in Ottawa after Mackenzie King, under Louis St Laurent from 1948 to 1957, Lester Pearson from 1963 to 1968 and Pierre Trudeau since 1968. After the 1921 election the Conservative Party held office briefly under Arthur Meighen's temporary Government for a few months before the 1926 election, under R. B. Bennett from 1930 to 1935, and under John Diefenbaker from 1957 to 1963. Neither the CCF (Cooperative Commonwealth Federation), nor its successor party the New Democrats, have ever governed in Ottawa, although they have won as much as 18 per cent of the popular vote and since September 1972 were in power in three of Canada's provinces. Usually the NDP captures no more than 10 per cent of the seats in the House of Commons. The Social Credit Party from 1935 to 1962 always won some seat in the Federal House, mostly from the west. Since 1962, however, the Social Credit Party has been transformed into the Ralliement de Créditistes in Quebec, with its appeal largely confined to rural areas and some smaller

Table 9
Prime Ministers Since Confederation, 1867

Rt Hon. Sir John A. Macdonald	Conservative	1 July 1867 – 5 November 1873
Hon. Alexander Mackenzie	Liberal	7 November 1873 – 16 October 1878
Rt Hon. Sir John A. Macdonald	Conservative	17 October 1878 – 6 June 1891
Hon. Sir John J. C. Abbott	Conservative	16 June 1891 – 24 November 1892
Rt Hon. Sir John S. D. Thompson	Conservative	5 December 1892 – 12 December 1894
Hon. Sir Mackenzie Bowell	Conservative	21 December 1894 – 27 April 1896
Rt Hon. Sir Charles Tupper	Conservative	1 May 1896 – 8 July 1896
Rt Hon. Sir Wilfred Laurier	Liberal	11 July 1896 – 6 October 1911
Rt Hon. Sir Robert Laird Borden	Conservative	10 October 1911 12 October 1917
Rt Hon. Sir Robert Laird Borden	Unionist	12 October 1917 – 10 July 1920
Rt Hon. Arthur Meighen	Unionist	10 July 1920 – 29 December 1921
Rt Hon. W. L. Mackenzie King	Liberal	29 December 1921 – 28 June 1926
Rt Hon. Arthur Meighen	Conservative	29 June 1926 – 25 September 1926
Rt Hon. W. L. Mackenzie King	Liberal	25 September 1926 – 6 August 1930
Rt Hon. Richard B. Bennett	Conservative	7 August 1930 – 23 October 1935
Rt Hon. W. L. Mackenzie King	Liberal	23 October 1935 – 15 November 1948
Rt Hon. Louis S. St. Laurent	Liberal	15 November 1948 – 21 June 1957
Rt Hon. John G. Diefenbaker	Conservative	21 June 1957 – 22 April 1963
Rt Hon. Lester B. Pearson	Liberal	22 April 1963 – 20 April 1968
Rt Hon. Pierre Elliott Trudeau	Liberal	20 April 1968 –

urban areas. It won nine seats in 1965, fourteen in 1968, and sixteen in 1972.

What are the differences between Canadian political parties? What kind of parties are they? Although clearly class voting exists, it can be misleading to press analogies of European or American ideological voting attitudes too far in Canada. We saw in chapter 1 how ideology in the European sense is flawed (or perhaps muted is a better word) in Canada. The centrist Liberal Party and the Conservative Party (officially known as the Progressive Conservative Party since 1942) do not appear to be clear ideological enemies, yet party competition remains intense. The most frequent explanation in most analyses of the Canadian party system and of Canadian voting behaviour has been to emphasize the impact of regionalism on voting behaviour. Although studies have indicated that there is significant class voting in some Federal constituencies and definitely in provincial elections, the dominant impression in the voting behaviour literature is that, on the whole, regionalism has greater impact on voting behaviour than class. Canada has seen minor regionally based parties arise to contest the dominance of the two major parties; the Progressives in 1921; in 1935 the Social Credit and the Cooperative Commonwealth Federation, and since the mid-1960s the Social Credit, then le Ralliement de Créditiste in Quebec. The single-member, single-plurality electoral system, also combines with regional preferences to produce heavy representation of one party in certain provinces, such as the near-monopoly of seats given to the Liberals in Quebec during most of this century, and the virtual capture of parts of the prairies by the Conservatives since 1958. Opportunity to build leverage for various regions is also afforded by the large representation of some regions in their Federal party caucus. This may also help to entrench regional affiliations within certain parties in Ottawa (for example, Quebec in the Liberal Party and Alberta in the Conservative). It has been suggested that although the socio-economic change that accompanies industrialization leads to more class voting, or what voting behaviour students in Western democracies call 'nationalization' or 'realignment', this process is not so evident in Canada because of a host of resistant factors. Prominent explanations for explaining this resistance are: the disinterest in cross-regional alliances of certain 'functional' social groups in Quebec owing to Quebec's concern with its own culture; other regional identities fostered in part by metropolitan centres oriented to provincial more than national economic growth, and the high visibility of provincial governments in their publicized struggles with Ottawa; and, to some extent, provincial boundaries reflect different types of economic activity and priorities in Canada. Let us review Federal voting.

Voting in Prince Edward Island, Newfoundland, New Brunswick and Nova Scotia is dominated by the Liberals and the Conservatives. These two parties together capture almost all of the votes. Except for the Diefenbaker landslide in 1958, Quebec since 1891 has delivered a particularly large majority of its seats to the Liberal Party. Since 1962, however, the Social Credit, now le Ralliement de Créditistes, has captured one-sixth to one-third of Quebec's seats. Ontario has provided the Liberals with a majority of its seats in eight of the fifteen elections since 1921, while the Conservatives have reaped a majority there seven times. (In 1921, however, the Progressives won twenty-four of the province's eighty-two seats. The CCF, now the NDP, have won between eleven and twenty-two seats in this province since 1945.) Manitoba delivered a majority of its seats to the Conservatives in most elections until 1921 when the Progressives won twelve of the province's fifteen seats. From 1935 to 1965 Manitoba delivered its majority of seats to the governing party. With three exceptions the CCF, now NDP, has attracted over 24 per cent of the vote in this province in all Federal elections since 1945. Saskatchewan in 1968 returned six NDP, two Liberals and five Conservatives, and in 1972, five NDP, seven Conservatives and one Liberal. It returned a heavy majority of seats to the CCF in the elections of 1948, 1953 and 1957, and to the Conservatives from 1958 to 1965. Alberta has been strongly Conservative since 1958. It returned a majority of its seats to the Social Credit Party from 1935 to 1957 and to the Progressives from 1921 to 1930. Generally speaking, British Columbia has split its seats among the CCF, Conservatives and Liberals since 1935. In the last two elections it swung considerably. In 1968 the Conservatives won no seats in this province, the Liberals sixteen and the NDP six. In 1972 the NDP won eleven, the Conservatives eight and the Liberals four.

Given these regional differences in voting behaviour and the amount of social and economic fragmentation in Canada, why isn't Canada similar to the Netherlands, where a vast number of parties win seats and majority Governments are now remote. The prevailing academic explanation for the cohesion and broad base of Canada's two major political parties has been their supposed ability, especially in the case of the Liberals, to act as 'brokers'. The brokerage theory suggests that a party attempts to balance and reconcile divergent interests by such strategies as regional compromises in policy outputs and by granting regional representation in the cabinet.

John Meisel's paper before the 1973 International Political Science Association is more sophisticated, however. He finds that:

Canadian parties do not try to exploit such advantages as they enjoy among particular groups in the population at the exclusion of more general appeals to a larger constituency. Nor does one or the other of the two groups comprising the various cleavages try to press its views through the medium of a narrowly representative party. But, some groups identify with given parties more than with others and this is of course reflected in, and no doubt related to, the predispositions the parties bring to national problems. But there is no French Canadian party, no Atlantic, Poor People's, Catholic, Pure Air, or Canada First party.

The particular physiognomy of each of the Canadian parties is well known and can be summarized quickly. The Liberal party receives disproportionately large numbers of votes from francophones, central Canada, individuals who are economically better-off and occupationally highly placed, Catholics, and from urban dwellers, both in the central provinces and at the peripheries. The Conservatives present almost a mirror-image of the Liberals although their general level of support is substantially lower; they attract above average support from anglophones, the Prairie and Atlantic provinces, Protestants, the economically less favoured, farmers and rural inhabitants in general. In its ethnic and religious support, the NDP resembles the Conservatives, and to some extent also in the degree to which it is preferred by people in lower income brackets, but it is by far the most nationalist of Canadian parties and in its Parliamentary posture is an outspoken champion of workers. Despite its main support now coming from urban Ontario, it is exceptionally sensitive to the interests of western Canada – a characteristic which preceded its capturing power in three provincial capitals. The Social Credit party has been decimated in its former western strongholds and has shrunk into a purely Quebec party. It is consequently overwhelmingly French, Catholic and located in a poor province. Not only its regional site, however, but also the individual condition of its voters make it Canada's party with, proportionately, the greatest appeal to the working and lower middle classes.

Canada's parties, taken together, do not reinforce and help freeze cleavages by providing strong institutional support for them, but at the same time they appear to be specialized enough in their appeal to give various groups a sense of having a reasonably effective partisan spokesman.

Meisel's outline suggests that Canada's parties are in part subordinate and in part superordinate to society. Hence the state is able to grow thanks to the peculiar nature of Canada's centre parties, which appeal to the mass in such a way as to permit the state system considerable autonomy. Part of the explanation for this may also lie in what Arendt Lijphart has called the 'operation of a cartel of elites', which although representing quite different interests agree to work together. This produces what Lijphart has called a 'consociational democracy'.[1] Its operation seems evident in Switzerland and in other fragmented political societies, and it helps to explain why these countries hold together when a national consensus is weak and mass social integration is lacking. Various business, agricultural, labour, educational and other key elites cooperate, and this in itself is sufficient. S. J. R. Noel explains the point further. Under a consociational system, agreements in a political society can be made and compromises reached among political leaders which would not be possible if they required popular ratification.

For it to function successfully, those who occupy positions of political leadership must understand the perils of political fragmentation and be committed to the maintenance of the national system; they must also be able, within their respective subcultures, to accommodate divergent interests and demands. For the masses, on the other hand, all that is required is that they be committed to their own subcultures and that they trust and support their respective elites. Since the more contact and interaction there is between the masses of the subcultures the greater likelihood of friction between them, Lijphart suggests, 'it may be desirable to keep transactions among antagonistic subcultures in a divided society ... to a minimum.' In theory, there is no reason why a consociational democracy could not function satisfactorily even if among the masses of the different subcultures there was absolutely no attachment to the national political system and no sense whatever of a national identity. In actual systems, however, some degree of popular national sentiment is invariably present. The distinguishing feature if a consociational political system is the relative weakness of popular national sentiment and the overcoming of this weakness through a process of elite accommodation.[2]

To some extent the integration of the state and the dependence of parts of society on the state is the structural outcome of this consociational collaboration. After a while, structures and policy programmes already in existence become a cause for more collaboration. Conditions allowing this collaboration can also be traced to the mass legitimacy of Canadian political parties.

To explain this it is necessary to introduce Jean Blondel's notion of 'mass legitimate' and 'group legitimate' parties to the Canadian scene.

In any political society, groups can be placed analytically on a continuum. At one end are communal groups which 'embody social relationships' and on the other associational groups which are those bodies 'constituted to pursue a goal'.[3] Associational groups resemble interest groups. Communal groups on the other hand are different. Churches, cultural associations, ethnic associations, immigrant associations, homogeneous local associations, even tightly-knit provincial societies are examples of communal groups. Communal groups can seldom be equated with interest groups. Since the 'aim' of the communal group is the well-being of its members, such groups translate, select and interpret the interests of the group. These interests may vary over time, and 'interpretation of what these interests are is likely to be left, to a great extent, to the leaders and to the pressure of circumstances'. Associational groups, however, are 'coexistensive with demands'.

The distinction between these two groups helps us to understand better the structure of Canadian parties and the role of parties in Canadian policy-making. One can easily find Canadian examples of these two types of groups, especially if one recalls their origins. The importation of new people into a community can give rise to a new communal group and/or change the goals of a previous group. For example the concentration in Canada of

Ukrainian and Italian immigrants gives rise to new communal groups, and in the first case perhaps changed the goals of what communal reality there was in 'Manitoba' as a communal group. Communal groups can also emerge from political or administrative structures. Provinces such as Alberta and Saskatchewan, which may have had little or no communal legitimacy at their birth, developed this as experience with provincial political institutions grew. The St Jean Baptiste Society in Quebec is probably a perfect example of a communal and associational group, its communal base resting, perhaps, on the characteristics of the larger communal group, a large minority of French Canadians in Quebec.

If the bond of allegiance between members and their group exists, in the case of communal groups, in the members themselves, and 'the goal' exists in the case of associational groups, both groups will allow transfers 'of support or of legitimacy' to a party in elections if the group is widely accepted by its members, and if its members recognize the importance of the group. For example, in Canada it may be possible for French Canadians, because of their high communal legitimacy, to shift support from one Federal party to another in the first fifty years after confederation without, in most cases, endangering the group. After confederation, Nova Scotian MPs (many of whom were against the terms of the confederation agreements) felt free to vote as they pleased, for the communal legitimacy of Nova Scotia was hardly in doubt.

When a party draws support from the electorate indirectly, through the allegiance which members have to the groups which have helped to constitute the party, there is, in Blondel's definition, no element of 'massness' at the basis of party support. A 'mass legitimate party' is one with direct mass support. Mass legitimate parties, however, are usually begun or 'put into orbit' by groups in the first place. Blondel notes that legitimate mass parties have tended to develop more quickly where parties have emerged from a class-based group. But, he notes, if parties have become legitimate before class-based loyalties have become strong, the legitimate mass party can spring from both associational and communal groupings (including even clientele organizations). For example, the Federal Liberal or Reform Party was launched by a number of associational, communal and clientele groups; the most prominent perhaps in Ontario was the 'Clear Grit' group and its associational attitudes, reflecting, in the opinion of one observer:

> ... a deep and abiding suspicion of the commercial and transportation monopoly of Montreal; and a belief in egalitarianism and rugged individualism, in free trade and free land, in representation by population, and in strict supervision of, if not limitation on government support to business enterprise. The Clear Grits were almost exclusively Protestant, and their latent anti-Catholicism found expression and stimulation in the writings of [their first leader] George Brown.[4]

The French Canadian part of this uneasy Reform coalition was comprised of cross-cutting communal and associational groups, made up primarily of those who were Catholic yet against the ultramontane attitudes of the clerical hierarchy, and of those who were suspicious of certain business interests and the Conservatives in general. The Conservative coalition was made up of spokesmen who emerged from the Montreal commercial and industrial interests, a major part of the ecclesiastical hierarchy which represented and led perhaps the largest communal group in Quebec (the Church-led communities of Quebec), the United Empire Loyalists, the Orange lodge, and moderate Reformers who earlier had followed Robert Baldwin. It is difficult to describe this collection of disparate forces as anything more than a coalition. The largest coalition also depended on floating MPs, mainly from the maritimes and the west, who would vote for the ministry, and any ministry would do if it proved profitable for the constituency and province.

For the first decade after confederation, Canadian parties were not therefore as mass legitimate as they were group legitimate. They were creatures of a host of associational and communal groups. The Conservative coalition was sustained in large measure by the astute leadership of Canada's first prime minister, Sir John A. Macdonald. In those days, when government was less complex and 'public policy' by definition was primarily patronage, Macdonald was able to disaggregate the stakes and keep his coalition together through the distribution of patronage – most regions and constituencies in the coalition were indulged. He also attempted to attach the budding associational labour groups to his party by supporting a progressive labour code. If he could avoid zero-sum decisions and keep attention on selected nation-wide needs, so as to capture the national imagination, he could sustain the coalition until the communal or associational groups changed. He did the latter through his audacious but courageous all-railway route to the west coast, and his 'National Policy' which, with the railway, provided tariff protection and other measures for an integrated transcontinental economy. The Riel Rebellion, however, was the zero-sum decision which eventually forced Macdonald to choose between the English and French. Macdonald decided to execute the Indian-French or Métis leader Louis Riel (because Riel under the authority of his self-pro-claimed 'provisional government' had executed an Orangeman acting as an Agent of the Dominion government). This began the erosion of Macdonald's support among French Canadian com-munal groups, even if it was not immediately condemned by the associational business and clerical groups in Quebec.

Even if the major parties were originally highly dependent on certain groups as intermediaries for their appeal to the mass, it is possible to argue that each major party eventually became increasingly 'mass legitimate' rather than merely 'group legiti-mate'. Macdonald's party to 1891, and then Laurier's from 1896 to 1911, were able to reach directly to the mass through the dispensation of favours and patronage, through the production of broad and sometimes nationally integrative policies. The ability of either one party or the other to gain support from most of the major newspapers in the country, and the monopoly of Parlia-ment by these two parties, may also have helped to shift public opinion to the view that these two parties were the viable national political parties.

As a result of these developments, it might be possible to say that Canada's two major parties were placed in orbit and a key parallel process of 'legitimacy transfer' took place. Once parties are launched, they are able to make appeals to the mass directly, and not simply through groups. When this occurs, Blondel sug-gests that broad communal groups begin to see that they must alter their strategy and not place their hopes in owning a political party but in supporting associations with their specific goals. For example, rural regions attempt to work through farm associa-tions. Parties then alter their strategy toward groups and begin to aim at 'aggregating' or mediating the interests represented by these associations, while not on the whole attempting to modify the goals of society. As they become increasingly independent of the broad communal groups, parties and associations will come to have an increasing number of specific reciprocal relationships. The pure type of a wholly legitimate party in Blondel's definition is one which ceases to have any 'special relationship with any communal group and 'comes to have relations with all associations on the basis of the intrinsic importance of their demands'.[5]

Today we see intimations of this in Canada. The two major Federal parties – especially the governing party – allow for almost constant contact of the Federal state with an immense array of associations, business, farm, professional, labour, and governmental (provincial and even municipal); contact with communal groups becomes less and less frequent. Communal groups in fact articulate increasingly through associational groups. The New Democratic Party has also developed more into a mass legitimate party than a simple 'group legitimate' (i.e. labour union supported) party. It too is in constant contact with a host of associations. It does, however, view itself in large measure as a 'particular type' of mass legitimate party, more reminiscent of European left-wing parties. Its Federal leader in 1972 puts it thus:

There is a mistaken view of the original purpose and concept of our party's association with labour unions. I have never believed that because a local union by majority decides to support the party ... that all its members would support the party in every election, or even that those who vote for affiliation will support the party in every election. To assume that is very naive. ...

I think the value of the association has been very definitely an identification of the average working man and woman in Canada with the New Democratic Party as being their party – even when they vote against us, they still admit the fact that the NDP is the worker's party. ...

That was the purpose of the association and that is still true.[6]

The essential condition which allows the two major parties to gain a fair degree of mass legitimacy is the presence of what is so often assumed to be absent in Canada: consensus. There is a broad (though not unanimous) consensus that the Canadian collectivist-capitalist system is not in need of dramatic change. Supporters for the major Canadian parties cannot be called supporters for dramatic social change if their opinions on policy issues in 1968 are any guide.[7] As Blondel suggests, when 'there is no, or little, conflict of goals in the political system, the dependence of groups on political parties will be small' (as in the United States) and 'the level of dependence at any given moment' can be measured 'by the extent to which the party is legitimate in the community'. Blondel's hypothesis suggests, therefore, that if there has been relatively little conflict in the majority of the political community about the proposition that the Canadian collectivist-capitalist system is not in need of revolutionary change, then the business community need not depend on one of the two major Federal parties but can support either, and it could, no doubt, survive a Government formed by the more left-wing third party, the New Democrats. Similarly, individuals or groups who do not believe in a radically different economic and social system (and this category could include a host of groups, including teachers, unionized and non-unionized workers, lower-middle class workers, etc.) no doubt also feel free to oscillate among the major parties. John Meisel's data show considerable correlation between certain statistical groups and certain parties. Hence only a minority of Canadians may oscillate in their voting preference. But it has been quite a sizable minority and it is crucial to victory. This part of the electorate may feel free to oscillate because it feels the major parties are open to communication with most groups when in power. S. H. Beer has explained, in his *British Politics In the Collectivist Age,* the openness of the British Labour and Conservative parties by pointing to the inherent necessity of state contacts with a host of 'functional' groups if the government is to manage Britain in the collectivist age. Something similar seems true for Canada. Most interest groups in Canada try to be reasonably non-partisan. Most of them also remain ready to communicate with the Federal Government of the day regardless of party. Their willingness to write briefs, to pass comment on embryonic legislative proposals, and to appear before parliamentary committees, give ample proof of this willingness, as well as the necessity for them to interact with the major parties, or with the state under the auspices of the major parties.

All this might also help to explain the curiously pragmatic and untheoretical character of Canadian politicians. It has been suggested by Dorothy Pickles in a study of French politics that 'over-indulgence in a national predilection for argument about ideas rather than about practical policies' is characteristic of political parties in that country. What a contrast this is to Canada! Of all the things that can be said to characterize Canadian political parties, a 'predilection for argument about ideas' is not one of them. The attraction in France for theories, doctrines and distinctions of principle is foreign to the world of Canadian political parties. The closest Canada comes to this French penchant for theoretical debate is in its publications on the left, especially in Quebec. Yet even here there is as much emphasis given to practical problems of public policy, to concrete examples – most of them markedly regional – of failures or abuses of the major parties as to theory. English-Canadian and much of the French-Canadian tradition of social science – especially historical – scholarship is heavily empirical, cautious about offering general explanations and well-known for its suspicion of almost all broad theories. In this respect it cannot be said that Canadian political parties lag behind the intellectual attitude of the most of the advanced thinking in the land. Canadian political parties almost never deduct their electoral policy platforms from an elaborate theoretical prolegomena. Canada's major parties appear to pride themselves on their 'pragmatism'. To foreign observers the more socialist New Democrats may also appear to be unusually pragmatic, considering their perennial opposition status at the federal level. This party is intensely empirical in its electoral strategy. The party platform seldom belabours theory, it concentrates on policy prescription.

(2) *Communication and Canadian Party Leadership*

It is no doubt true that leaders and leadership groups in most party systems are the main channels through which parties are linked to the people. This, of course, is not to say that party leaders and leadership groups are the main channels through which all public policy is made. As we have seen in other chapters, the complex and systematic work of the public service, boards and commissions makes them probably more important in countless areas of policy than political leaders. But political leaders are important for linking parties to the people. This is true for group dependent, as well as mass legitimate, parties. All party leaders no doubt have dark moments of doubt about how closely their party is involved in the real world of community concerns. At least annually they exhort their party to participate more in the life of local communities, to seek 'roots closer to the people'. Yet when election time comes in Canada, the relationship of the mass to the leader and to leadership groups in the party become vitally important in the formation of popular perceptions of political issues and political parties.

This is especially true for mass legitimate parties which, because of their perceived independence from any communal group and their readiness to communicate with all associations on the basis of their intrinsic demands, are thereby considered not to be group-dominated, and are able to emphasize the party leader, or leadership group, as the object of attention. His or their utterances, attitudes and styles then become important for defining the nature of the party. This may be part of the explanation for the heavy emphasis given to the personality and style of the party leader in the mass media, and why party publicists respond with similar personality-oriented appeals in their campaign strategies. This type of politics is intrinsic to the nature of mass legitimate parties, rather than evidence of a contrived restriction of political debate by party publicists frightened of the public's hunger for something else. When parties are able to be perceived as mass legitimate, a symbiosis emerges between public notions of what is relevant and what party leaders say and do. This symbiosis, of course, will always strike that part of the electorate which is alienated from the mass legitimate parties as empty and cruelly irrelevant; hence perhaps the despair and cynicism of a large minority of the population who vote for the smaller parties or the 25 per cent who do not vote at all. Yet the business of mass-legitimate parties as defined by Blondel is to gain political power, and thus their mode of appeal will centre instead on the constituency which can provide this.

The business of building a direct appeal to the mass makes modes of communication through the press, radio, television, parliamentary debate, and party campaign literature vital to all parties but especially to mass legitimate parties. 'Direct contact with the mass' becomes heavily dependent on how political messages are communicated. The ways in which the mass media define and publicize issues, the way they ignore some issues and concentrate on others, are matters of considerable importance to mass legitimate parties. (If the mass media are hostile, the mass legitimate party, like the group legitimate party, will have to depend heavily on its party canvassers, volunteers and advertising to overcome this handicap.) Still, leaders of the major three parties are not without considerable exposure in the mass media. At one time Canadian newspapers were stridently partisan, and many urged their party choice on their readers from the front page. It is fair to say that although most Canadian dailies now suggest their choice on the editorial page, they at least give better than token coverage to what all the major party leaders say and do during an election campaign. The Canadian Press wire service also strives to report in a balanced way and this service is used by most Canadian newspapers. The Canadian Broadcasting Corporation supplies time on television for the major parties each week and after its reporting of Federal Government statements it usually allows time for Opposition opinion to be expressed as well. All this helps to facilitate communication from the major Federal parties to the mass and thereby helps them in their efforts to become increasingly mass legitimate. There are some disquieting features, however, about the concentration of media ownership in Canadian communities, and this may narrow somewhat the diversity of political opinion heard in various communities. The first volume of the Senate Special Report on the mass media (1970) found in 103 surveyed communities, as many as sixty-one where groups or independents own two or more of their community's media outlets, thirty-four communities where groups own two or more radio outlets, and thirty-one where groups have common interests in both radio and television stations. Although radio and television licences are granted under a fairly independent licensing commission, there have been rumours of political influence.

Another feature of Canadian political life which may help major parties to dominate disparate and unorganized political dissent and opinion is the dialectic of Parliament which (with its orchestration of debate and the importance given to statements made by party leaders) can cut down on the diversity of views the electorate is able to hear. (Although the loosening of the Government's control over some committee activity may be increasing diversity to some extent.) Finally, the more successful a party looks likely to be, the greater is its ability to raise enough money for its advertising and for campaigning. It is argued, therefore, that dependence on the financial contributions of businesses to maintain the party apparatus between elections and to wage election campaigns makes them less mass legitimate than they seem. (The chairman of the Federal Liberal party's finance committee stated on CTV television on 30 April 1972, that the bulk of his party's funds for operating the central office of the Federal party between elections came from ninety-five firms, and from about 350 firms for Federal election campaigns.) It is a well known but as yet unproven axiom in Canadian politics that many large businesses split their contribution to the Liberals and Conservatives, with slightly more going to the governing party. (For more documentation on the dynamic and history of party finance in Canada, see the publications of the Advisory Committee on Election Expenses, Ottawa, 1966.) Analytically, however, this question of sources of party funds can be understood only crudely as an indication of the degree of dependency of those parties on certain parts of the business world. This question can be placed in analytical perspective by realizing that these sources of funds enable the two major parties to finance a nation-wide appeal which becomes far more than a partisan appeal on behalf of one part of society. Just as the New Democrats claim that their dependency on union funds does not make their party only a party for labour unions, business-financed parties claim a similar catholicity. In fact, as we have suggested earlier, it is imperative for the three major parties to reach beyond the partisan interests of their benefactors if they are to grow increasingly mass legitimate and to attain, or remain in, office. Only if a society is significantly split between the advocates of capitalism and its enemies, will the partisan benefactors insist on pure partisan use of governmental power. Even that insistence could prove suicidal to the party that provides it. It is difficult to maintain that there is in Canada a high level of consciousness of such a split in society as a whole. Generally, the major parties have been careful not to emasculate their mass legitimacy by fostering a perception of such a split.

The peculiar mass legitimacy of Canada's major parties has some important implications for party leadership and policy-making. Although the iron law of oligarchy limiting the number of key decision-makers may exist in mass legitimate parties, the more a party becomes mass legitimate, the greater is the openness in the choice of leaders and the more frequent is the rotation of leaders. The three major parties have chosen their leaders by convention since 1919 in the case of the Liberals, since 1927 for the Conservatives, and since the founding of the party in the case of the CCF-NDP. The choice of leaders by convention rather than by the parliamentary caucus helps to make leadership selection more open if one assumes that parliamentary caucuses would have been disposed to choose leaders with long records of Federal elective office. Of the ten leaders chosen by convention, three (Bracken, Drew and Stanfield) were provincial premiers with no Federal legislative experience; three others (King, St Laurent and Trudeau) had six years or less in the House of Commons; and only two – Manion and Diefenbaker – were in relative terms parliamentary veterans.

For example, John Diefenbaker was chosen as Conservative Party leader in 1956, though his support was greater outside the identifiable party oligarchy than within it. Equally instructive were the soundings made by the Federal Conservative Party Association's president with the party outside the party leader's apparatus in Ottawa. These enabled him to discover the demand for, and later to organize the engineering of a party convention request for a leadership convention. This was done in the teeth of the wishes of the incumbent party leader from 1966 to 1967. Although mass legitimate parties in Opposition often appear to be more open in leadership choice than mass legitimate governing parties, it is by no means evident that this need always be true. National leadership can exhaust men. For example, Lester Pearson voluntarily stepped down after five years as prime minister and twenty years in the cabinet. Furthermore, the exercise of government can diversify a party's direct contact with the mass. In short, the party headquarter's national apparatus and the party caucus cannot monopolize the contacts with the electorate or with active party supporters. A host of other agencies, offices and manifestations of governmental power build up contacts with various clienteles as well. It is interesting to note therefore that Liberal leaders, since that party first began to govern with longevity under Laurier from 1896 to 1911, have been chosen from the cabinet. Equally interesting is the way the Conservative party, which has been in opposition for forty-two of the fifty-four years since 1921, has chosen leaders from outside the Federal caucus, to lead the party in three of its four leadership conventions since 1942.

The powers of leaders of mass legitimate parties frequently give rise to allegations of dominance oligarchic. But the notion of the mass legitimate party helps us to understand the tendencies of the leaders of the Federal Liberals and Conservatives (and to some extent the NDP) to insist on their right to make vital policy decisions and to control the party apparatus. These traits are not unique to Canada but are characteristic of mass legitimate parties everywhere. It is true that leaders do not exercise power in a vacuum. They must accept the broad, non-revolutionary goals of the party and must tailor their policies to the influence of electoral defeats and to deeply felt divisions in the party over policy. In office (as we have seen in chapters 2 and 5), they are also limited by the traditions of collective cabinet government, by the rigidities of bureaucratic structures, and by Federal-provincial relations. These restraints on an Opposition leader may be weaker but also the incentives to make hard policy may be weaker and the temptation to remain at rhetorical generalities stronger than on a Prime Minister.

These restraints and imperatives on leaders are real yet in Canada's Federal Liberal and Conservative Parties, as in mass legitimate parties in other countries, the leader can seldom allow party congresses, party policy conventions, or party 'thinkers' conferences' (now a regular feature of all three major parties) to dictate party policy. Blondel has asserted that for mass legitimate parties everywhere,

It may be shown that leaders are often, particularly in large parties of a competitive type, nearer to the views of the mass of supporters than the most extreme and more ideological regulars who speak on party platforms ... even if in practice, party policy comes to be more representative because party leaders 'flout' Congresses, the fact of flouting congresses is far from being uncommon and is only relatively rare because leaders appear sufficiently skilful in pre-venting internal opposition from becoming overt or at least from assuming significant proportions.[8]

For example, by the end of 1971 the Federal Conservative

party in its annual meeting, and the Federal Liberals one year before, completed what was probably the most extensive process of formulating policy resolutions in either party's history. From the summer of 1968 to their November 1970 policy convention, the Liberals (and some non-Liberals) formulated policy papers and debated them in policy seminars organized by constituency, regional and district associations. These papers and debates set the stage for the Liberals' 'National Policy Rally' or Convention in November 1970. The result, 'Directions for the Seventies', was distilled from more than four hundred resolutions dealt with at the convention. The Conservatives also produced a 'votation book' of 260 resolutions for vote at its December 1971 policy meeting. Delegates debated the resolutions, then marked 'yes, no, or undecided' by every resolution in the 47-page votation book, and the results of the voting were released early in 1972. Delegates to these two conventions were chosen from constituency and other local associations and by the party headquarters. Most, but not all, delegates were party supporters. As one reporter noted, however, 'many members are still confused about the ultimate purpose of this technique' of passing opinions on policy.[9]

Little confusion was evidenced by party leaders about the purpose, however. The Liberal leader and prime minister, Pierre Trudeau, agreed that his Government would be glad to come before party conventions and account for its actions if certain resolutions were not implemented; but he made it clear that 'in respect of some [resolutions], the Government will not be able to proceed in accordance with the delegates' wishes'. The Conservative party's leader, Robert Stanfield, took a similar position before his party's policy convention. 'We still have much to do before our final programme is ready', he told the delegates. In fact, the first page of the votation book warned that 'resolutions presented here are not intended to be statements of party policy', but are voted on 'to assist the leader and caucus by ascertaining the opinion of delegates'.[10]

Nor does the operation of the Liberal or Conservative parliamentary caucus ensure anything like complete control over the leadership. Full caucus meetings seldom vote on policy. Instead they are set up to provide an occasion for back-bench advocacy of policies or of political strategies before the party leader and (in the case of the governing party) the cabinet ministers. Caucus committees have become active since the mid-1930s under King for the Liberals, and since 1942 under John Bracken for the Conservatives, but these have always had to defer to the leader and to the full caucus. Liberal caucus influence may have increased since 1968, owing to the requirement that ministers consult with the appropriate caucus committee before legislation is presented to the House, yet complaints persist that ministers are not greatly affected by the process. One Liberal back-bencher has suggested that caucus meetings are so 'loaded' with ministers' legislation that there is no time to discuss 'general directions of the party'. The NDP claims to operate with less leader dominance of its caucus (similar perhaps to the British Labour Party), but its small parliamentary membership affords a much greater opportunity for the leader and the other caucus members to discuss policy informally. The three major parties also maintain permanent party headquarters in Ottawa which, especially in the case of the Opposition parties, churn out policy research. They are sometimes deployed as intellectual allies of certain forces in the party. Notable about the Conservative research work under George Drew, John Diefenbaker and Robert Stanfield as leaders of the Official Opposition, is the fact that there is very close liaison of the research office with the party leader and his office, rather than with the caucus.

In Canada, a party leader as prime minister has six weapons by which he can assert his supremacy. He has the power to dismiss, appoint and shuffle ministers. He can manage, within very few limits, the agenda of the full cabinet and to some extent the cabinet committees. He organizes and controls a great deal of the patronage decisions of government. He can shuffle the personnel at top levels of the public service. He can appoint to key positions on boards, commissions, task forces and parliamentary committees. The Canadian prime minister may, if he wishes, run a loose ministerial form of government. This seems to have been Lester Pearson's style. Or he can insist on a large number of collective cabinet decisions (this, on a number of issues, was John Diefenbaker's style). Or he can move to varying degrees of prime ministerial government based on heavy policy control from his Privy Council Office staff, and close political monitoring from the Prime Minister's Office (as under Pierre Trudeau).

A prime minister cannot always exercise all of these options, however, not because his will has failed, or because his colleagues have mounted a spontaneous mutiny (although both seem to have happened twice in Canadian history, once in the last year of Mackenzie Bowell's prime ministership in 1895, and once in the last year of John Diefenbaker's in 1962). Instead, the failure to exercise his options and powers more frequently comes when he has lost the authority deriving from personal popularity in the country or from the popularity of the Government's actions. To some extent, the same may be true for Opposition party leaders, although the indicators of popularity are frequently less reliable. It is the prime minister's position as the key link between the mass (not simply the groups within it) and the state that is significant. It is not his power to make policy in detail which defines the prime minister's role. (Policy work is done in detail by public servants, by ministers, and sometimes by MPs.) It is the tendency of mass legitimate parties to push the essential decisions on vital political judgements to the prime minister, especially on contro-versial national issues, and the concomitant tendency of the electorate to look to the prime minister for responses in crises, which make him the symbol around which the mass reacts to the Government of the day. Before this pivotal and symbolic stage can be attained, however, a party leader must keep his party mass legitimate by maintaining its perceived independence from a handful of communal or associational groups. He can do the first primarily through orchestration of the representation in his cabinet. This is a time-honoured necessity for all Canadian prime ministers. Due representation must be given to Quebec, and so on. Yet in an age when the growth of the state and of provincial visibility demands more extensions of the same principle he must now go further. The prime minister, therefore, gives positional power to various representatives of communal and associational groups through appointments to other key administrative posi-tions. He will also indicate a willingness to acknowledge group interests not simply though policies, but through Federal-provincial conferences, speeches, personal visits, and so on.

That the Federal cabinet ought to be representative of Canada's major regions is a long-standing imperative in Canada. Yet this may be of more symbolic than policy-making importance given the many forces that operate in Ottawa against instituting a system of regional strongmen centred in the cabinet. Thanks in part to jet travel and television the leaders of the Federal parties are able to communicate directly to regional electorates without going through Federal regional power brokers. Federal departments are organized less to emphasize regional interests than to emphasize industrial, social and other clientele structures which are seldom completely coterminous with regional interests. Ministers, as spokesmen for departments and working through cabinet committees with functional mandates, for 'economic policy', 'social policy', 'external policy', 'technology, etc., are, in effect encouraged to supersede regionalism. All of this helps to make the Federal party in power and the public service agents of state direction somewhat superordinate to many regional imperatives.

All this must be intelligently orchestrated in Canada if the prime minister is to keep his party relatively mass legitimate. (In fact, the failure of successive Liberal prime ministers to do this intelligently for the west in Canada since 1953 has decreased the extent of the governing party's mass legitimacy there.) All these are obvious preconditions. If this is done adequately, the prime minister can find himself in a position of sufficient independence from such groups that he and his administrative machine can then approach associational groups (with their cutting edges of specific demands) on the basis of their intrinsic utility for the prime minister's political strategy and the policy-making imperatives of the administrative apparatus.

A group legitimate party leader supported by a majority of the society, such as a labour or farmers' party, need do little but forward the group's interests. This may be possible in some provinces. But federally, where such a majority group consensus does not seem to exist, the prime minister then has the most crucial role of all, that of giving cognitive leadership to the public on key issues, persuading the public to accept the state's inclinations and his own. This points to his most influential role in the state's relation to society, that of shaping public cognitions. It is a role also played to a lesser degree by the leaders of the other parties.

Government plays an important function in shaping cognitions about political issues and public policy problems. There are several conditions that facilitate governmental influence upon cognitions. Two important conditions are the public's difficulty in examining a source of anxiety empirically, because it involves a situation expected to occur in the future; and 'conspicuous, publicized governmental actions either explicitly assert or clearly imply a factual state of affairs'[11] and the public can never be sure if the assertions are accurate. Canadians become especially aware of these conditions during the FLQ crisis in October 1970. During this crisis the allegations about the extent of the uprising, the size of the FLQ and the potency of the War Measures Act went far to shape the views of Canadians during this crisis. The power of the prime minister to contribute to the shaping of public opinion on political issues is not, however, confined to such dramatic occasions. In fact almost weekly the second condition is exploited by the prime minister (and by the other Federal party leaders.) This is perhaps one of the most potent powers of the state. Its exploitation and implementation by the prime minister of Canada is perhaps one of his most powerful tools for helping to shape public perceptions.

In the long run, the extent of the state system's penetration of society may not depend greatly on which type of party dominates Canadian political life. Both contribute to penetration. The group dependent party does so in a group-engineered way. The mass legitimate party that has a detailed policy mandate would do so in a way based on the political energy of the cabinet and the caucus. The mass legitimate party without a detailed policy mandate would penetrate in a way congenial to the imperatives of the public service and to the political executive's assessment of what outputs are needed to maintain or to enhance the party's mass legitimacy as the need arises.

All this leads to a recognition of the function of mass legitimate parties in Canada to foster considerable political stability and integration. The ability of the mas legitimate parties to communicate directly with the mass, their openness to communication with almost all associational groups, especially when the party is in office, and the party's basic intelligence and soundings of communal grievances, have all helped the governing party of the day to achieve a fair measure of mass legitimacy. This gives it the ability to appeal directly to the mass, primarily through the leader. This can contribute to stability because it can allow the public servant in Ottawa to communicate with all associations necessary to ease the state into new activity and to monitor the needs of these groups. It also gives the Federal state an aura of mass legitimacy and support to rival the legitimacy given to provincial state systems. All this has given Ottawa confidence to expand its relationships with the provinces and thereby to help integrate the state system.

Some observers suggest however that the conditions giving rise to all this may be weakening somewhat. On the morning of 1 November 1972 Canadians woke up to hear that they had elected their fifth minority government in the last seven Federal elections. To many it was becoming increasingly clear that majority Government, the staple diet of Canadians before 1957, could very well be the exception, no longer the rule, in the coming few decades. The once politically stable Canadian system seemed to have come permanently unstuck.

Yet, as a European will quickly point out, there is a great difference between European brands of political instability and the Canadian variety. In the Netherlands or in Italy, for example, no single party ever comes close to getting a majority or realistically expects to. What is remarkable about Canada is that, for all its internal divisions, at least the two major parties do expect to be able to put together a majority if they play their cards right. Also significant is the evidence that a large number of Canadians are willing to vote for a political party primarily because they think it is important to have a majority Government. Both attitudes are evidence that Canadian parties still contain great potential for contributing to political stability and that the Canadian people, as always, continue to believe in the importance of strong, yet sensitive, state leadership.

The role of the state system as super-order, as a network with its own specificity and dynamic which cannot be understood solely as a reflection of class forces, is vital for understanding the amount of political stability and integration in the country today. It can be argued that the mass legitimate Federal party system with three-quarters of the vote usually split fairly evenly between the Liberals and the Progressive Conservatives (except in unusual elections such as those in 1958 and 1968), leaving around 18 per cent to the NDP and less than 10 per cent to other parties, is as potent a result for accelerating state penetration of society as would a politics based more explicitly on group-based parties, as in Europe for example. The latter might afford more sustained and detailed control of the policy process by the parliamentary caucus but also partisan cooptation of select interest groups. The former, especially under majority Governments, probably allows the public service's assessments to prevail more often and, under either majority or minority Governments, it probably enables Ottawa to suck a greater range of groups into collaborating with the state, be these groups farm, educational, business, labour or professional.

We have noted in this chapter and in the other chapters the forces creating a strong state presence in Canada. The tradition of parliamentary sovereignty with a central initiating executive; the history of state action to define provincial communities and the nature of federal society; the growing coexistence and collaboration between levels of government; the skill and resources of the public service, boards and commissions to monitor, mediate, advise and regulate. When these forces are joined to the pattern of the perhaps incoherent, but catholic, political leadership of mass legitimate parties, we see how the state network in Canada increasingly penetrates society and hence slowly, but progressively, encourages dependence on this network and its integration.

Canada, therefore, is of special interest to anyone interested in the ability of states in Western industrial societies to grow and to penetrate society. The phenomenon of growing state superordination is not restricted to totalitarian or one-party states. Canada, with its societal cleavages, its far from unitary system of government, its tradition of common law and human rights, may be less penetrated by the state than other Western democracies. Yet this should not deter us from recognizing the potency of the state in Canada and its key role in defining and organizing society since confederation.

Notes

Chapter 1: The Canadian State: Its Development and Influence

1 S. H. Beer, *British Politics in the Collectivist Age,* New York, 1966.
2 Department of the Secretary of State, *The Canadian System of Government,* Ottawa, 1970.
3 L. Hartz, *The Founding of New Societies,* New York, 1964.
4 P. Waite, 'The Edge of the Forest', *Canadian Historical Association Papers,* 1969, pp. 1–13.
5 M. Schwartz, *Public Option and the Canadian Identity,* University of California Press, Berkeley, 1967.
6 L. F. S. Upton, 'In Search of Canadian History', *Queens Quarterly,* Winter 1967, p. 682.
7 Quoted in *ibid.*
8 Allan Smith, 'Metaphor and Nationality in North America', *Canadian Historical Review,* September 1970.
9 See S. D. Clark, *The Developing Canadian Community,* Toronto, 1962, p. 218.
10 R. I. Cheffins, *The Constitutional Process in Canada,* Toronto, 1969, p. 10.
11 *Ibid.,* p. 57.
12 *Financial Post,* 13 May 1972, p.7.
13 *Ibid.*

Chapter 2: Collaboration and coexistence: The State Network for Province-Building and Nation-Building

1 Federal Government Budget Papers (appendix to the *House of Commons Debates,* 18 June 1971, pp. 122–4).

2 *Ibid.*

3 *Ibid.,* p. 36.

4 E. R. Black and A. C. Cairns, 'A Different Perspective on Canadian Federalism', *Canadian Journal of Public Administration,* March 1966, p. 38.

5 Statistics Canada, *Canada Year Book, 1972,* Ottawa, 1972, p. 167, 171.

6 J. M. S. Careless, 'Limited Identities in Canada', *The Canadian Historical Review,* March 1969.

7 Quoted in *Encounter,* Spring 1971, p. 82.

8 Black and Cairns, p. 40.

9 Dominion Bureau of Statistics, *Survey of Production 1969,* Cat. 61-202. (Ottawa) pp. 18, 19.

10 Federal Provincial Constitutional Conference, February 1968.

11 See The Economic Council of Canada, *Fifth Annual Review,* Ottawa, 1968, p. 154.

12 Canadian Tax Foundation, *Provincial Government Finance: Revenue and Expenditure, 1969,* November 1969.

13 D.B.S., *Manufacturing Industries of Canada, Section D, Province of Ontario, 1967,* Ottawa, February 1971, p. 7.

14 D.B.S., *Asbestos,* vol. 440, no. 12, Cat. 26–001, p. 1.

15 I am grateful to Ken McRoberts' chapter in T. A. Hockin *et al, The Canadian Condominium,* Toronto, 1972, which I follow for this summary of Quebec's social pattern.

16 *Ibid.*

17 J. W. Fesler, *The Fifty States and Their Local Governments,* New York, 1967, p. 28.

18 See the note in *Canadian Forum,* July 1964, p. 84.

19 Black and Cairns, p. 30.

20 *Ibid.,* p. 32.

21 Garth Jones, *Planned Organizational Change: A Study in Change Dynamics,* London, 1969.

22 See D. V. Smiley, 'Two Themes of Canadian Federalism', *Canadian Journal of Economics and Political Science,* vol. 31, 1965.

23 Gordon Robertson, 'The Changing Role of the Privy Council Office', *Canadian Journal of Public Administration,* Winter 1971, p. 497.

24 *Financial Post,* 14 August 1971.

25 Richard Simeon, *Federal-Provincial Diplomacy : The Making of Recent Policy in Canada,* Toronto, 1972.

Chapter 3: The Growth of Government in Canada

1 S. F. Wise, 'Conservatism and Political Development: the Canadian Case', *South Atlantic Quarterly*, Spring 1970, pp. 233–4, 234–5.
2 J. A. Corry, *The Growth of Government Activities Since Confederation*, Ottawa, 1939, p. 3.
3 *Ibid.*
4 *Ibid.*, p. 4.
5 G. Grant, *Lament For a Nation*, Toronto, 1970.
6 D. G. Creighton, *The Empire of the St Lawrence*, Toronto, 1956.
7 See A. W. Curry, *Canadian Transportation Economics*, Toronto, 1967, pp. 404, 406.
8 Corry, *op cit.*, p. 91.
9 *Ibid.*, p. 84.
10 See *How Your Tax Dollar is Spent*, Ottawa, 1972.
11 See *Budget Papers, 1971*.
12 UNESCO, *Survey of Education*, vol. 4, Paris, 1964.
13 See *Statutes of Canada*, 1923, c9.
14 See the *Estimates of the Government of Canada, 1971–72*, Ottawa, 1971, pp. 22 ff.
15 *Ibid.*, pp. 11–14.
16 *Financial Post*, 6 November 1971.
17 See his discussion in *Political Studies XIII*, i, 1965, pp. 22–44.
18 *Ibid.*, p. 25.
19 See the Federal Department of Labour's 1971 *Annual Report*, Ottawa, 1971, p. 15.
20 S. Jamieson, *Times of Trouble: Labour Unrest and Industrial Conflict in Canada 1900–1966*, Federal Task Force on Labour Relations Ottawa, 1968, pp. 472–3.
21 *Annual Report*. Footnote 19 above.
22 *Globe and Mail*, 6 January 1972, p. 8.
23 Stanley Ryerson, *Unequal Union*, Toronto, 1967.
24 Jacques Ellul, *The Autopsy of Revolution*, New York, 1971, pp. 165–7.

Chapter 4: Canada in the World.

1 See the Science Council Study Number 15, *Innovation in a Cold Climate*, 1971.
2 See K. Holsti's chapter in S. L. Spiegel and K. N. Waltz, *Conflict in World Politics*, Cambridge, Mass., 1971.

3 *Survey of Current Business,* vol. L. no. 11, US Department of Commerce, November 1970, pp. 16–17.
4 See the letter of G. R. Reuber, *Globe and Mail,* 27 January 1971, p. 7.
5 John Gellner in the *Commentator,* September 1971, p. 22.
6 See the Annual Report for 1971 of Canada's Commission for International Development Assistance.

Chapter 5: The Federal Public Service: Mediator, Adviser, Policy-Maker

1 J. E. Hodgetts, *The Public Service of Canada: A Physiology of Government 1867–1970,* Toronto, 1973 is not only an excellent description and analysis of the Federal public service, it is also attentive to the relationship of the public service to its environment.
2 *Ibid.,* p. 11.
3 See note 5, chapter 2.
4 Hodgetts, p. 66.
5 *Annual Report of the Public Service Commission,* 1971.
6 *Canadian Forum,* July 1964, p. 84, and *Globe and Mail,* 29 January 1972, p. 7.
7 A. G. Irvine, 'The Delegation of Authority to Crown Corporations', *Canadian Public Administration,* Winter 1971, p. 557.
8 *Ibid.,* p. 559.
9 *Ibid.,* p. 556.
10 See folded insert in the *Canada Year Book 1970–71,* Ottawa, 1971.
11 *Annual Report 1970* of the Dept of Regional Economic Expansion, Ottawa, 1971.
12 Jean Blondel, *Introduction to Comparative Government,* New York, 1969, p. 405.
13 See Robert Presthus, *Elite Accommodation in Canadian Politics* (Toronto 1973).
14 R. Crossman, *The Myths of Cabinet Government* (Cambridge, Mass., 1971).
15 Blondel, *op. cit.* p. 400.
16 N. Fera, 'Review of Administrative Decisions Under the Federal Court Act, 1970', *Canadian Public Administration,* Winter 1971, p. 585.

17 See his paper published in S. D. K. Kernaghan (ed.), *Bureaucracy in Canadian Government* (Toronto, 1970).

18 *Globe and Mail,* 22 May 1971, p. 3.

19 Gordon Robertson, 'The Changing Role of the Privy Council Office', *Canadian Public Administration,* p. 489.

20 See Bruce Doern's essay on this in B. Doern and P. Aucoin, *The Structure of Policy-Making in Canada* (Toronto, 1971).

21 Robertson, p. 493.

22 Government of Canada, *Planning and Budgeting Guide* (Ottawa, July 1968) p. 2.

23 *Globe and Mail,* 19 November 1970, p. 5.

24 See T. Lowi, *The End of Liberalism* (New York, 1969).

25 *Debates,* 1971, pp. 67–8.

26 See 'Executive Patterns in the Public Service', *Executive,* February 1969, p. 28.

27 R. M. Dawson, *The Civil Service of Canada,* London, 1929.

28 Hodgetts, p. 79.

29 *Globe and Mail,* 25 November 1972, p. 1.

30 *Ibid.,* 28 January 1972, p. 5.

Chapter 6: Parliament as Catalyst

1 For a thorough discussion of this, see the chapter on the House of Commons in R. M. Dawson and N. Ward, *The Government of Canada,* Toronto, 1970.

2 Escott Reid, 'The Rise of National Parties in Canada', in H. G. Thorburn, *Party Politics in Canada,* Toronto, 1963, p. 19.

3 See table 8 (page 191).

4 *Ibid.*

5 *Ibid.*

6 A. H. Birch, *Representative and Responsible Government,* London, 1964, p. 138.

7 *Ibid.*

8 See W. F. Dawson, *Procedure in the Canadian House of Commons,* Toronto, 1962.

9 T. Hockin 'Reforming Canada's Parliament: the 1965 Reforms and Beyond', *University of Toronto Law Journal,* 1966.

10 *Ibid.,* pp. 325–35.

11 For a good discussion of the Public Service Bills, see J. R. Mallory and B. A. Smith, 'The Legislative Role of Parliamentary Committees in Canada: The Case of the Joint Com-

mittee on the Public Service Bills', *Canadian Public Administration,* Spring 1972.

12 For a more extended background on this, see C. E. S. Franks, 'The Dilemma of the Standing Committee in the Canadian House of Commons', *Canadian Journal of Political Science,* December 1971. See also T. Hockin, The Advance of Standing Committees in Canada's House of Commons', *Canadian Public Administration,* Summer 1970, p. 192.

13 Hockin *Ibid.*

14 See Franks *op. cit.*

15 Dorothy Byrne, 'Some Attendance Patterns Exhibited by Members of Parliament During the 28th Parliament, *Canadian Journal of Political Science,* March 1972 p. 136.

16 *Ibid.* p. 139.

17 D. Hoffman and N. Ward, *Bilingualism and Biculturalism in the Canadian House of Commons,* Ottawa, 1970, p. 15.

18 Byrne, p. 140.

19 F. H. Underhill, *In Search of Canadian Liberalism,* Toronto, 1961, p. 11.

20 Charles Taylor, *The Pattern of Politics,* Toronto, 1970, chapter 1.

21 See F. Engelmann's chapter on parliamentary opposition in Austria in R. Dahl (ed.), *Political Opposition in Western Democracies,* New Haven, 1966.

22 For the theoretical framework used to delineate contemporary disciplined parliamentary opposition from earlier styles of opposition in Westminster, see my 'Parliamentary opposition in the British House of Commons; Three Historical Paradigms', *Parliamentary Affairs,* Winter 1971.

23 S. C. Patterson and M. Jewell, *The American Legislative System,* New York 1965 (the first and last chapters).

Chapter 7: Political Parties, Political Leadership and the Executive

1 See A. Lijphardt, 'Cultural Diversity and Theories of Political Integration', *Canadian Journal of Political Science,* March 1971.

2 See S. J. R. Noel's 'The Prime Minister's Role in a Consociational Democracy', in Hockin (ed.), *Apex of Power,* pp. 104–5.

3 Blondel, *Introduction to Comparative Government,* chapter 5.

4 George Hougham, 'The Background and Development of

National Parties', in H. Thorburn (ed.), *Party Politics in Canada,* Scarborough, Ont., 1967, p. 5.

5 Blondel, p. 129.
6 *Globe and Mail,* 21 January 1972, p. 7.
7 See John Meisel, *Working Papers on Canadian Politics,* Montreal, 1972.
8 Blondel, p. 136.
9 *Toronto Star,* 9 December 1971, p. 9.
10 *Ibid.,* 1 April 1972, p. 16.
11 Murray Edelman, *Politics As Symbolic Action,* Chicago, 1971, p. 174.

Appendix

From the British North American Act: Sections 91, 92, 93 of the 'Distribution of Legislative Powers'

VI.—Distribution of Legislative Powers

Powers of Parliament.

91. It shall be lawful for the Queen, by and with the Advice and Consent of the Senate and House of Commons, to make Laws for the Peace, Order, and good Government of Canada, in relation to all Matters not coming within the Classes of Subjects by this Act assigned exclusively to the Legislatures of the Provinces; and for greater Certainty, but not so as to restrict the Generality of the foregoing Terms of this Section, it is hereby declared that (notwithstanding anything in this Act) the exclusive Legislative Authority of the Parliament of Canada extends to all Matters coming within the Classes of Subjects next hereinafter enumerated; that is to say,—

1. The amendment from time to time of the Constitution of Canada, except as regards matters coming within the classes of subjects by this Act assigned exclusively to the Legislatures of the provinces, or as regards rights or privileges by this or any other Constitutional Act granted or secured to the Legis-

Source: The British North America Act, consolidated with amendments, as Appendix I in P. E. Trudeau, *A Canadian Charter of Human Rights,* Ottawa, 1968 pp. 56–61.

lature or the Government of a province, or to any class of persons with respect to schools or as regards the use of the English or the French language or as regards the requirements that there shall be a session of the Parliament of Canada at least once each year, and that no House of Commons shall continue for more than five years from the day of the return of the Writs for choosing the House: provided, however, that a House of Commons may in time of real or apprehended war, invasion or insurrection be continued by the Parliament of Canada if such continuation is not opposed by the votes of more than one-third of the members of such House. (39)

1A. The Public Debt and Property. (40)
2. The Regulation of Trade and Commerce.
2A. Unemployment insurance. (41)
3. The raising of Money by any Mode or System of Taxation.
4. The borrowing of Money on the Public Credit.
5. Postal Service.
6. The Census and Statistics.
7. Militia, Military and Naval Service, and Defence.
8. The fixing of and providing for the Salaries and Allowances of Civil and other Officers of the Government of Canada.

(39). Added by the *British North America (No. 2) Act, 1949,* 13 Geo. VI c. 81 (U.K.).
(40) Re-numbered by the *British North America (No. 2) Act, 1949.*
(41) Added by the *British North America Act, 1940,* 3–4 Geo. VI, c. 36 (U.K.).

5.—ONTARIO, QUEBEC, AND NOVA SCOTIA.

89. Each of the Lieutenant Governors of Ontario, Quebec and Nova Scotia shall cause Writs to be issued for the First Election of Members of the Legislative Assembly thereof in such Form and by such Person as he thinks fit, and at such Time and addressed to such Returning Officer as the Governor General directs, and so that the First Election of Member of Assembly for any Electoral District or any Subdivision thereof shall be held at the same Time and at the same Places as the Election for a Member to serve in the House of Commons of Canada for that Electoral District.

9. Beacons, Buoys, Lighthouses, and Sable Island.
10. Navigation and Shipping.
11. Quarantine and the Establishment and Maintenance of Marine Hospitals.
12. Sea Coast and Inland Fisheries.
13. Ferries between a Province and any British or Foreign Country or between Two Provinces.
14. Currency and Coinage.
15. Banking, Incorporation of Banks, and the Issue of Paper Money.
16. Savings Banks.
17. Weights and Measures.
18. Bills of Exchange and Promissory Notes.
19. Interest.
20. Legal Tender.
21. Bankruptcy and Insolvency.
22. Patents of Invention and Discovery.
23. Copyrights.
24. Indians, and Lands reserved for the Indians.
25. Naturalization and Aliens.
26. Marriage and Divorce.
27. The Criminal Law, except the Constitution of Courts of Criminal Jurisdiction, but including the Procedure in Criminal Matters.
28. The Establishment, Maintenance, and Management of Penitentiaries.
29. Such Classes of Subjects as are expressly excepted in the Enumeration of the Classes of Subjects by this Act assigned exclusively to the Legislatures of the Provinces.

And any Matter coming within any of the Classes of Subjects enumerated in this Section shall not be deemed to come within the Class of Matters of a local or private Nature comprised in the Enumeration of the Classes of Subjects by this Act assigned exclusively to the Legislatures of the Provinces. (42)

(42) Legislative authority has been conferred on Parliament by other Acts as follows:
1. The *British North America Act, 1871,* 34–35 Vict., c. 28 (U.K.).
2. The Parliament of Canada may from time to time establish

new provinces in any territories forming for the time being part of the Dominion of Canada, but not included in any Province thereof, and may, at the time of such establishment, make provision for the constitution and administration of any such Province, and for the passing of laws for the peace, order, and good government of such Province, and for its representation in the said Parliament.

3.   The Parliament of Canada may from time to time, with the consent of the Legislature of any Province of the said Dominion, increase, diminish, or otherwise alter the limits of such Province, upon such terms and conditions as may be agreed to by the said Legislature, and may, with the like consent, make provision respecting the effect and operation of any such increase or diminution or alteration of territory in relation to any Province affected thereby.

4.   The Parliament of Canada may from time to time make provision for the administration, peace, order, and good government of any territory not for the time being included in any Province.

5.   The following Acts passed by the said Parliament of Canada, and intituled respectively,—'An Act for the temporary government of Rupert's Land and the North Western Territory when united with Canada'; and 'An act to amend and continue the Act thirty-two and thirty-three Victoria, chapter three, and to establish and provide for the government of "the Province of Manitoba," shall be and be deemed to have been valid and effectual for all purposes whatsoever from the date at which they respectively received the assent, in the Queen's name, of the Governor General of the said Dominion of Canada.'

6.   Except as provided by the third section of this Act, it shall not be competent for the Parliament of Canada to alter the provisions of the last-mentioned Act of the said Parliament in so far as it relates to the Province of Manitoba, or of any other Act hereafter establishing new Provinces in the said Dominion, subject always to the right of the Legislature of the Province of Manitoba to alter from time to time the provisions of any law respecting the qualification of electors and members of the Legislative Assembly, and to make laws respecting elections in the said Province.

The *Rupert's Land Act 1868*, 31-32 Vict., c. 105 (U.K.) (repealed by the *Statute Law Revision Act, 1893*, 56–57 Vict., c. 14 (U.K.) had previously conferred similar authority in relation to Rupert's Land and the North-Western Territory upon admission of those areas.

2. The *British North America Act, 1886*, 49–50 Vict., c. 35, (U.K.).

1. The Parliament of Canada may from time to time make provision for the representation in the Senate and House of Commons of Canada, or in either of them, of any territories which for the time being form part of the Dominion of Canada, but are not included in any province thereof.

Exclusive Powers of Provincial Legislatures.

92. In each Province the Legislature may exclusively make Laws in relation to Matters coming within the Classes of Subject next herein-after enumerated; that is to say,—

1. The Amendment from Time to Time, notwithstanding anything in this Act, of the Constitution of the Province, except as regards the Office of Lieutenant Governor.
2. Direct Taxation within the Province in order to the raising of a Revenue for Provincial Purposes.
3. The borrowing of Money on the sole Credit of the Province.
4. The Establishment and Tenure of Provincial Offices and the Appointment and Payment of Provincial Officers.
5. The Management and Sale of the Public Lands belonging to the Province and of the Timber and Wood thereon.
6. The Establishment, Maintenance, and Management of Public and Reformatory Prisons in and for the Province.
7. The Establishment, Maintenance, and Management of Hospitals, Asylums, Charities, and Eleemosynary Institutions in and for the Province, other than Marine Hospitals.
8. Municipal Institutions in the Province.
9. Shop, Saloon, Tavern, Auctioneer, and other Licences in order to the raising of a Revenue for Provincial, Local, or Municipal Purposes.
10. Local Works and Undertakings other than such as are of the following Classes:—

(a) Lines of Steam or other Ships, Railways, Canals, Telegraphs, and other Works and Undertakings connecting the Province with any other or others of the Provinces, or extending beyond the Limits of the Province;

(b) Lines of Steam Ships between the Province and any British or Foreign Country;

(c) Such Works as, although wholly situate within the Province, are before or after their Execution declared by the Parliament of Canada to be for the General Advantage of Canada or for the Advantage of Two or more of the Provinces.

11. The Incorporation of Companies with Provincial Objects.

12. The Solemnization of Marriage in the Province.

13. Property and Civil Rights in the Province.

14. The Administration of Justice in the Province, including the Constitution, Maintenance, and Organization of Provincial Courts, both of Civil and of Criminal Jurisdiction, and including Procedure in Civil Matters in those Courts.

15. The Imposition of Punishment by Fine, Penalty, or Imprisonment for enforcing any Law of the Province made in relation to any matter coming within any of the Classes of Subjects enumerated in this Section.

16. Generally all Matters of a merely local or private Nature in the Province.

Education

93. In and for each Province the Legislature may exclusively make Laws in relation to Education, subject and according to the following Provisions:—

(1) Nothing in any such Law shall prejudicially affect any Right or Privilege with respect to Denominational Schools which any Class of Persons have by Law in the Province at the Union:

(2) All the Powers, Privileges, and Duties at the Union by

3. The *Statute of Westminster, 1931,* 22 Geo. V. c. 4, (U.K.).

3. It is hereby declared and enacted that the Parliament of a Dominion has full power to make laws having extra-territorial operation.

Law conferred and imposed in Upper Canada on the Separate Schools and School Trustees of the Queen's Roman Catholic Subjects shall be and the same are hereby extended to the Dissentient Schools of the Queen's Protestant and Roman Catholic Subjects in Quebec :

(3) Where in any Province a System of Separate or Dissentient Schools exists by Law at the Union or is thereafter established by the Legislature of the Province, an Appeal shall lie to the Governor General in Council from any Act or Decision of any Provincial Authority affecting any Right or Privilege of the Protestant or Roman Catholic Minority of the Queen's Subjects in relation to Education :

(4) In case any such Provincial Law as from Time to Time seems to the Governor General in Council requisite for the due Execution of the Provisions of this Section is not made, or in case any Decision of the Governor General in Council on any Appeal under this Section is not duly executed by the proper Provincial Authority in that Behalf, then and in every such Case, and as far only as the Circumstances of each Case require, the Parliament of Canada may make remedial Laws for the due Execution of the Provisions of this Section and of any Decision of the Governor General in Council under this Section. (43)

(43) Altered for various provinces since 1867.

Further reading

This is not a bibliography, even 'select'. It is a list of some of the more obvious and accessible books through which the reader may follow up the subjects dealt with in this volume. Included also is a short list of other general introductions to Canadian government.

The Canadian Constitution and Formative Political Influences

R. M. Bird, *The Growth of Government Spending In Canada*, Canadian Tax Foundation, Toronto, 1970.

G. W. Brown (ed.), *Canada*, United Nations Series, University of California Press, Los Angeles, 1950.

R. I. Cheffins *The Constitutional Processs in Canada*, McGraw-Hill, Toronto, 1969.

J. A. Corry and J. E. Hodgetts, *Democratic Government and Politics*, University of Toronto Press, 1959.

R. M. Dawson, *The Government of Canada* (revised by Norman Ward), University of Toronto Press, 1970.

A. R. M. Lower, *Canadians In The Making*, Longmans, Toronto 1958.

K. A. MacKirdy, J. S. Moir and Y. F. Zoltvany, *Changing Perspectives in Canadian History*, Dent, Toronto, 1967.

C. Martin, *Foundations of Canadian Nationhood*, University of Toronto Press, 1955.

W. L. Morton, *The Kingdom of Canada*, McClelland and Stewart, Toronto, 1963.

S. B. Ryerson, *Unequal Union*, Progress Books, Toronto, 1968.

M. Wade, *The French Canadians 1760–1945*, Macmillan, Toronto, 1955.

S. F. Wise and C. Brown, *Canada Views The United States*, University of Washington Press, Seattle, 1967.

Federalism and Federal-Provincial Relations

D. G. Creighton, *The Road to Confederation: The Emergence of Canada 1863–1867*, Macmillan, Toronto, 1964.
R. H. Leach (ed.), *Contemporary Canada*, University of Toronto Press, 1968.
J. P. Meekison (ed.), *Canadian Federalism: Myth or Reality* Methuen, Toronto, 1968.
R. Simeon, *Federal-Provincial Diplomacy: the Making of Recent Policy in Canada*, University of Toronto Press, 1972.
D. V. Smiley, *The Canadian Political Nationality*, Methuen, Toronto, 1967.
D. V. Smiley, *Conditional Grants and Canadian Federalism*, Canadian Tax Foundation, Toronto, 1963.
D. V. Smiley, *Canada In Question: Federalism In The Seventies*, McGraw-Hill Ryerson, Toronto, 1972.
P. E. Trudeau, *Federalism and the French-Canadians*, Macmillan, Toronto, 1968.
K. C. Wheare, *Federal Government* (4th ed.), Oxford University Press, London, 1963.

Parliament

W. F. Dawson, *Procedure In the Canadian House of Commons*, University of Toronto Press, 1923.
D. Hoffman and N. Ward, *Bilingualism and Biculturalism in the Canadian House of Commons*, Queen's Printer, Ottawa, 1970.
A. Kornberg, *Canadian Legislative Behavior: A Study of the 25th Parliament*, Holt, Rinehart and Winston, New York, 1967.
A. Kornberg and L. D. Musolf (eds), *Legislatures In Developmental Perspective*, Duke University Press, Durham N.C., 1970.
F. A. Kuntz, *The Modern Senate of Canada, 1925–1963: A Reappraisal*, University of Toronto Press, 1965.
N. Ward, *The Canadian House of Commons: Representation*, University of Toronto Press, 1950.
N. Ward, *The Public Purse: A study in Canadian Democracy* University of Toronto Press, 1962.

Political Parties and Elections

R. R. Alford, *Party and Society: The Anglo-American Democracies*, Rand McNally, Chicago, 1963.

J. M. Beck, *Pendulum of Power: Canada's Federal Elections,* Prentice-Hall, Scarborough, Ont., 1968.

F. Engelmann and M. Schwartz *Political Parties and the Canadian Social Structure,* Prentice-Hall, Scarborough, Ont., 1967.

J. L. Granatstein, *The Politics of Survival: The Conservative Party of Canada 1939–1945,* University of Toronto Press, 1967.

G. Horowitz, *Canadian Labour in Politics,* University of Toronto Press, 1968.

W. E. Lyons, *One Man – One Vote,* McGraw-Hill, Toronto, 1970.

J. Meisel, *The Canadian General Election of 1957,* University of Toronto Press, 1962.

J. Meisel (ed.), *Papers on the 1962 Election,* University of Toronto Press, Toronto, 1964.

J. Meisel, *Working Papers on Canadian Politics,* McGill-Queens University Press, Montreal, 1972.

K. Z. Paltiel, *Political Party Financing in Canada,* McGraw-Hill, Toronto, 1970.

T. H. Qualter, *The Election Process,* McGraw-Hill, Toronto, 1970.

P. Regenstreif, *The Diefenbaker Interlude: Parties and Voting in Canada,* Longmans, Toronto, 1965.

Report of the Committee on Election Expenses, Queens Printer, Ottawa, 1966.

M. Robin (ed.), *Canadian Provincial Politics,* Prentice-Hall, Scarborough, Ont., 1971.

M. Stein, *The Dynamics of Right-wing Protest: Social Credit in Quebec,* University of Toronto Press, 1973.

C. Taylor, *The Pattern of Politics,* McClelland and Stewart, Toronto, 1970.

H. G. Thorburn (ed.), *Party Politics In Canada* (3rd ed.), Prentice-Hall, Scarborough, 1972.

F. H. Underhill, *In Search of Canadian Liberalism,* Macmillan, Toronto, 1960.

W. D. Young, *The Anatomy of a Party: The National CCF 1932–1961,* University of Toronto Press, 1969.

The Bureaucracy and the Political Executive

C. A. Ashley and R. G. H. Smails, *Canadian Crown Corporations,* Macmillan, Toronto, 1965.

B. Doern and P. Aucoin (eds.), *The Structures of Policy-making in Canada,* Macmillan, Toronto, 1971.

B. Doern, *Science and Politics in Canada*, McGill, Queens University Press, Montreal, 1972.

F. W. Gibson (ed.), *Cabinet Formation and Bicultural Relations: Seven Case Studies*, Queen's Printer, Ottawa, 1970.

M. Hamelin (ed.), *The Political Ideas of Prime Ministers of Canada*, University of Ottawa Press, 1970.

T. Hockin (ed.), *Apex of Power: The Prime Minister and Political Leadership in Canada*, Prentice-Hall, Scarborough, Ont., 1971.

J. E. Hodgetts, *The Public Service in Canada*, University of Toronto Press, 1972.

Planning, Programming, Budgeting Guide, Queen's Printer, Ottawa, 1968.

J. Porter, *The Vertical Mosaic*, University of Toronto Press, 1965.

W. D. K. Kernaghan, *Bureaucracy In Canadian Government*, Methuen, Toronto, 1969.

K. J. Rea and J. McLeod (eds.), *Business and Government in Canada: Selected Reading*, Methuen, Toronto, 1969.

B. Thordardson, *Trudeau and Foreign Policy*, Oxford University Press, London, 1972.

A. M. Willms and W. D. K. Kernaghan (eds.), *Public Administration in Canada: Selected Readings*, Methuen, Toronto, 1968.

Other General Introductions to Canadian Government and Politics

R. M. Dawson, *The Government of Canada*, revised by Norman Ward, University of Toronto Press, 1970.

P. Fox (ed.), *Politics: Canada*, McGraw-Hill, Toronto, 1970.

O. Kruhlak *et al* (eds.), *The Canadian Political Process*, Holt Rinehart and Winston, Toronto, 1970.

R. H. Leach (ed.), *Contemporary Canada*, University of Toronto Press, 1968.

J. R. Mallory, *The Structure of Canadian Government*, Macmillan, Toronto, 1971.

J. White, R. Wagenberg and R. Nelson, *Introduction to Canadian Politics and Government*, Holt, Rinehart and Winston, Toronto, 1972.

R. J. Van Loon, M. S. Whittington, *The Canadian Political System; Environment, Structure and Process* (2nd ed.), McGraw-Hill Ryerson, Toronto, 1975.

Index

18